THE GREAT WAR OF OUR TIME

*The CIA's Fight Against Terrorism—
From al Qa'ida to ISIS*

Michael Morell

with Bill Harlow

TWELVE

New York   Boston

Twelve
Hachette Book Group
1290 Avenue of the Americas
New York, NY 10104
twelvebooks.com
twitter.com/twelvebooks

Originally published in hardcover and ebook by Twelve in May 2015.
First Trade Paperback Edition: August 2016

Twelve is an imprint of Grand Central Publishing.
The Twelve name and logo are trademarks of Hachette Book Group, Inc.

The publisher is not responsible for websites (or their content) that are not owned by the publisher.

The Hachette Speakers Bureau provides a wide range of authors for speaking events. To find out more, go to www.hachettespeakersbureau.com or call (866) 376-6591.

Library of Congress Cataloging-in-Publication Data

Morell, Michael J.
  The great war of our time : the CIA's fight against terrorism—from al Qa'ida to ISIS / Michael Morell with Bill Harlow. — First edition.
    pages cm
  Includes index.
  ISBN 978-1-4555-8566-3 (hardback) — ISBN 978-1-4555-8961-6 (large print hardcover) — ISBN 978-1-4555-9055-1 (international trade paperback) — ISBN 978-1-4789-5463-7 (audiobook)   1. Morell, Michael J.   2. United States. Central Intelligence Agency.   3. United States. Central Intelligence Agency—Officials and employees—Biography.   4. Qaida (Organization)   5. Terrorism—United States—Prevention.   6. War on Terrorism, 2001–2009.   I. Harlow, Bill.   II. Title.
  JK468.I6M665 2015
  363.325'1630973—dc23

                        2014049799

  ISBNs: 978-1-4555-8567-0 (trade paperback), 978-1-4555-8568-7 (ebook)

Printed in the United States of America

RRD-C

10 9 8 7 6 5 4 3 2 1

To the men and women involved in CIA's fight against terrorists—
the finest public servants you will never know

Contents

The Spread of al Qa`ida and its Affiliates

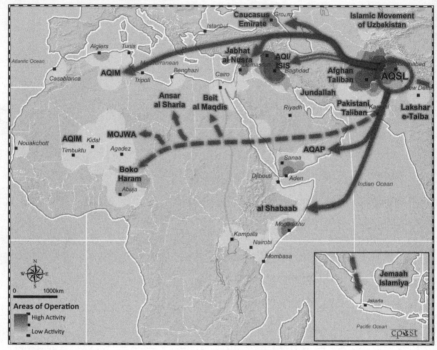

Associates ➤

These groups have sworn loyalty to al Qa`ida's senior leadership (AQSL) and are recognized by AQSL as part of the core network.

- **al Qa`ida in the Arabian Peninsula:** formed in 2009, operates in Yemen and Saudi Arabia but has tried to attack the US.
- **al Qa`ida in the Islamic Magrib:** operates across North Africa, association starts in 2006.
- **al Shabaab:** controlled significant territory in Somalia, pledged allegiance to al Qa`ida in 2012.
- **Caucasus Emirate:** operates in Chechnya and the North Caucasus, official affiliation begins as early as 2008.
- **Jabhat al Nusra:** formed in 2012 as al Qa`ida's branch in Syria.

Former Associates ═════➤

These groups have officially broken their ties with AQSL.

- **al Qa`ida in Iraq:** now the Islamic State of Iraq and Syria (ISIS), association began in 2004 but was broken in 2014.

Affiliates ▬ ▬ ▬ ▬➤

These groups are ideologically aligned with al Qa`ida and may receive support but have not sworn loyalty.

- **Afghan Taliban** (Afghanistan)
- **Ansar al Sharia** (Libya)
- **Ansar Beit al Maqdis** (Egypt)
- **Boko Haram** (Nigeria)
- **Islamic Movement** (Uzbekistan)
- **Jemaah Islamiya** (Indonesia)
- **Jundallah** (Iran)
- **Lakshar e-Taiba** (India/Kashmir)
- **Movement for Oneness and Jihad in West Africa** (Mali, Niger, Algeria)
- **Pakistani Taliban** (Pakistan)

Map current as of early 2015

cpost.uchicago.edu

Credit: Courtesy of the Chicago Project on Security and Terrorism at the University of Chicago.

Introduction to the Paperback Edition

An ISIS affiliate in Egypt in October 2015 placed an explosive device aboard a Russian charter plane departing from the Egyptian resort city of Sharm al Sheikh, killing 224 people. It was only the third time that an aircraft had been brought down by a bomb in a quarter of a century. It was the largest loss of life in the downing of an airliner by a bomb since Pan Am 103 in 1988.

The ISIS leadership in Syria (the Islamic State of Iraq and the Levant or ISIL) conceived, planned, and directed an attack on the streets of Paris in November, killing 130. It was the largest terrorist attack in Western Europe since the Madrid bombings in 2004. It was the first ISIS-directed attack in the West ever.

Just a month later, two individuals inspired by ISIS went on a rampage in San Bernardino, California, that killed fourteen people. In terms of fatalities, this was the largest terrorist attack in the US since 9/11—bigger than the Boston Marathon bombings and slightly bigger than the 2009 shootings at Fort Hood, Texas.

And then, in March 2016, the terror network that ISIS has established in Europe struck again—this time in the Brussels airport and subway station, killing thirty-two. All told, ISIS is conducting attacks at a pace much faster than al-Qaʻida ever did.

As of this writing, a year has passed since the publication of the hardcover edition of this book. Unfortunately the predictions outlined in the penultimate chapter of the book are proving accurate—even faster than I anticipated. The terrorist threat to the United States and to US interests abroad is getting worse. The ISIS threat has grown significantly. And, with everyone's focus on ISIS, al Qa'ida is on the rebound.

* * *

As I wrote in *Time* magazine in the immediate aftermath of the Paris attacks, the nature and significance of the ISIS threat flows from the fact that it is—all at the same time—a terrorist group, a state, and a revolutionary political movement. We have not faced an adversary like it before.

As a terrorist group, ISIS poses a threat to the homeland. In mid-2015 that threat was largely indirect—ISIS's ability to radicalize young American men and women to conduct lone-wolf attacks here. That indirect threat remains today. There are thousands of ISIS sympathizers in the United States—more than al Qa'ida ever had. The FBI has roughly 1,000 open investigations into homegrown extremists—the vast majority radicalized by ISIS and a large number of whom may be plotting attacks here. Such attacks have already occurred in the United States, including the attack in San Bernardino. Other ISIS supporters have been arrested before they could act.

Today we face an additional threat from ISIS—a direct threat—stemming from ISIS's ability to plan and direct attacks in the homeland from the group's safe havens in Iraq and Syria. Just as it did in Paris. How would such an attack play out? Most likely by a group of European operatives taking advantage of the Visa Waiver Program, getting on a plane, and flying to the United States.

What is the difference between a direct and an indirect threat? A lone-wolf attack, while horrific, is likely to produce fairly limited casualties—on the order of the Boston Marathon bombing in 2013 (three killed) or the shootings at Fort Hood in 2009 (thirteen killed). A directed attack, however, carries the potential to be more complex and sophisticated—multiple simultaneous attacks, for example—and therefore more deadly, again just as in Paris (130 killed), or in London in 2005 (fifty-six killed), or even on 9/11 itself.

The attacks in Paris and Brussels were the first manifestation of ISIS's effort to put together an attack capability in Europe— an effort that it had begun less than a year before. More attacks in Europe are a certainty. The head of the UK's domestic security agency has warned that ISIS is planning mass-casualty attacks in Britain. ISIS has said that it wants to conduct attacks in the United States. Now that it has an attack capability in Europe, it is almost certainly working to achieve the same here.

ISIS is also a quasi state—a state in every sense of the word, except one. It does not have foreign recognition or relations with other states. But it does have an executive, it has an army, it has a police force, it has a set of laws, it has a judiciary, it provides social services, it takes care of the poor, and it levies taxes.

Why does it matter that ISIS is a quasi state? It matters for two reasons. One is that, as a state, it can use all the resources—human and otherwise—within the area it controls in the pursuit of its aims. The best example? Using the chemistry labs at Mosul University to make bombs and chemical weapons. And two is that statehood will make it more difficult to dislodge them. Yes, we have successfully taken territory from them in Iraq and Syria, but ISIS is deeply rooted in the areas it controls.

As a state, ISIS also poses a threat to regional stability—a threat to the very territorial integrity of the current nation-states there, a threat of inflaming the entire region in sectarian war. All this in a part of the world that still provides almost a third of the world's oil supply; a region that is home to one of America's closest allies, Israel; and a region that is home to a set of close American allies—the Gulf Arab states—that are a bulwark against Iran's push for regional hegemony.

And, as a revolutionary political movement, ISIS is gaining affiliates among extremist groups around the world. They are signing up for what ISIS desires as its objective—a global caliphate in which day-to-day life is governed by extreme religious views. In the mind of ISIS, this global caliphate would extend to the US itself.

When they join ISIS, these affiliates evolve from focusing on local issues to focusing on establishing an extension of the caliphate themselves. And their targets evolve from local to international ones. This is the story of the bombing of a Russian airliner in the Egyptian Sinai by an ISIS group.

ISIS has gained affiliates faster than al Qa'ida ever did. From nothing two years ago, there are now militant groups in nearly twenty-five countries that have sworn allegiance to ISIS. They have conducted attacks that have already killed Americans, and they carry the potential to themselves grab large amounts of territory. Libya is the furthest along—ISIS has between 4,000 to 6,000 fighters there, it has training camps there, it has conducted attacks in North Africa, and it is plotting attacks in Europe.

To degrade and ultimately defeat ISIS will require both removing the leadership from the battlefield and shrinking and eventually eliminating the safe havens. The former will be easier than the latter. The former requires good intelligence and the military assets to turn that intelligence into action. The latter requires a complex military operation in both Syria and Iraq. And that requires a political solution in Syria to the problem of President Basher al-Assad and a political solution in Iraq to the problem of the disenfranchisement of the Sunnis. This is very complicated.

* * *

The attacks in Paris and Brussels and the bombing of a Russian airliner over the Sinai are news stories that have focused the world's attention on ISIS—and rightfully so. But there is another story that should also have our attention—but that does not as of the writing of this introduction. It is the story of the rebound of al Qaʿida, a story that the former under secretary of defense for intelligence, Mike Vickers, and I told in *Politico* late in 2015.

That story is twofold—involving the emerging rebirth of the al Qaʿida leadership in South Asia, so-called core al Qaʿida, as well as a significant rebound of the most important al Qaʿida affiliate, al Qaʿida in the Arabian Peninsula (AQAP), the al Qaʿida entity in Yemen.

Intense US counterterrorism operations beginning in the fall of 2008 pushed core al Qaʿida to the brink of defeat. Only a few of core al Qaʿida's top leadership remain at large, namely the group's leader, Ayman al-Zawahiri, and its general manager, Abdul Rehman al-Maghribi, Zawahiri's only surviving son-in-law.

Since late 2010 the group has largely been in survival mode, hunkering down in its Pakistan safe haven in hopes of outlasting the US onslaught. Its ability to conduct attacks in the West has consequently been severely degraded.

While core al Qaʿida is down, it is not defeated. And, most significantly, it is beginning to stage a comeback. Why do I say this?

The group's senior leadership ranks were recently bolstered by Iran's release of three management council members: Abu Khayr al-Masri, Zawahiri's designated successor, Abu Mohammed al-Masri, and Saif al-Adel. All were held for over a decade in Iran. All are veteran jihadists, whose experience in the group dates back two decades.

The group's alliances with key safe haven providers—the Haqqani Network, which is under the protection of Pakistan's security forces, and the Pakistani Taliban—remain intact and have recently been strengthened. The new Afghan Taliban leader, Mullah Akhtar Mansour, recently affirmed his organization's alliance with al Qaʿida.

Perhaps most importantly, core al Qa'ida is expanding its presence in Afghanistan.

For several years al Qa'ida has maintained a small presence in eastern Afghanistan under the leadership of Farouq al-Qahtani, and that presence has been growing. Qahtani has made clear his intent to strike the West.

More significantly, al Qa'ida recently established training camps in Afghanistan's southeast—the group's first training camp in Afghanistan since it was pushed out of the country in the weeks after 9/11. US and Afghan forces recently struck some of these camps—because of concern about them.

Core al Qa'ida has also shifted its targets. Once focused exclusively on large, symbolic, 9/11-style targets, the group has become enamored of "Mumbai-style" attacks, akin to what ISIL just did in Paris. Core al Qa'ida sees itself in a competition with ISIL for leadership of the global jihad, and it knows it needs to stage some bold attacks if it is going to retain its position as the vanguard of global jihad.

Yemen lies some 1,500 miles south-southwest of Afghanistan, and it is home to AQAP, the most dangerous al Qa'ida group on the planet today. Its capabilities were degraded by US counterterrorism operations too, but nowhere near as much as those of core al Qa'ida.

Now AQAP is gaining considerable strength—thanks to the war between the legitimately elected government of Yemen and an insurgent group called the Houthis.

That war has created a vacuum that AQAP is filling. The group now has more territory under its control than at any other time. The group has more fighters under its banner than ever before—as it is drawing Sunni recruits motivated to fight the Shi'a Houthis. AQAP also has more money than ever before—thanks to its success in overrunning a branch of the Yemeni Central Bank.

AQAP, which already has the most sophisticated bomb technology of any extremist group in the world and has been trying to attack the United States since at least 2009, will use its newfound strength to enhance its capability to strike the West.

The bottom line: Do we need to worry about an ISIL-directed attack in the United States? Absolutely. Do we also need to worry about an al Qa'ida–directed attack here? Absolutely.

* * *

The reaction to the hardcover publication of *The Great War of Our Time* was very positive—it got strong reviews, became a *New York Times* best-seller, and, most importantly, the book has helped define the public debate about terrorism in a way that is very satisfying to me. One radio host, Hugh Hewitt, liked the book so much that he said he would send a copy to every candidate running for president.

The reaction to the very detailed chapter devoted to pushing back on those who criticize the CIA and me for our actions with regard to Benghazi was also positive and satisfying to me. For example, Ross Kaminsky, a respected journalist for the conservative magazine *National Review*, wrote that "Morell's explanation of his and the CIA's role in the Benghazi talking points offers a believable vindication of himself and senior officials at the agency." Kaminsky went on, "I find Morell's account [of Benghazi] credible and exculpatory despite picking up the book with pre-existing notions about this messy story."

In September 2015, five months after the publication of the book, I testified before Congress for the fifth time on Benghazi. On this occasion I appeared before the House Select Committee on Benghazi. I spent nine hours in private with the committee answering many questions from both Republicans and Democrats. In preparing for this session, I had reviewed many documents. In doing so I discovered additional facts that I have added to this version of the book. The bottom line remains the same—CIA as an organization and CIA officers, including me, in no way allowed politics to influence any of our actions or decisions with regard to Benghazi.

Most satisfying to me, though, were those readers who told me that the book provided unique insight into how important intelligence is to our national security, what it is like to be a CIA officer, the dedication and commitment of those officers, and the sacrifices those officers and their families make in defense of the nation. People told me that stories about the effect of my job on my own family were both enlightening and entertaining. To me the most important chapter of the book remains the last one.

While reactions to the book were almost universally positive, there were some significant critiques. Senator Dianne Feinstein of California, currently the ranking member of the Senate Intelligence Committee and previously the committee's chairman, put out a public statement when the book was published saying that there was nothing new in my criticism of her committee's study on CIA's post-9/11 enhanced interrogation program, and that my arguments simply repeated those in the CIA's rebuttal to her staff's report.

Feinstein is a staunch advocate of national security, and she is not known for playing politics. Certainly I never saw her play politics. She truly believes that her staff's study on the CIA's detention and interrogation is accurate. I truly believe that it is not accurate.

In early May 2010, just after I was named deputy director of the Agency, I paid a courtesy call on Senator Feinstein. In that meeting she outlined her expectations of me. At the top of her list was to "always, always tell the committee exactly what you think. Do not spin, do not hold back, for any reason." That is exactly what I did throughout the book—including in the chapter on enhanced interrogation techniques.

Feinstein's public statement about the book was quickly followed by a fifty-four-page detailed rebuttal to my thirty-five-page chapter, drafted and made available to the public by her committee's staff—largely those who worked on the study. The staff made sixty-six separate critiques.

Because it is so important to me that I get my facts and analysis right, I studied the staff's rebuttal in detail. In doing so I made roughly twenty edits to the chapter, often only adding or deleting a word or two for accuracy. It is important to note that those edits, while making the book's discussion on enhanced interrogation techniques more accurate, do not, in any way, change my bottom line about the committee's study—that it is a deeply flawed document.

I should also note that I believe I made more changes to my thirty-five-page chapter based on the committee's critique of it than the committee made to its six-thousand-page study based on CIA's comments on it.

Two other reactions to the book are worth noting. The first came from Philip Zelikow, the executive director of the 9/11 Commission and professor of history at the University of Virginia. Philip, a leading thinker on many issues related to national security, questioned my criticism of the commission's finding that 9/11 was a "failure of imagination." He did not do so publicly, rather via private communications with me. After rereading the commission's report and discussing the issue with him, I concluded that Philip was correct, and the language has been adjusted.

The second came from a former senior CIA official. That critique had to do with my characterization of what occurred inside CIA, prior to the Iraq War, with regard to our understanding of the credibility of the key source for our judgment that Saddam Hussein had a mobile capability to produce biological weapons. Again, this officer was correct, and the language has been adjusted. As was the case with the hardcover, any remaining errors in the paperback are mine and mine alone.

* * *

In early December 2015, during a debate in the British House of Commons over whether Parliament should authorize British air strikes against ISIS in Syria, the Labor Party's shadow minister for foreign affairs, Hilary Benn, gave a remarkable speech. Some of his colleagues called it one of the greatest speeches in the history of the British House of Commons.

Benn, breaking with his own party leader and supporting the air strikes, said, "We are here faced by fascists—not just their calculated brutality but their belief that they are superior to every single one of us in this chamber tonight and all the people that we represent. They hold us in contempt. They hold our values in contempt. They hold our belief in tolerance and decency in contempt. They hold our democracy...in contempt."

He went on. "What we know about fascists is that they need to be defeated.... It's why this entire House stood up against Hitler and Mussolini.... We must now confront this evil."

It is very rare in the British House of Commons for a speech to receive applause. Benn's speech did. And it was very right that it did, because Benn's points are exactly correct.

Michael Morell
Washington, DC
April 2016

Preface

The drinks had not even arrived before the first phone call. It was August 4, 2013, and my wife, Mary Beth, and I had taken our daughter Sarah to dinner to celebrate her twentieth birthday. We were sitting outside in the garden of one of the D.C. area's finest restaurants. L'Auberge Chez Francois is located along the Potomac River in the rolling treelined hills of Great Falls, Virginia. It was a beautiful evening—low seventies and low humidity—and Sarah was beaming. She was with her mom and dad—the latter of whom also just happened to be the deputy director of the Central Intelligence Agency.

In the span of the next two hours, senior officials from CIA's Counterterrorism Center (CTC) called my cell phone nine times. Each time, I would walk into a field adjacent to the garden for privacy. Several times I had to follow up a call from CTC with my own call—either to CIA Director John Brennan or to President Obama's White House Counterterrorism Advisor Lisa Monaco. At first Mary Beth and Sarah were frustrated with the calls, saying things like "Not tonight. Not during a birthday dinner." But as more and more calls came, it became comedic, and the frustration turned to laughter. I would sit down after talking on the phone for five minutes, and then thirty or sixty seconds later, the phone would ring again. Although my phone was on vibrate so as not to bother the other patrons, my frequent walks through an archway into the field garnered the attention of all. No one, not even Mary Beth and Sarah, knew that each phone call I received that evening related to the most serious terrorist threat to face the United States since al Qaʻida's plot in August 2006 to bring down multiple airliners over the Atlantic Ocean. We ordered the birthday cake to go.

* * *

The birthday dinner took place on the Sunday evening before my last week as deputy director. Five days later I would step down from my three-and-a-half-year assignment as the Agency's deputy director, enter CIA's Transition Program, and prepare to retire from the Agency after thirty-three years of service.

For the previous fifteen years, I had been obsessed with al Qaʻida and the threat it posed. In the late 1990s, I monitored increasingly worrisome intelligence coming in about the then-obscure terrorist group. At the time I was the executive assistant to Director of Central Intelligence George Tenet. Like Tenet, I was frightened by what I saw and concerned that few in or outside government shared our alarm.

Then, in early 2001, I began an assignment as the daily intelligence briefer for the newly elected president of the United States, George W. Bush. Again and again I would deliver warnings in the President's Daily Brief that were both ominous in their potential and frustrating in their lack of actionable specificity. You could not have lived through the day of 9/11 at the president's side and looked down from Air Force One at the smoldering ruins of the Pentagon, as I did, without becoming obsessed by the issue of terrorism or vowing to do everything possible to prevent the recurrence of such a tragedy.

In the decade that followed 9/11, the United States and its premier intelligence agency, CIA, had enormous successes in their fight against terrorism, and a few significant failures. I was part of both—from CIA's failure to correctly assess Iraq's capabilities regarding weapons of mass destruction to the operation that brought Usama bin Ladin to justice. I also had to deal with the political backlash that occurred against the aggressive counterterrorism programs put in place in the aftermath of 9/11. One issue in particular was CIA's use of harsh interrogation techniques to acquire information from captured senior al Qa'ida operatives. A second was the NSA's operations to ensure that terrorists could never again take advantage of the pre-9/11 seam that had existed between overseas intelligence collection and domestic law enforcement.

* * *

In early October 2013—just weeks after my retirement—I received a phone call from a good and trusted friend. He asked me to consider writing a book. I said, "No, that is not what professional intelligence officers do," but as I thought about the phone call, I changed my mind. Three things led me to this conclusion—and to this book. First, I wanted to tell the remarkable story of CIA's fight against the group that killed nearly three thousand people on that beautiful sunny morning in September 2001. No department or agency has done more to keep the country safe than CIA, and I wanted Americans to know that.

Second, without putting our operations at risk, I believed more can and should be shared with the American people about what the Agency does every day. This is important because popular culture creates many myths about the Agency. One is that the Agency is all-powerful—that there is no secret it cannot steal or discover, no threat it cannot disrupt, and no adversary it cannot defeat. This is the "Jack Ryan" myth from countless Tom Clancy novels. Then there is the opposite view, that the Agency is incompetent, made up of people who screw up everything they touch. This is the "Maxwell Smart" myth from the 1960s TV series *Get Smart* and the 2008 movie with the same title. Finally, and most perniciously, is the notion that CIA is a rogue agency—sometimes succeeding, sometimes failing, but always pursuing its own agenda, all without the authority, direction, or control of America's elected leaders. This is the "Jason Bourne" myth, from the wildly popular book and film series.

The truth is that all these myths are wrong. CIA gets many things right and a few things wrong. And in my experience CIA officers always did what they thought was best for the country, and they undertook operations only with the approval, authorization, and direction of our nation's elected leaders. Creating an accurate picture of CIA is important because the Agency is a secret organization operating in a democracy, and the American people need to have confidence that the Agency is functioning both effectively and within the Constitution and laws of the United States.

Third, and most important, I wanted to tell Americans how deeply concerned I am about the threat that remains to our country from al Qa'ida and various groups associated with it. The threat of terrorism has not gone away. It did not die in Abbottabad along with Bin Ladin. It is going to be with us for decades to come, and as a nation we must be prepared. If we are not, we will, with certainty, face another devastating attack on our homeland.

Taken together, these three reasons are why I decided to write a book and why I decided to focus it on the Agency's fight against terrorism—the great war of our time.

* * *

In July 2013, the threat reporting coming out of Yemen skyrocketed. The intelligence was clear—al Qa'ida in the Arabian Peninsula (AQAP), the al Qa'ida franchise most closely tied to the al Qa'ida leadership in Pakistan and the one posing the greatest threat to the United States, was planning attacks against American interests. The reporting pointed to multiple targets and attacks of significance. But, as is almost always the case, the intelligence was frustratingly lacking in details—about targets, locations, and timing.

The hope of a quiet last few weeks on the job turned out to be wishful thinking. I had to cancel many of the visits I had planned throughout the Agency to say thank you to the women and men of CIA for all the hard work that they do for the country and all the work they had done for me as deputy director (and twice acting director). My days, evenings, and nights—including the birthday dinner—were now consumed with the new threat reporting.

Our counterterrorist experts briefed me multiple times a day, and I took their information and analysis to the National Security Council's Deputies Committee—a policy-making forum of the number two officials from the most important national security departments and agencies in the US government. The Deputies Committee is where departments and agencies share information to understand issues, develop strategies to deal with them, and make policy recommendations to the "principals"—the heads of their agencies—and ultimately to the president. I told my colleagues, "This is the most serious threat reporting I have seen during my three and a half years as deputy director."

They paid attention. The deputies recommended actions to our bosses on the Principals Committee and to President Obama. The president made decisions to protect our diplomats and to disrupt the terrorists. He ordered embassies in the region closed for a number of days—with some sending their employees home to make the US footprint smaller.

And he ordered a flurry of drone strikes in Yemen. The targets of the drones were those AQAP members the United States knew were at the center of the attack plotting. This action was successful. The plot, which turned out to be simultaneous AQAP attacks against US diplomatic facilities in Yemen as well as Yemeni military facilities, was disrupted. It was called off because many of the key operatives involved in the plot had been killed by US air strikes. Hundreds of lives were saved. It was another in a line of unheralded intelligence and military successes in the war against al Qaʿida. And it was the last issue in which I was involved as an intelligence officer—my final engagement in a war that had defined my career.

*   *   *

What follows is the story of CIA's fight against al Qaʿida told from the perspective of someone who always seemed to find himself in the middle of history-making events and who has always been nonpartisan—seeking and reporting the truth no matter what policy-makers wanted to hear—serving six different presidents, three Republicans and three Democrats. There are, of course, many things related to this story that I cannot recount because they are and should remain secret. What I can promise is that I will offer an intimate, insider's look at how we at CIA have faced the biggest threat to our nation since the darkest days of the Cold War.

CHAPTER 1

Opening Salvos

On Friday, August 7, 1998, Molly Hardy was a CIA officer operating under cover in Nairobi, Kenya. Molly was from Georgia, and she had single-handedly raised a daughter as she traveled the world over a lengthy career. Molly was a finance officer, and a good one. Her job was handing out and keeping track of the money that CIA uses to pay its sources for the information that keeps America safe. She dealt largely in cash—in many different currencies and many different denominations. In August 1998 she was fifty-one and a grandmother, and she was looking forward to returning home to see her granddaughter.

For a number of weeks over the summer of 1998, intelligence sources had been picking up chatter among terrorists about a looming attack, about coming "good news." But the talk was non-specific about target, location, and timing. All of those missing details would become clear on the morning of August 7.

At ten thirty a.m. Molly, among many others at the embassy in Nairobi, heard gunfire and a small explosion from a grenade. It was the breach of the embassy security barrier by al Qaʻida suicide bombers. The noise attracted employees to the windows—including Molly. Molly, sensing what was about to happen, warned others to stay away from the windows and to "get down." As she did, a massive truck bomb exploded—destroying a large part of the embassy as well as much of an adjacent building. Over two hundred people were killed—including twelve Americans. More than four thousand were injured. Molly's last words were heroic ones, saving the lives of many of her embassy colleagues. Molly was among CIA's first casualties at the hands of Bin Ladin.

* * *

In Washington, eight thousand miles from Nairobi and Dar es Salaam—where there was a near-simultaneous attack against our embassy in Tanzania—it was the middle of the night. My wife, Mary Beth, and I, along with our three children, were fast asleep in our small three-bedroom house in Arlington, Virginia. It was the type of house a mid-level intelligence officer could afford. Our two older children, Sarah and Luke, had their own bedrooms, but Peter, our baby, was sleeping in a crib in the master bedroom. At the time I was the executive assistant to the director of central intelligence, George Tenet, and one of the requirements of my job was that I have a special STU-III secure telephone at home so I could discuss classified information at any time. Because our house was cramped, the secure phone was on the floor of the master bedroom, under Peter's crib, and that night, as usual, it was also buried under a pile of laundry.

The ringing jolted me awake. I scrambled to find the phone and answer it before it woke Mary Beth or Peter. I failed on both counts, and Peter loudly expressed his displeasure. I had taken my share of calls in the middle of the night, but this one was not typical. The senior duty officer from the CIA Operations Center, the Agency's most senior officer after hours, told me that a DOD (Department of Defense) satellite system had detected two enormous explosions in East Africa. He added that other reports, most important from the State Department Operations Center, had confirmed large explosions at the US embassies in Nairobi and Dar es Salaam, and that these were quite clearly terrorist attacks. I told the officer to wake Director Tenet and tell him everything—one of only two times I woke him during my two years as his executive assistant (the other being when CIA-provided information led NATO to accidently bomb the Chinese embassy in Belgrade). I quickly showered, jumped in my car, and headed to work.

* * *

At this point in my career, I was an eighteen-year veteran of CIA, an organization that has three primary missions: collecting secrets clandestinely, conducting all-source analysis for the president and his senior advisors, and undertaking actions covertly to further US foreign policy objectives. No one who had known me as a young man would have even predicted that CIA would hire me. I did not get serious about education until I was a senior in high school. I lived at home during college, never traveled overseas, and did not speak a foreign language.

I majored in economics, and my aspiration was to go to graduate school, earn a PhD, and teach. But one of my professors had a different idea. "You ought to send a résumé to the CIA," he said, stressing that the Agency hired economists and that it might be a good fit for me. My professor knew that economics is one of a handful of academic disciplines that teaches critical thinking—the number one skill needed to be a successful intelligence analyst.

To be honest, I had little understanding of CIA or what an economist would do there, and even less interest in joining its ranks. But on a lark I sent off an application and was surprised a few months later to be invited for a visit. I had never been to Washington, D.C., and after four austere years living at home while going to college, I figured it would be a treat to see the sights. I set off for our nation's capital with no intent of accepting a job offer from CIA.

What I found when I arrived, however, was a group of amazingly talented people who were enormously dedicated to an important mission. I found an Agency that was helping the nation address a world of challenges, including an ongoing hostage crisis in Iran and the Soviet invasion of Afghanistan. It needed young men and women to help unravel some enormously complex issues. It was enticing, but I told my recruiter that I really had my heart set on graduate school. "No problem," he said. "Come here. Do a good job. We'll eventually send you to grad school on our dime" (a promise on which the Agency would make good). I accepted an entry-level job paying fifteen thousand dollars a year and began my career as an intelligence analyst.

As an analyst I was fortunate to be involved in some important work early on. For example, I led a small team that statistically demonstrated—using a combination of information provided by intelligence sources and the Philippine government's publicly released election results—that President Ferdinand Marcos had stolen the presidential election in 1986 from Corazón Aquino. Marcos had used a new technique—the systematic disenfranchisement of millions of voters in areas expected to vote in large numbers for Aquino. Our analysis showed that Marcos's 54–46 victory would have been a victory for Aquino by a wide margin in a fair election. CIA's findings played a role in the Reagan administration's decision to distance itself from Marcos after the election, which helped lead to his fall from power only weeks later in the peaceful "People Power Revolution." It was exhilarating to be a young analyst and to see my work have such impact. I was hooked. And then, in the early 1990s, I was involved in a larger team effort that uncovered the nascent North Korean nuclear weapons program, which remains a serious threat to this day. Our work included supporting the initial US diplomatic negotiations with the North Koreans on the issue—analysts providing real-time assistance to the US negotiating team.

Most of my time, however, was spent on East Asian economic issues—significant matters but not the stuff of spy novels. In 1996, however, an unexpected part-time assignment changed the course of my career. At the time, CIA Director John Deutch and his deputy, George Tenet, were fielding complaints from the secretary of the treasury, Robert Rubin, and his deputy, Larry Summers, about the intelligence community's collection of information on economic matters. (This followed the French declaring persona non grata a senior Agency official in Paris for allegedly stealing information on French trade policy.) Rubin and Summers believed that much of the effort the intelligence community was expending to obtain economic data on other countries, as well as other nations' plans for economic policy, was unnecessary and could become counterproductive to our diplomatic relationships with those countries. Tenet, whom I had met briefly on several occasions, asked me to lead an interagency team to examine the question.

The bottom line of my study was that Rubin and Summers were right. Much of what the intelligence community was collecting on economic issues was available through public means, or what is internally referred to as "open-source" information. Even though the study went against the status quo, it was well received, particularly by Tenet, who told me that he liked the rigor of the report and the clarity with which the results were conveyed. Not surprisingly, Rubin and Summers liked the answer as well, with Rubin writing a letter to Deutch complimenting the study.

Just eighteen months later, Director Deutch stepped down as

DCI and was succeeded by Tenet. On December 11, 1997, I was at Arlington Hospital in Virginia waiting for Mary Beth to deliver our third child, Peter. A phone rang—not in the waiting room and not at the nurses' station but in the delivery room. Mary Beth, in the initial stages of labor, did not look pleased. Neither did the attending nurse who answered, then handed me the phone, saying with some sarcasm, "It's for you." On the other end of the line was a friend, Greg Tarbell, who at the time was the daily intelligence briefer for Director Tenet and who would later become my chief of staff when I served as deputy director and acting director. Being resourceful, Tarbell had tracked down the phone number in the delivery room.

Tarbell said with some excitement, "I know you are busy, but I thought you'd want to know—Tenet told me this morning that he remembered the good work you did on that economic intelligence study and that he is considering asking you to be his new EA." Being tapped to serve as the director's executive assistant would be a significant career opportunity, but with my mind understandably elsewhere, I ended the call by simply saying, "That's interesting." Mary Beth asked, "Who was that?" I gave her the standard answer that an Agency officer provides to a questioning spouse, "Oh, it was nothing," and I went back to my primary job of delivering ice chips on demand.

A few days after Peter's birth, I was back at work. Tenet called me to his office to offer me the job. As I crossed the threshold of his long, rectangular office, he handed me a cigar from his private stash to offer congratulations on Peter's arrival. Excited, I accepted the position on the spot.

Exciting, however, is not the word I would use to describe the first few weeks on the job. *Overwhelming* was more like it. I had never had a job anything like it before. It was 24/7 and totally consuming. I was the director's only executive assistant at the time; now there are two or three, depending on the director. I was reluctant to get up from my desk to walk down to the cafeteria for lunch, or even to visit the men's room, for fear that the stack of new e-mails in my inbox would double during even a brief absence. On top of this, I had, at first, no earthly clue what people were talking about. Tenet and his senior subordinates from across the agency often spoke or wrote in the kind of shorthand that only people who have worked an issue for a long time can understand. And there were so many cryptonyms (code words) to learn that my head was swimming. Furthermore, the breadth and scope of the issues coming at me were unlike anything I could have imagined.

After I had been on the job for a few weeks, Tenet said as I handed him a report, "Are you OK?" I fibbed and told him everything was fine. But as time went on I caught up to the pace of the work and also learned the lingo. I kept my head well above water, and I settled into one of the best jobs of my life.

One of the things that made the job special was the chance to work with Tenet, the most down-to-earth, approachable senior government official I have ever met. The son of Greek immigrants, who learned hard work busing tables in his father's diner in Queens, Tenet has an everyman quality about him that makes him impossible to dislike. He is brilliant in an unthreatening way, and kings and cafeteria workers thought he was their best friend. And they were right. Ranging from slightly to very rumpled in appearance, Tenet set an informal mood in the office, where he would frequently burst out in Motown hits like Aretha Franklin's "Respect," do spot-on imitations of foreign leaders (he did an incredible Yasser Arafat), or dribble a basketball in the hallways of the Agency. Tenet never took himself too seriously, a vital trait in a place where the work, which he attacked vigorously, was often a matter of life and death (literally).

I loved working for him. There were four main parts to the

job—any one of which might have kept me fully occupied. First I was to review every piece of information coming into the director's office—whether in a letter, memo, e-mail, cable, phone call, or personal visit—and make a snap decision on whether Tenet needed to know it or not and, if so, whether he needed to know it immediately or it could wait for that evening's nightly "Read Book." Information was flooding in every minute from many different sources. If I passed too much of it to the boss, he would be overwhelmed and unable to focus on the most critical matters. If I kept some critical bit of intelligence from the director, something could go badly wrong.

The second duty was to review and organize decisions that he needed to make—in the form of official brown folders from various parts of the organization asking the director for a formal judgment on a wide range of issues, informal questions to which someone needed an answer, and letters drafted by others for the director to sign and send. If I decided something was routine—if I was confident that I knew how Tenet thought about the issue—I could have a machine (called an autopen) sign it. I would then put a copy of what had gone out in the director's name in his overnight reading materials. This autopen was to become the source of my first mistake as EA.

A senior Agency officer named Joan Dempsey—who had just finished a stint as Tenet's chief of staff—handed me a letter that she said needed to be signed right away and sent to the secretary of defense. The subject, an intelligence community technical issue, was incomprehensible to me, but she assured me it was no big deal and I should simply have the guys down the hall crank up the machine and affix the "George J. Tenet" signature to the letter she had drafted. Trusting her judgment, I did just that and put a copy of the resulting letter in Tenet's thick pile of materials to read at home that night, telling him in a note that I had sent the letter to the "SECDEF." The next morning I got the letter back with Tenet's distinctive scrawl all over it. At the top he had written, "Never ever, ever, ever...," and the *ever*s continued across the top of the page... down the right side, upside down across the bottom, and up the left-hand margin. After the final *ever*, he'd written, "autopen a letter to a cabinet member!"

Properly chagrined, I affixed a Post-it note to the letter: "Your instructions are not clear to me. Would you please clarify?" I put it in the night's reading file. He accepted my riposte in good humor, which tells you a great deal about the kind of boss he was.

My third responsibility was to make sure that when Tenet was scheduled to have a meeting he had everything he needed in advance. This was perhaps the toughest part of the job, because some materials that came forward from lower levels of the Agency and intelligence community were poorly written, badly argued, confusing, or just too long. So I would have to rewrite a lot of stuff on the fly—particularly talking points for his use at White House meetings. Often I did a good job, but sometimes not. Once he read a page of talking points and, not thinking much of it, asked, "Who was the idiot who wrote this?" I raised my hand and said, "That would be me."

The final part of the job was to do whatever else he asked of me. I was a messenger, a deliverer of good news and bad, a source of information on morale in the building, a traveling companion, the butt of many jokes, and the participant in much humor. Tenet once threatened to give me as a gift to a world leader who had a special interest in young men, going so far as to quickly leave a dinner with the leader while I was visiting the restroom. Luckily I jumped into the last car as the director's motorcade left the presidential palace. On another occasion, in a large meeting in the director's conference room, we were discussing a request from another foreign leader for six helicopters as "payment" for operational support that that country had just undertaken on behalf of the Agency. Tenet responded to the leader's request by saying, "How about we give him three helicopters and Morell?" The room exploded in laughter.

But I had my moments. Tenet was in his office with his senior leadership team late one morning, just before leaving for a particularly important testimony in front of the Senate Intelligence Committee—to explain how CIA had failed to predict India's May 1988 test of a nuclear weapon. Tenet asked for one piece of advice from everyone and started around the room. I quickly calculated that I would be last, but I didn't know if Tenet planned to ask me, since I was the most junior officer in the room. But when the circle ended with me, Tenet did ask, "Any thoughts?" I said, "Pull up your zipper!" I had noticed when we entered the room that his fly was down. The room broke into laughter, and Tenet said, "Finally, a fucking piece of advice that is actually useful." Tenet had a way with colorful language.

* * *

The global array of problems that the director of central intelligence had to worry about was mind-boggling. At the start of each calendar year, the Agency's director was obliged to appear before the Senate and House intelligence oversight committees and lay out what concerns him. In January 1998 Tenet did just that, and he had no shortage of things to discuss. Each of the five main areas of challenge he talked about was suddenly something on which I had to quickly come up to speed. At the top of his list of worries were transnational issues that threatened all Americans. Included in this category were the proliferation of weapons of mass destruction, international terrorism, drug trafficking, information warfare (what we would call cyber warfare today), and, interestingly, the fallout from a financial crisis that had befallen Asia.

Close behind those worries was a second major category—the threat posed by major powers like Russia and China. The two traditional foes of the United States were on very different trajectories—Russia down and China up—and both were trying to navigate difficult political and economic transformations. Next was the threat from rogue nations like Iraq, North Korea, Libya, and Iran. Fourth on Tenet's list were regional trouble spots like the Middle East, South Asia, and Bosnia. And finally he mentioned humanitarian emergencies caused by natural disasters, ethnic conflict, and foreign government mismanagement—any one of which could suddenly place heavy demands on US military and economic resources.

That was quite a list, and the director could not afford to ignore any part of it. But I can tell you there was one entry on that parade of threats that dominated his days and thus mine—and that was international terrorism. This was a revelation to me. Throughout my prior time at the Agency I had had little involvement in that arena, and the vast majority of my colleagues at Langley would have told you that counterterrorism—or "CT"—was not a front-burner issue. But Tenet didn't see it that way. For years before 9/11, the terror threat was the single issue that would keep him up at night. He was focused on it, laser-like.

The counterterrorism arena had a dizzying array of bad guys—Lebanese Hezbollah, responsible for several mass attacks against the United States and for more American fatalities than any terrorist group prior to 9/11; Egyptian terrorist groups al-Gama'a al-Islamiyya and the Islamic Jihad, the latter responsible for the assassination of Egyptian president Anwar Sadat in 1981; Palestinian groups responsible for multiple attacks against Israel; and many others outside the Middle East—ranging from the Irish Republican Army in the United Kingdom to the Sendero Luminoso or "Shining Path" in Peru. But the one group on which Tenet was intensely focused—and the one that caught my attention as I read and listened—was a group called "al Qa'ida," under the leadership of a man named Usama bin Ladin.

* * *

Bin Ladin was born in 1957 in Riyadh, Saudi Arabia, the son of one of the kingdom's richest men. Usama, meaning "lion," attended King Abdulaziz University. While he took practical courses in construction engineering and business administration, undoubtedly under pressure from his family, his true passion was religion, studying the Koran and what it meant for how Muslims should live their lives. At school, Bin Ladin became close to members of the Muslim Brotherhood, an Islamic organization intent on imposing Koranic law throughout Muslim societies. He loved poetry, black stallions, and soccer. He was an avid follower of English football.

After college Bin Ladin was drawn to the war in Afghanistan. He felt a religious duty to support the Afghan freedom fighters, and he went to South Asia in the early 1980s. As he traveled back and forth between Afghanistan and Pakistan, his role was one of funding and organizing the flow of foreigners into Afghanistan to fight the Soviets. (Despite many stories over the years to the contrary, CIA never worked with Bin Ladin in the Agency's own efforts to drive the Soviets out of Afghanistan in the 1980s.) Bin Ladin's time in South Asia convinced him that ideologically motivated insurgents can defeat a much better-equipped and -trained military force. It was the defining experience of his life.

Bin Ladin had two advantages as he moved through life—a

piece of his family's wealth, which helped him in his early years, and, even more important, charisma. His personality was magnetic. This was not an American-style appeal consisting of a dominant personality that could take over a room. It was an Arab-style charisma made of a soft-spoken, poetic voice and a gentleness of movement in the manner of the Prophet Muhammad.

* * *

CIA's interest in Bin Ladin began during his time in Sudan, from 1991 to 1996, when he combined business ventures with jihad. Bin Ladin established terrorist training camps in Sudan and financed the travel of hundreds of Afghan War veterans to Sudan to attend those camps. In late 1992, Bin Ladin financed the bombing of a hotel in Aden, Yemen, housing US servicemen, and in 1996 he sent his operatives to Somalia to work as advisors to the warlord Mohammed Farrah Aidid, responsible for the tragedy commonly referred to as "Black Hawk Down." These were Bin Ladin's opening salvos against the United States, but we learned of his role only years later. We also learned later that during this time Bin Ladin acquired what would be an enduring interest in acquiring weapons of mass destruction.

Bin Ladin's early activities create an interesting dichotomy. As far as most Americans are concerned, the fight against al Qa'ida began in 1998 in East Africa or on 9/11. But from Bin Ladin's perspective, he had been at war against the United States dating back to 1992.

CIA knew that Bin Ladin relocated to Afghanistan from Sudan in late 1996, taking many operatives with him. What we did not know at the time was whether Bin Ladin was just a financier of terrorists or the head of a terrorist organization himself. Because his name was popping up in the intelligence so much, CIA decided to find out. The Agency in 1996 created a special unit to follow Bin Ladin, called Alec Station. Unlike a typical CIA station, this one was based in the United States, within driving distance of CIA headquarters. (The code name Alec was taken from the unit chief's oldest son.) Its initial objective was to find out who Bin Ladin really was.

By 1997, Alec Station had its answer. CIA had learned and had told policy-makers that Bin Ladin was the head of a terrorist organization whose goal was the establishment of a global caliphate. And we had learned and reported that, to Bin Ladin, the United States was the key to his goal—and therefore the prime target or, as al Qa'ida referred to us, the "far enemy." To achieve his caliphate he had to drive the United States out of the Middle East and then overthrow what he saw as the US-supported apostate leaders currently sitting atop the countries in that region, al Qa'ida's so-called near enemies.

Not only did the intelligence make that known, but so did Bin Ladin himself, publicly. He announced his intentions to attack the United States with great clarity. In at least five public statements between mid-1995 and early 1998, Bin Ladin professed his hatred for America and everything it represents. He directly announced his intent to force us to retreat from the Muslim world. And he stated his plan to acquire and use weapons of mass destruction, which he called a "religious duty." In international relations, sometimes the best indicator of what someone is going to do is what he tells you he is going to do. And, since it is a religious obligation in Islam to warn your enemies in advance, there was reason to pay particular attention to what he had to say. While the intelligence community did so, Bin Ladin's public statements generated little interest among the American media—even though some of his pronouncements were made directly to US news outlets.

To put teeth behind his rhetoric, Bin Ladin, under the protection of the Taliban, was increasing his capabilities. Al Qaʻida built training camps in Afghanistan, attracting recruits from all over the world and turning out committed jihadists by the thousands. Bin Ladin built a document forgery capability and mechanisms to move money securely.

CIA was not just collecting information on Bin Ladin and his activities; it was actively trying to undermine him. Alec Station was working hard on a program to disrupt his finances, arrest the operatives he sent abroad, and bring him to justice. Thanks to Tenet, we were not sitting on our hands, but the rest of the Agency, with the exception of Alec Station, did not take al Qaʻida as seriously as did its director.

Significantly, Alec Station, arguably one of the most important CIA operational units at the time, was led by an analyst. As a career analyst myself, I strongly believed that people from my career path could make enormous contributions. But I couldn't get over that the leader of Alec Station—an officer by the name of Mike Scheuer— was not a trained operations officer and that few operations officers played a significant role in the unit.

Alec Station also did not get the support it needed to do its job. Part of this was due to Scheuer's personality. He was a zealot. In the years before 9/11, I don't think anyone knew more or cared as much about al Qaʻida. His analytic assessments were always on the mark, but he also had a penchant for angering anyone who didn't see things exactly as he did. Scheuer was constantly getting into fights with the FBI, the NSA, and his own bosses within the Directorate of Operations. (Mike got a chance to vent when he anonymously published a couple of books, but he eventually left the Agency bitter and questioning our commitment to the fight.) But I am convinced that the Agency did not give him enough support in part because Scheuer was an analyst. At the time there were strong divisions between the operational and analytic sides of CIA. When

I started in 1980, the two organizations were on different sides of the building and their officers ate in different cafeterias. There was a strong "not invented here" culture in the Directorate of Operations. I believe the DO, as we called it, rejected Scheuer because he was not one of its own.

The lack of support also reflected the fact that not all levels of management understood the source of the passion Alec Station's officers brought to the job. And not all CIA managers understood that because the threat had not yet manifested itself. They could not see it and feel it (this was also an issue in the broader government and in the country at large). One of the analysts in Alec Station was once counseled that she was spending too much of her career on Bin Ladin.

Scheuer frequently complained about the lack of support. For example, he believed he did not receive the backing he needed from the Agency's geographic operational units (the "owners" of our overseas stations), from other agencies in the intelligence community, or from foreign intelligence services. And Scheuer believed that his superiors in CIA did not push those organizations hard enough to be more forthcoming. Some of this was hyperbole, but some of it reflected reality. Scheuer was a frequent visitor to my office after a meeting in the director's suite and would share his frustrations with me. I wondered to myself if an operations officer, as chief of Alec, would have received more support. I thought so, and would occasionally share this view with Tenet.

Perhaps one of the best examples of this lack of support was the reaction of the leadership of the Directorate of Operations—headed at the time by a gruff Cold Warrior named Jack Downing—to a plan from Alec Station to capture Bin Ladin. The plan, put together in the fall of 1997 under the presidential authorities we had at the time to undermine and degrade terrorist groups, called for members of a particular Afghan tribe, codenamed TRODPINTS and with an undistinguished record of fighting, to ambush Bin Ladin, capture him alive (despite his being under constant heavy guard by highly trained gunmen), whisk him off, and hide him in a cave for up to a month until a US military aircraft could swoop in clandestinely and spirit him out of Afghanistan. The plan from Scheuer and his team, presented to Tenet in the spring of 1998, was imaginative and aggressive, but it had little chance of succeeding. This was an overly complicated paramilitary operation. The more moving parts in such an operation, the greater the risk of failure, and there were a lot of moving parts in the Alec Station plan. There was also an issue regarding collateral damage, as Bin Ladin seemed constantly surrounded by his wives and children. The Covert Action Review Group, the board of senior officers at the Agency that reviews all covert action proposals, gave the operation only a 30 percent chance of success. All in all, it was a poorly conceived plan.

But what struck me most about the Alec Station proposal was that it ever showed up in the director's office. Not a single person in Scheuer's chain of command thought his plan was wise. Typically the Directorate of Operations would protect its people and not let them see the boss unless everyone was supportive of whatever plan they had in mind. But in this case they brought Scheuer in, allowed him to do the briefing, then, once Scheuer left the room, told Tenet (correctly, in my view) that the plan was implausible.

I asked myself why Scheuer's bosses would let him hang out there like that. The answer, it seemed to me, was that he was a mere analyst they did not respect and to whom they owed nothing. And yet they did not seem to respect Alec Station's mission sufficiently to put one of their own in the job—until after the threat became real, after the East Africa bombings, when Scheuer was replaced with one of the best operations officers of his generation.

One of the consequences of the way Alec Station was managed in the early years was that we did not have al Qa'ida penetrated with spies to the extent that we should have. While we knew a bit from spies on the periphery about the organization and its plans and intentions, we had few human sources—fewer than a handful—with access to the leadership of al Qa'ida itself. This significantly lowered the chances that we would detect an attack in preparation and disrupt it. This was the fundamental responsibility of Alec Station, and its failure helped lead to the bombings of our embassies in East Africa; this failure did not even start to get remedied until the leadership of Alec Station changed and a career operations officer was placed in charge and until the East Africa bombings galvanized the rest of the Agency.

The bottom line is that Mike Scheuer should have been in Alec Station as the senior analyst—but he should not have been running the show. That job should have gone to an experienced operations officer from the very beginning. And the rest of the clandestine service should have been pushed harder to support the work of Alec Station. These were failures on the part of Downing and his leadership team.

*　*　*

My drive to work on the morning the embassies in Kenya and Tanzania were bombed brought me to the office at five a.m. Tenet was already there. I gathered all the materials on the bombing, read them carefully, and highlighted key passages for the director, who was on and off the phone with a number of his colleagues around government. At eight a.m. we assembled the relevant players in the director's conference room to go over what we knew, what we did not know, and what we needed to do. Tenet walked into the conference room, sat in his usual spot—in the middle of the table rather than at the head, a gesture that is respected by the workforce in the egalitarian CIA—and immediately asked the assembled representatives "Who did this?" Scheuer, sitting directly across from the director, responded almost instantaneously, "This is al Qa'ida; no doubt about it." Although we did not yet have a shred of intelligence linking al Qa'ida to the attack, no one questioned Scheuer because everyone in the room knew he was right.

By Sunday evening, just two days after the bombing, we had intelligence from a human source that confirmed Scheuer's instinct. That night we gathered in Tenet's office, and I listened as he spoke on a secure telephone with President Clinton, National Security Advisor Sandy Berger, Secretary of State Madeleine Albright, Secretary of Defense Bill Cohen, and other members of the National Security Council (NSC) in a conference call about the attacks. Tenet briefed them on the intelligence pointing strongly to Bin Ladin's responsibility for the deaths of twelve Americans, including CIA's Molly Hardy. The entire country, for the first time, was now aware of Bin Ladin and al Qa'ida.

Tenet taught me an important lesson in leadership that evening. We were waiting for the talking points for the director's call with the president, and they were late. I was becoming impatient, wondering aloud, "What the hell are they doing down there?" Tenet counseled me, saying, "Calm down. They are doing the best they can." He went on to say that in a crisis situation, everyone is working all out and there is no need to push, that doing so would actually be counterproductive. "In the normal day-to-day situation—in the absence of a crisis—is when folks need a swift kick in the butt," he said.

In the immediate aftermath of the embassy bombings, Tenet went to visit the troops in Alec Station to bolster their morale, and I went along. It wasn't an unusual event for him. He regularly "went walkabout" and enjoyed popping in unannounced to offices all over the headquarters complex. He relished bantering with Agency officers of all ranks much more than he liked rubbing elbows with senior administration officials. But this occasion was not at all enjoyable.

After he made brief informal remarks, one of the analysts, a woman who was among those intensely loyal to Mike Scheuer, raised her hand and said, "Mr. Director, I hope you know that if you had let us proceed with the plan to capture Bin Ladin some months ago the attacks on the embassies would not have happened." She was blaming Tenet for the attacks and the deaths of Americans. I found it to be a stunning, disrespectful, and inaccurate thing to say. Such an outburst was also highly unusual in Agency culture, but many of her coworkers seemed to agree with her fully. To his credit, Tenet did not respond harshly but simply said something about everyone having a right to his or her opinion. In fact, the plan to go after Bin Ladin had had a minimal chance of success, and we later learned through intelligence sources that the plots to blow up our embassies had been under way long before the proposed capture of Bin Ladin. And later, when the TRODPINTS were given the green light to go after Bin Ladin, they failed miserably to put together any workable plan.

Once we were certain that al Qaʻida was responsible for the embassy attacks, President Clinton wanted to hit back hard. Al Qaʻida training camps in Afghanistan were an obvious target, and we were fortunate enough to intercept an al Qaʻida communication that told us Bin Ladin and other senior al Qaʻida leaders were likely to be meeting at one of the group's training camps near Khost, Afghanistan, a few days hence. That became target number one. But the president and others wanted to strike at least two targets, since two embassies had been hit, and he wanted to hit somewhere outside

Afghanistan to demonstrate a willingness by the United States to go beyond the group's sanctuary. From a list of other potential sites, a pharmaceutical plant in Khartoum, Sudan, that was suspected of producing chemical weapons for al Qaʻida was selected.

Early on the morning of August 20—the day of the US military response—Tenet was woken by a two a.m. phone call from President Clinton, who asked if he was comfortable with the plan. Tenet later told me that he advised the president that the attack on the training camp near Khost was a "no-brainer," but that he was less convinced about the plan to hit the al-Shifa pharmaceutical plant. Tenet told me that the president said something like, "That's OK; I want al Qaʻida, if they are going to attack us, to wonder a bit how I am going to respond."

As it turned out, the US counterattacks—our opening shot in the new war against al Qaʻida—were not a great success. The strike on the training camps killed only a handful of terrorists, as Bin Ladin and his al Qaʻida leadership had left Khost a short while before seventy-five cruise missiles hit. While we were never able to prove it, I strongly suspect that someone tipped him off. The United States had sent General Joe Ralston, vice chairman of the Joint Chiefs of Staff, to Pakistan to let its government know that US cruise missiles would soon be transiting Pakistani airspace en route to Afghanistan. There had been plenty of time for some sympathizer within the Pakistani government to warn Bin Ladin, and I suspect someone did.

The attack on the pharmaceutical plant was worse. As it turned out, the plant was not involved in the production of chemical weapons. The key intelligence that had driven the decision to attack the facility—that CIA had collected a soil sample outside the plant that contained a precursor for chemical weapons (O-ethyl methylphosphonothioic acid, or EMPTA)—was shaky at best. And we were wrong in our assessment that the owner of the factory was a person associated with Bin Ladin. He was not.

Rather than viewing the failed attack on the al Qaʻida training camp as a near miss, I am convinced that Bin Ladin and his associates saw it and the strike on the pharmaceutical factory in Khartoum as victories. First of all, Bin Ladin had narrowly escaped—garnering even more status among extremists as a result—and second, he was convinced that we had embarrassed ourselves in the eyes of the world by blowing up what critics of the strike called an "aspirin factory." There is no doubt that this had an emboldening effect.

One of the key consequences of the East Africa bombings was an even more determined director of central intelligence. On the flight home from a December 1998 meeting with our British counterparts in London—during which the discussion had been dominated by the threat from al Qaʻida—Tenet took out a pad of legal paper and handwrote the first draft of a letter to the leadership of CIA and the leaders of all the agencies of the intelligence community. (At the time, in addition to leading his own agency, the CIA director also provided leadership for all the agencies of the intelligence community. In April 2005 the position of director of national intelligence took over that role as a result of the passage and signing of the Intelligence Reform and Terrorism Prevention Act in late 2004.) Tenet wrote furiously for forty-five minutes, and when he finished, he ripped the pages from the pad and handed them to me. He simply said, "Here." As I read what he had written, I was struck by the language. The director made clear that we should consider ourselves at war with al Qaʻida and that no effort or resource should be spared in prosecuting the war.

For CIA, the "we are at war" memo, as it was called, became an early 1999 directive to the Agency's operational arm to review CIA strategy against al Qaʻida and to suggest enhancements. There was a similar memo for the rest of the intelligence community. Then, in the spring of 1999, as the intelligence grew that Bin Ladin was planning another operation and as our efforts to locate the al Qa'ida leader and remove him from the battlefield were going nowhere, Tenet asked for a new strategy—one not constrained by resources or authorities. In response the Counterterrorism Center in the fall of 1999 produced what was called "the Plan." The Plan involved a major shift in resources to the al Qa'ida problem and greater integration of the Agency with the rest of the intelligence community, particularly the NSA. This work had some real successes, namely the disruption of a number of attacks during the pre-millennium period, both inside the United States and overseas (Tenet had told President Clinton to expect five to fifteen attacks). But these successes did not get us any closer to Bin Ladin.

In the aftermath of the embassy bombings, increased attention was also given at the White House to the Bin Ladin problem. New covert action authorities— called Memorandum of Notifications (MONs), additions to an overall 1986 presidential finding on counterterrorism—were approved to give CIA increased authority to go after Bin Ladin.

A common misconception is that the Central Intelligence Agency conducts covert action on its own authority. This is not true. Covert action can be proposed by the Agency or initiated by the most senior national security officials at the White House. But only with White House approval can CIA put together an actual plan. The policy objective for the plan comes from the White House, and the Agency builds a program designed to meet that objective, producing either a draft finding or a draft MON— essentially a set of authorities giving approval to the Agency to conduct specific activities. That draft is vetted within the Agency and throughout the interagency, including by the Department of Justice; it is approved by both the principals and the deputies of the National Security Council, and it is formally approved by the president via his signature. In keeping with its legal obligations, CIA then notifies the leadership of Congress, the Senate and House intelligence committees, and the two defense appropriations subcommittees from which CIA gets its funding. While Congress is technically only "notified," in reality it can withhold money from the operation and therefore prevent it from getting off the ground. As a participant in this process, I can tell you that it would be very wrong to assume that there is any "rubber-stamping" during any part of it.

People might wonder, with all those steps required—how does anything stay secret? And the answer is that, for the most part, things do not. Most covert actions leak. But, contrary to conventional wisdom, it is not Congress that leaks (there are exceptions). It is generally the White House—as officials there want, for political reasons, to show the American people that it is doing something about a particular national security threat—or officials in executive branch agencies who leak secrets to try to get a leg up in a policy debate.

In the aftermath of the East Africa bombings, President Clinton signed a number of new MONs related to Bin Ladin. Prior to the East Africa bombings, CIA had been permitted only to capture Bin Ladin, and the use of lethal force had been expressly prohibited. The draft of this new MON allowed CIA, using its Afghan surrogates, to kill Bin Ladin if it judged that capture was not feasible during an operation. It was a significant step—essentially allowing CIA to kill a terrorist. The Clinton administration's position, which has remained consistent throughout both the Bush and Obama administrations, was that under the Law of Armed Conflict, killing a person who poses an imminent threat to the United States and who cannot be captured is self-defense, not an assassination.

Sandy Berger, the national security advisor, sent the draft MON to President Clinton on the morning of Christmas eve, 1998. The White House had told us that the president would sign the MON that day, and it fell to me to wait around the office until he did so. My job was to obtain confirmation that the president had signed the document, so that our headquarters officers could send the president's instructions out to the field. Everyone else in the front office had gone home or was on annual leave, but there I was sitting by the phone waiting. Mary Beth was home with her parents and brother, who were visiting, along with the three kids, all under the age of six at the time, waiting for Daddy and Santa, not necessarily in that order. They were all frustrated by my absence, but I could not tell them that I was waiting for an order from President Clinton to kill Bin Ladin.

Late on the afternoon of Christmas eve, the president walked into the White House Situation Room, read the document, and signed it. The White House Situation Room called me, and I, in turn, called the director, the Agency's general counsel, and our director of congressional affairs to inform them. I asked the latter to inform the relevant members of Congress, which he did that evening and the next day. I then sent word to the Counterterrorism Center, so that it could relay instructions to our officers in the field, where it was already the early-morning hours of Christmas day. I got in my car and went home to Christmas eve celebrations, feeling that we were hitting back now more than at any time in al Qa'ida's history.

But the truth was that we were still not fully engaged. There was much more that could have been done on the military and paramilitary fronts. Certainly more covert actions would be signed and more pressure would be put on Bin Ladin and his host the Taliban, but the United States still was not doing everything it could to go after al Qaʻida or to defend against the kind of attacks we were worried about. Even a focused, determined, and popular president, as Bill Clinton was, faced constraints on how far he could go. An attack against two embassies—with twelve Americans killed, including Molly—was not enough to bring the American people to the point where they would support all-out action. That would have to wait for two and a half more years.

CHAPTER 2

The President and the Sheikh

I f you are a Little Leaguer, you fantasize about playing in the World Series. If you are a piano student, you aspire to perform in Carnegie Hall. And if you are a young CIA analyst, your dream job is to be the daily briefer for the president of the United States. I was no different. I grew up in CIA admiring the officers who briefed presidents—including an officer named Chuck Peters, nicknamed Pete, who briefed President George H. W. Bush and was a legend at the Agency for completely rewriting PDB (President's Daily Brief) articles drafted by the analysts, or even writing his own PDB pieces and calling surprised analysts to his office to sign off on them. There was also an officer and friend named John Brennan, now the director of CIA, who was President Bill Clinton's first intelligence briefer.

My dream came true in December 2000 when I was selected to be the briefer for the newly elected George W. Bush. My boss at the time, the Agency's head of analysis, Winston Wiley, called me into his office and offered me the job, saying, "There is no one else who can do this as well as you can."

Although I knew there was hyperbole in what Wiley said, if he thought that this was good for the Agency, then that meant a great deal to me. When he asked me about the briefer job, he and I had just returned from a conference in Hawaii on Asian issues. My five-year-old son Luke was working on a Flat Stanley project for kindergarten class. The project involves a cutout doll—Flat Stanley—and the goal is to get photographs of Stanley taken in as many places around the world as possible. With that objective in mind, I had brought Stanley along with me to Hawaii. When Wiley heard about this, he'd insisted on driving Stanley and me around Oahu and Maui, snapping pictures on the sides of steep volcanoes, stunning green valleys, and beautiful sandy beaches. Luke's project had hit pay dirt. Wiley was the kind of boss who earned total loyalty from his people.

I said yes to Wiley's offer on the spot. He was asking me to walk into the Oval Office every morning. Being a presidential briefer is a huge honor but an even greater responsibility, because what a briefer chooses to show to a president and what he says about it helps shape a commander in chief's view of the world and therefore the decisions he makes on important national security issues. This, of course, is widely known across the senior ranks of the national security team, which pays close attention to what a briefer says to a president. Paul Wolfowitz, the deputy secretary of defense, once sent a letter to George Tenet complaining that something I had told President Bush regarding Taiwan's relationship with the United States was not accurate and he wanted the record corrected. When Tenet showed me the letter, it hit home just how big a deal this job was. Just a couple of months later the importance of the job was again driven home—this time by Steve Hadley, the president's deputy national security advisor. Tenet and I gave Hadley a ride to Camp David on a Saturday morning, and he and I had a conversation about the PDB and the president. I learned a lot from the conversation that would help me in the months ahead but I particularly remember Hadley saying, "The Agency's analysis shapes the president's view of the world. He makes decisions based on your analysis. So you have a huge responsibility to get everything right, every day."

After talking to Wiley about the job, I walked across the suite and met with Wiley's principal deputy, Jami Miscik, who had just returned from a few days of briefing President-elect Bush at the governor's mansion in Austin, Texas. What Miscik said scared the hell out of me. "You will really need to be prepared every day," she said. "He will fire questions at you at a rapid pace and he expects you to be able to answer most of them. He will test you to see how much you know, and he will test you to see if you are willing to say you don't know when you have reached the limits of your knowledge. He doesn't want you guessing or speculating if you don't know. In short, get ready for a challenging assignment." All of a sudden, I was having second thoughts.

By the time I got home that night, I had mostly pushed the second thoughts out of my mind. I told my wife, Mary Beth, the news. Although I have this bad habit of accepting jobs and talking about it with her after the fact, she was OK with the decision. This not only made sense professionally but it also seemed to both of us to make sense from a family perspective. At the time our children were seven, five, and three, and we figured that starting work in the middle of the night and coming home about noon, I would be able to pick the kids up at school, help them with their homework, and just be around more.

With only a week of preparation, I was on my way to Texas to be introduced to the president-elect as his dedicated intelligence briefer. I walked into the kitchen of the Governor's Mansion in Austin where the president-elect had just finished getting a haircut. George W. Bush stood from the chair and with a firm handshake, looking me straight in the eye, said, "Welcome to Texas. Grab a cup of coffee and let's go upstairs to my study."

* * *

The job was another baptism by fire. The first day I watched Wiley do most of the briefing, although he had me walk through one piece about Chinese military modernization "to get my feet wet." The second day I did the entire briefing myself, with Wiley observing. I asked the president-elect if he wanted a Saturday briefing and he said, "No, but call me if you think I need to know something. Otherwise, I will see you on Monday." From then on I would be flying solo.

The second day provided an indication of the high expectations of our new "First Customer," as CIA analysts call the president of the United States. At the end of the briefing, Wiley explained that CIA planned to change the presentational format of the PDB. After a few sentences of detail, the president-elect interrupted him. "Winston," he said, "I don't care about the format. I don't care if you bind it at the top, on the side, hold it together with a paper clip or even spit. What I care about is the content." The president-elect then went on to speak for thirty minutes about his expectations for the intelligence community. He said, "There are people out there who want to hurt the United States. I want you to find out what they are trying to do and tell me. And I don't want to hear that it is hard to do; I know it is hard, but I expect you to do it." I thought to myself, "Not a bad mission statement for the collectors of intelligence." The president added, "And I am going to be making many tough decisions as president on national security, and I expect that you will fully inform every one of those decisions." I thought, "Great mission statement for our analysts." I also thought, "I really like this guy." Then came the punch line: the president-elect said, "I guess when I am president I will start seeing the good stuff." It struck Winston and me that the president-elect thought we were holding back, not showing him the Agency's most sensitive secrets. But we were already showing him "the good stuff." The president-elect had just raised the bar sky-high. We went back to the office we were working out of in Austin, called Director Tenet, and reported, "We just had an oh shit moment."

President Bush had this way of always raising the bar, always challenging you to do better. Once, on Air Force One, I showed him an intelligence report based on the comments that a Middle Eastern leader had made to our chief of station. After reading the report, the president said, "Michael, that is interesting. But what I really want to know is not what the leader is saying to me through CIA but what he is saying behind my back to Saddam Hussein."

Along with the very high bar, though, came one of the most enjoyable experiences of my life—getting to know the forty-third president of the United States. He treated me with respect and affection—like a member of his family, like a son. Before briefings at the ranch in Crawford, we would have cereal together, talk about the previous night's baseball games, and wash and dry the breakfast dishes together (a requirement of the First Lady). On my first visit to the ranch, the president-elect insisted on giving me a tour. Into a golf cart we jumped, and with the Secret Service in tow, Bush drove through the ranch, describing the different environs and the flora and fauna in great detail.

What struck me quickly about the president was that he was a normal guy—informal and approachable. During one briefing at the ranch in January 2001, the phone rang, and the president-elect answered and simply said, "Of course." When he finished the call, he explained to me that the First Lady was doing some work on the new home they were just finishing on the ranch and that she'd asked that he bring some light bulbs over when the briefing was done. He then said, "Pal, the most important thing you are going to do today is not let me forget those light bulbs when we're done here." On another occasion in Crawford, I walked into the house to find the president tidying—picking up newspapers, straightening pillows, that sort of thing. I said to him, "Mr. President, it is sure good to know that even presidents have to do housework." He responded, "Pal, you don't know my wife!" All of this, of course, made me very comfortable around the president, and my biggest concern was that I would one day slip up and call him George instead of Mr. President.

Starting Monday, January 8, it was my job to deliver the PDB—five days a week during the transition and six days a week after the inauguration. I'd start work at four a.m., sifting through the most critical pieces of current intelligence and analysis, deciding which ones to present and in what order, cramming additional information on each topic into my head in case the president or any of the others in the room—almost always Vice President Dick Cheney, National Security Advisor Condoleezza Rice, and White House Chief of Staff Andy Card—had additional questions, as they almost always did. The president told me once, "I'm easy. It is the other folks in the room that you have to worry about." It was like preparing to orally defend several graduate school dissertations every day, six days a week.

And there was a new twist with this president, something we had never done before with any president—travel with him. The president's first trip was to Mexico to see President Vicente Fox, and the day before the president was to depart, he asked me if I was coming along. Thinking that we had never done this before and having no idea how we would do it, I actually responded, "I think it is a long way to go just for a thirty-minute briefing." As Tenet and I walked out of the Oval Office, Tenet whispered to me, "I can't believe you just blew off the president of the United States." Not surprisingly, the president got his way about the travel, and never again did my response to a presidential query carry so little tact. If nothing else, I am a fast learner.

I traveled with the president wherever he went—on day or overnight trips around the country, on foreign trips, and on vacations, which turned out to be either at his father's home in Kennebunkport, Maine, or, much more often, at the ranch in Crawford, Texas. The president spent Memorial Day weekend in 2001 at the Kennebunkport estate, and as I walked up the driveway for the briefing, he was playing fetch with his beloved dog Barney. As he threw a tennis ball across the lawn and with Barney in hot pursuit, the president said, "Michael, I have a question for you and this is a test." "Oh, God," I thought, "not a test!" The president continued, "Should we spend the month of August here, where it will be a beautiful seventy degrees, or in Crawford, where it will be one hundred degrees?" I knew the "right" answer, of course, but I went the other way. "Mr. President, no doubt about it. We should be right here." "Wrong," the president said, adding with a grin, "Michael, I am disappointed in you."

A briefing would generally include seven or eight items, each of them placed in a three-ring blue leather binder with the words "President's Daily Brief" and the president's name embossed on the cover. Copies were made for the others in the room, although each of them, except Card, had already received his or her own briefing before the session with the president. If Rice or the vice president had had an issue with a particular piece, the briefers tried to alert me before I went into the Oval Office so that I would not be blindsided.

It was up to me to decide both what to show the president and how to brief complex issues so that he took away the key points. Typically I would "tee up" each item in the briefing book with a few words—for example, reminding him of the last thing we had told him about the topic, telling him how this new piece advanced the story, and giving him a preview of the key points. The president would then read the item, often quite carefully. But sometimes, with a complicated or poorly constructed piece, I would have to do more. One morning I found on my desk a two-page piece containing a detailed chart on the Palestinian intifada. After reading the piece several times, I could not see the bottom line. After more reading and a detailed study of the chart, I concluded that the key point was that, despite the very high levels of violence in the West Bank, the vast majority of it was occurring in only three towns. Interesting, I thought, so I simply asked our cartographers to put all the violent incidents on a map, which showed three main clusters, and I showed the president only this map, making the main point orally.

After reading a piece or listening to me brief it, the president would either ask me questions about the item's substance or, more frequently, ask the senior officials in the room questions about the policy implications of the intelligence. When the discussion ended on the first topic we would move to the next item in the binder. Although thirty minutes were usually allotted for the briefing, more often than not it ran much longer.

Bush entered office with a strong-willed and strong-minded national security team including Vice President Dick Cheney and National Security Advisor Condoleezza Rice. But he personally did not have a particularly deep background in foreign affairs. One thing that made him stand out, however, was that he was the son of a former president who was also a former CIA director. The president told me that his father, George H. W. Bush, had stressed to him the importance of his daily intelligence briefing. He had clearly taken that advice to heart, and I found him incredibly interested in the broad range of subjects I would bring to him each morning. The president was very quick to understand the essence of an issue, and I found his gut instincts on policy to be right on the mark. Sometimes I thought the president too quick to make a decision, but I also know from my own experience as a leader that a quick decision is better than a late decision or no decision.

Some of the most special moments for me were when President George H. W. Bush, aka "41," would join the briefing, which he did fifteen or so times during my year as briefer. As a former president, he had that right; as a national security expert and a former CIA director, he was very interested; and as a man who commanded deep respect inside the Agency, he was more than welcome. One morning, just days before the inauguration, 41 joined us for the briefing, which was being held in Blair House (the president's official guesthouse). In the middle of a discussion about the steps Russian president Vladimir Putin was taking to rebuild the Russian military after a decade of decay, the former president said to the president-elect and the rest of us, "I've done this before. You guys deal with this. I'm going to play with the grandkids."

43 asked many questions—just as Miscik had predicted. One of the things he was interested in knowing was how we knew what we knew. For a piece of information provided to us by a human spy, he would want to know the source's position so he could judge for himself the credibility of the information—perhaps the informant was an aide in the prime minister's office who had been at the meeting when the issue was discussed, or a friend of the aide who'd heard the information secondhand. When the intelligence was derived from intercepted communications, he would want to know exactly who was communicating with whom and how—by phone, e-mail, fax, etc. In response, I developed separate mechanisms with CIA operations directorate and with the National Security Agency to get the information I needed. I was now sharing with the president and the others in the room some of the most sensitive information anywhere inside the US intelligence community or even the entire US government.

For the first briefing I did following the inauguration, I was accompanied by George Tenet, who had been director of central intelligence since 1997 under President Clinton. After that, Tenet came only sporadically, and I was on my own most of the time. This ended in the second week of February when President Bush, at the end of a briefing, asked me, "Does George understand that I would like to see him here with you every day?"

"He will, as soon as I get back to the Agency," I responded.

"Good," said the president. That had never been the practice, but Tenet, as any Agency director would have been, was happy to comply. It was awkward at first, since the Bush team had not told Tenet whether it planned to keep him on or not, a decision it did not make until late February.

I asked Tenet how he wanted to handle the sessions and he quickly decided that I was to continue doing the "play-by-play" and he would jump in periodically to do the "color commentary." It proved successful. When the president traveled, only I would be with him, but when he was in Washington, I had Tenet as my wing-man. It's a bit odd having your boss watch you do your job every day, like being named starting quarterback and finding your coach in the huddle. But I had been his executive assistant for two years; Tenet and I were close, and he helped my performance by regularly giving me useful tips and critiques.

Tenet and I would meet every morning in his "downtown" office in the Old Executive Office Building at the White House. There we would plan the briefing, with Tenet deciding which pieces he wanted to remark on. Then, at 7:55 a.m., we would walk across West Executive Avenue to be outside the Oval Office at precisely eight a.m. for the briefing. The president was almost never late.

Tenet's presence in the room was extremely helpful to the president. For almost any national security issue that came up, Tenet was able to explain the history of the issue, how the Clinton adminis-tration tried to deal with it, what had worked, and what had not. I was worried at first about Rice's reaction to Tenet's talking about policy, but she too seemed appreciative of the background. There was an early tendency on Bush's part to be leery of any of Clinton's approaches to issues—investing US credibility in trying to find an accommodation between the Palestinians and the Israelis, for example—but Tenet's commentary seemed to ease that tendency. Tenet provided a continuity in national security policy that most presidents do not get.

The briefings during those first few months were tough sledding, not because of the president or anyone else in the room, but because the Agency was not producing a sufficiently high-quality product to meet the president's expectations. Tenet would routinely pull pieces from the book—sometimes at my urging—judging them to be not good enough for the president, either because they told him something he already knew or because the analysis was not insightful enough. Our Middle East analysis was most often the victim—the analysts for that region frequently produced pieces that did not advance the president's thinking. Occasionally one of these pieces would slip by, and after reading it, the president would look at me and say, "Duh, no shit." *That* is customer feedback. But to its credit, the analytic side of the Agency worked hard to improve its game and the number of pieces pulled by Tenet or criticized by Bush declined sharply over time.

There were a number of international incidents during the first few months of the Bush administration that dominated the briefings. The biggest crisis in those early months was when a US Navy EP-3 surveillance aircraft had a midair collision with a Chinese fighter over the South China Sea and was forced to land at a Chinese military base on Hainan Island. A tense ten-day diplomatic crisis ensued, and I think our analysis proved extremely helpful to the president. One piece that seemed particularly useful was a comparison of China's public statements about the United States regarding the EP-3 incident with its statements during the Taiwan Strait crisis in 1996 (when the Chinese moved military assets in response to an independence-minded Taiwanese president and the United States responded by moving an aircraft carrier into the Taiwan Strait). This comparison showed that the Chinese were much less concerned about the EP-3 incident than they had been about Taiwan, and spoke to the need for patience on the part of the United States. Bush was indeed patient and the crisis ended peacefully.

While the briefings were filled with analysis and discussions about serious issues, the sessions were not without their lighter moments. I particularly remember the president's dog Barney chewing on the tassels on Tenet's loafers as the CIA director struggled mightily to give Bush the impression he didn't mind. I also remember the president's telling a not particularly funny joke one morning in the Oval Office. When no one laughed, the president turned to me and said, "Michael, your job is to laugh at my jokes—even if they are not funny."

And during a briefing at Camp David as the president, George Tenet, Steve Hadley, and I were sitting around a coffee table discussing a PDB article, Barney got a piece of plastic stuck in his throat. The president was the first to notice. Both the president and I pushed the briefing books from our laps and tried to reach the dog, who was under the table. The president grabbed Barney, and the piece of plastic popped out of his mouth onto the floor. I quickly grabbed it, and when I did, I said proudly, "Mr. President, I got it." The president responded by saying, "Good job, Michael." And during this entire time, Tenet and Hadley continued their substantive discussion. The president looked at them with wry irritation.

* * *

When it came to al Qa'ida and Bin Ladin, the early 2001 briefings focused on two issues. The first surrounded responsibility for the October 2000 terrorist attack on the USS *Cole*. President Clinton had left office with no clear intelligence linking the al Qa'ida leadership with the bombing that had killed seventeen of the ship's crew and wounded thirty-nine. On January 25 we wrote a piece for the new president outlining our preliminary assessment, that the plot had been directed from Afghanistan by the al Qa'ida leadership. Because we could not nail down responsibility with certainty and because President Bush believed that the "pinpricks" of cruise missile strikes did not serve any real military objective, there would be no US response to the *Cole* bombing pending development of a more robust response to al Qa'ida, which in the spring and summer of 2001 was in the process of being put together.

The second issue with regard to al Qa'ida in the early months was bringing pieces to the president designed to educate him about the group. We provided the president with analytic pieces on the group's training camps in Afghanistan, its fund-raising capabilities and networks, its complex relationship with the Taliban, and the Taliban's multifaceted relationships with some of our allies. In short, I wanted to give the president as much as we could provide about what CIA believed was the leading national security threat facing the United States.

In retrospect, I think it would have been helpful had the intelligence community produced a National Intelligence Estimate (NIE) for the new administration on the threat posed by al Qa'ida. An NIE is the community's premier product—the authoritative voice of the analysts throughout the IC on an issue. It is discussed and approved by the leadership of the community. I think such a document would have helped put al Qa'ida in context for the new administration and helped it understand the seriousness with which intelligence officials took al Qa'ida.

I should add, however, that during the transition and during those first three months, there was little to no specific threat reporting on what al Qa'ida was plotting. That changed dramatically in the spring. In fact, starting in the spring and through early summer, the bulk of my time in the Oval Office was taken up with wide-ranging and increasingly frightening reports about terrorist threats from al Qa'ida. From late April until early July we were picking up very worrisome intelligence, with al Qa'ida members telling each other of "very good news to come," and that "significant victories" were on the horizon. None of the reports were specific in terms of location, timing, or method of attack, but all were shared with the president and his entire national security team.

On the morning of April 18, I walked, as I did every morning, into Tenet's "downtown" office at the Old Executive Office Building. As soon as he saw me, he said, in a tone that I knew meant there would be no debate, "I'm taking over the briefing today." The night before, at his daily CT update, our officers had briefed Tenet on credible information that Bin Ladin was planning multiple significant attacks. The analysts were writing a piece to put this information together and explain it, but Tenet was not going to wait to tell the president. He switched seats with me to place himself closer to the president and vice president—the only time he did that in my entire year of briefing—and he did both the play-by-play and the color commentary in vintage Tenet style. And there was a lot of color that morning. When Tenet gets rolling it can be an amazing thing to witness. He is an outstanding briefer who speaks with great clarity and with a conviction that commands the room, and that morning he expressed in words, tone, and body language his deep concern that al Qa'ida was going to hit us. While he had the floor in the Oval Office, I was watching the reactions of the president and his senior advisors. It was not clear to me at the time if the tactic was working, however. I could see that they did not know what to make of Tenet's passion, which made sense in the context of what the previous administration had been through—the East Africa bombings, the attempted attacks during the pre-millennium period, and the *Cole* attack. The piece produced by the analysts the next day, on April 19—based on the same information that Tenet had orally presented the previous morning—was titled "Bin Ladin Planning Multiple Operations." The 9/11 Commission would later title one of the chapters of its report with a quote from Tenet about this period: "The system was blinking red."

After the one-time event of Tenet leading the briefing, we went back to our usual format. The threat reporting continued—other pieces were titled "Bin Ladin Attacks May Be Imminent" and "Bin Ladin Planning High-Profile Attacks"—but I sensed some skepticism about it. The vice president one morning asked me whether all this threat reporting might not be deception on the part of al Qa'ida—purposely designed to get our attention and to get us to needlessly expend resources in response. We were getting the same question from Donald Rumsfeld's staff at the Defense Department. Steve Cambone, at that time a special assistant to the secretary of defense, visited Tenet in his office to tell him that the Pentagon's view was that this was all deception. Tenet told Cambone, "I want you to look in my eyes. I want you to hear what I have to say. This is not deception. This is the real deal." Still, the vice president deserved an answer. So I had CIA analysts consider that possibility, and they came back with a report titled "UBL Threats Are Real." When I finished briefing that piece—that day on Air Force One—the president jokingly said to me, "OK, Michael. You've covered your ass." I tell this story only to ensure that the history of this period is recorded with accuracy, as word of the president's comment spread and it was mistakenly referred to as a response to the now-famous August 6 briefing that I will address shortly. Most important, the president said it to me as a joke. It was not a serious comment on the piece or on the warnings that CIA was providing about an al Qa'ida attack, which he took seriously.

In mid-July the threat reporting suddenly dried up, with some intelligence even suggesting that the major attacks had been delayed.

At the time we could not explain the lull, nor can we fully explain it today. We do know that a good bit of the reporting we saw in the late spring and early summer resulted from Bin Ladin's going from training camp to training camp giving pep talks to his troops. During these talks the Sheikh, as he was known to his followers, would speak of "good news to come" and "preparations to strike the idol of the world." Not surprisingly, this kind of talk spread and we picked up some of it. Why it stopped in mid-July is hard to say. My best guess is that, as the hijackers were moving into position and lying low, Bin Ladin and his leadership stopped talking about attacks even in general terms. They were practicing operational security. As the time for their strike approached, they went silent in an effort to make sure nothing interfered with their murderous plans. There are two times when you need to worry about terrorists: when you pick up their chatter and when you don't—which means, of course, that you worry all the time.

In August the president went off on an extended vacation to his ranch in Crawford, and I went with him. Earlier in the summer, I had met with each analytic office in the Agency to discuss what it might want to write during the "summer doldrums"—the weeks of late July and August when it was hard to get the number of good PDB pieces we needed because so many people were on vacation. So we did as much preparation as we could. When I met with the terrorism analysts, I asked them to write the now-famous August 6 PDB titled "Bin Ladin Determined to Strike in US." I asked for this piece because earlier in the year, whenever Tenet and I would brief the president on the al Qa'ida threat, the president would directly ask us, "Is there any indication that this threat is aimed here at the United States?" He was clearly very worried about that possibility. My answer to that question—supported by Tenet—was always the same: "Mr. President, while there is no *specific* information to suggest that these attacks we are hearing about are aimed at the homeland, Bin Ladin would like nothing more than to bring the fight here to our shores." Given the president's frequent question, I wanted to have the analysts dig deeper into the subject.

The resulting piece later became the first PDB item ever declassified and released. A casual reading makes clear that we thought the threat from al Qa'ida to the homeland was very real. The threat was not limited to attacks on US interests abroad. But a careful reading also shows that nothing in the item told the president where, when, or how al Qa'ida might strike our country—or even that we thought there was a link between the threat reporting of spring and early summer and a catastrophic attack on the homeland. Later some analysts would claim—some of them to the 9/11 Commission—that they had intended the piece to convey such a linkage. However, the words on the piece of paper we read that morning simply did not do so.

The August 6 briefing took place in the living room of the president's ranch. There was only one other person present, Steve Biegun, the executive secretary of the National Security Council, who was filling in for Rice and her deputy, Steve Hadley, who themselves were taking turns spending time with the president at the ranch that August. I teed up the piece by explaining why we had written it. The president then read it closely. I do not recall any further discussion of the piece; we moved on to the next item. I did not treat it as a "hair on fire" or action-forcing piece, and the president did not read it that way either.

* * *

During this period of heightened threat, CIA was not just collecting the intelligence chatter and passing it on to policy-makers. It was also working to disrupt whatever plotting might be under way. As a briefer, I did not have visibility into these operations, but I later learned they included Tenet's contacting dozens of his foreign counterparts and urging action. Thanks to these efforts, a number of terrorist suspects were arrested and detained in almost two dozen countries. We helped halt, disrupt, or uncover weapons caches and plans to attack US diplomatic facilities in the Middle East and Europe.

But this level of operational intensity is hard to maintain for a long period, and particularly difficult in the absence of specific threat reporting. So after a period of intense action, we returned to the status quo—still deeply concerned about the next possible attack but no longer on the trigger the way we had been for several months. Without additional intelligence to guide us, there was simply no other place to go.

CHAPTER 3

The Darkest Hours

I slept fitfully in my hotel room in Sarasota in the early-morning hours of September 11, eyeballing the hotel alarm clock as it ticked toward three thirty a.m., the time I would get up to go to work. My recurring nightmare was oversleeping and standing up the president of the United States.

It was the second week of September, and the president was on a two-day trip to Florida for events focused on his new education policy. As had become standard practice, I had come along to deliver to him the latest intelligence.

As I was stirring in Sarasota, two young men were checking out of the Comfort Inn in Portland, Maine, the same hotel I had stayed in two months earlier when the president spent a long weekend at his father's ocean-side summer home in Kennebunkport. As I was showering and dressing in Florida, fifteen hundred miles away, these men took a short drive to the Portland International Jetport, where they boarded a six a.m. flight to Boston, connecting to American Airlines Flight 11, bound for Los Angeles. Their names were Mohamed Atta and Abdulaziz al-Omari.

Because we were traveling, only one of the other usual senior participants, Chief of Staff Andy Card, was scheduled to sit in on the president's briefing that morning. Navy Captain Deborah Loewer, the director of the White House Situation Room, was also to be present to receive policy-related questions the president might raise and, more important, to communicate items of interest to Condoleezza Rice and her deputy Steve Hadley back in Washington.

At 7:55 a.m., Loewer and I went up the stairs to the presidential suite at the Colony Beach & Tennis Resort. We passed through Secret Service checkpoints and waited in the hallway outside the president's room. The president had just returned from a four-and-a-half-mile run and was dressing. While we waited and chatted with one of the president's personal aides, American Airlines Flight 11—a Boeing 767 with ninety-two passengers and crew members aboard—took off from Boston's Logan Airport. It was the first of the four hijacked flights to take to the air.

A little after eight a.m., Chief of Staff Card opened the door and motioned us in. We found President Bush seated at a table with a cup of coffee and a newspaper. He seemed surrounded by pastries, none of which he had touched. When he saw us, he asked if we had enjoyed our night at the beach. I told the president I had *heard* some waves but had not actually *seen* any. "Michael, you need to get a new job," he joked. He put down the newspaper and asked, "Anything of interest this morning?" On the most important day of President Bush's tenure, his intelligence briefing was unremarkable, focusing on the most recent developments in the Palestinian uprising against Israel. Contrary to some media reports, there was nothing regarding terrorist threats in the briefing.

An intelligence report about a phone conversation that the United States had intercepted between two (non-allied) world leaders that I had placed in the president's binder caught his attention and caused him to pick up the phone to call Dr. Rice in Washington. They talked for only a couple of minutes. The briefing was over by 8:25 a.m. Only six minutes earlier one of the flight attendants on Flight 11 had contacted American Airlines ground personnel to say, "I don't know, but I think we are getting hijacked." And just one minute earlier Mohamed Atta, the lead hijacker, was trying to communicate with the cockpit on Flight 11 but had actually contacted air traffic control, saying, "We have some planes. Just stay quiet and you will be okay."

I left the presidential suite and took the elevator down to take my place in the motorcade that would carry the president to the Emma E. Booker Elementary School in Sarasota, where he was scheduled to speak. Soon joining me in the van were several senior White House officials, including political advisor Karl Rove, Press Secretary Ari Fleischer, and Director of White House Communications Dan Bartlett. I had become friendly with both Rove and Fleischer during the previous eight months. Fleischer and I would often talk sports, and Rove and I would frequently banter about the PDB. (He was not among the handful of White House officials cleared to see it.) "You don't have anything in that briefcase that CNN doesn't have," he would tease me. "Karl, if you only knew what I know," I would respond.

During the drive to the school, at 8:46 a.m., American Airlines Flight 11 slammed into the north side of the North Tower of the World Trade Center, between the ninety-third and ninety-ninth floors. It was traveling at 490 miles per hour.

Just as we were pulling up to the school, Fleischer's cell phone rang. He listened for a few seconds and flipped his phone closed. He turned to me and asked, "Michael, do you know anything about a plane hitting the World Trade Center?" I said, "No," but told him I would make some calls. As the motorcade came to a stop, I said, "Ari, I sure hope this is an accident and not terrorism." He paused for a second or two—the word *terrorism* hanging in the air—and said, "I sure hope so too."

My guess at the time was that a small plane had lost its way in bad weather and, by accident, had crashed into the World Trade Center. From just outside the classroom, I called CIA's Operations Center. When I got the duty officer on the line he quickly told me that the plane in question was a large commercial airliner. My hope that this was not terrorism started to fade.

As I flipped my phone shut and walked into the senior staff room, I looked at my watch. It was nine a.m. Booker Elementary had placed a television in the room, and everyone was glued to the coverage coming out of New York. At 9:03 we watched as United Airlines Flight 175, a Boeing 767 with sixty-five passengers and crew members on board, slammed into the south side of the South Tower of the World Trade Center between the seventy-seventh and eighty-fifth floors. At impact, UAL Flight 175 was traveling at nearly six hundred miles per hour.

There was now no question—this was a deliberate act of terrorism. In the classroom next door, Andy Card made his way to the president, who was listening, along with sixteen second graders and a large number of reporters and others, to a story about a girl and her pet goat. At 9:05 a.m. Card whispered in the president's ear, "A second plane has hit the World Trade Center. America is under attack."

Back at CIA headquarters, one of the many odd coincidences of the day was playing out. While I was briefing the president, several senior CIA officers were having a long-planned breakfast with Commander Kirk Lippold, the commander of the USS *Cole* when it was attacked in Yemen. The group was lamenting that the American public was not sufficiently seized with the threat of terrorism, and Lippold suggested that it would take some "seminal event" to get the public's attention. Minutes later news of that event reached the room. The Agency officers quickly turned to their duties, and Lippold rushed back to the Pentagon—arriving just in time to see American Airlines Flight 77 slam into the building.

In Alec Station the reaction was a grim realization. When reports of the second plane's hitting the World Trade Center reached the Station, everyone instantly thought and said the same thing: "So this is what al Qa'ida was planning. This is what we were waiting for."

The president finished the session with the students and joined the senior staff. He made a number of calls on a secure phone that is always with the president for such a contingency. He spoke with the vice president and national security advisor. During one of these calls, on a nearby television, one of the networks played a recording of the second plane hitting the South Tower. A staff member called the president's attention to the footage, a moment his photographer captured in an unforgettable image that would be published in hundreds of newspapers and magazines. I am in the far left of the photo, holding my briefcase.

I could only stand and watch as the president spoke on the phone and as Ari Fleischer sat at a nearby table writing out the first draft of remarks that the president would soon deliver to the nation. Standing there, being photographed, I was growing increasingly concerned about the president's safety as well as the safety of others at the school. The fact that the president would be at Booker Elementary at this hour, on this day, had been public knowledge for days. I wondered when a plane might come crashing into the school. I thought about mentioning this to the head of the president's Secret Service detail, but I figured that he'd probably thought of that, as he looked as nervous as I felt.

At nine thirty a.m. President Bush went back to a classroom to speak to the nation. Surrounded by students, teachers, and reporters, he said the country had suffered an apparent terrorist attack and promised to hunt down those who had committed the act, adding that "terrorism against our country will not stand."

At 9:37 a.m., a few minutes after the president concluded his remarks, American Airlines Flight 77, a Boeing 757 carrying sixty-four passengers and crew members, crashed into the west side of the Pentagon. One of CIA's professional drivers, a gentleman with whom I had become well acquainted during my briefing assignment, was waiting at the Pentagon's River Entrance for a colleague who was delivering the PDB to Secretary of Defense Donald Rumsfeld. He said the impact of the crash lifted his vehicle off the ground.

The father of some of my children's closest friends since pre-school, a teacher in Arlington County, Virginia, home to the Pentagon, told me later that the plane passed directly over the trailer in which he was teaching. Tom said the roar made it seem as though the jet's landing gear might touch the school's roof. It was a sound he had never heard before. He said to a colleague or a student, "Wow, that's really low!" He then went back to teaching. It was only a few minutes later that a student coming in late to class said that a plane had crashed into the Pentagon. "Sure," Tom said to this boy, thinking that the student was simply being silly. "Sit down and open your math book." A few minutes later, Tom apologized to the boy as the trailers were being evacuated.

While the president was still speaking at Booker Elementary, the Secret Service told those of us in the staff area to take our places in the motorcade as quickly as possible. They said that once the president was finished speaking and was in his limousine the motorcade would wait for no one. I climbed into the back of the senior staff van. Within minutes we were speeding to the Sarasota-Bradenton International Airport, just three and a half miles away.

When we arrived at the airport we received news of the attack on the Pentagon. Dire speculation took hold: how many planes had been hijacked and how many more targets might there be? I also thought of my family. I wondered if Mary Beth, who was at home, even knew yet what horrors had been unleashed on New York City and Washington. My children were at school in Fairfax County, Virginia, and I prayed that they would not be too frightened by what was going on—or too concerned about my safety. After all, I was about to board the most secure aircraft in the world.

Once everyone was aboard, Air Force One's engines roared to life. The aircraft accelerated down the runway and began a rapid climb—one steeper than I had ever imagined a wide-bodied aircraft could achieve. It was ten a.m.

We were off and I asked the president's military aide—the keeper of the nuclear "football" (a briefcase containing the codes needed by the commander in chief to launch a nuclear war)—where we were going. He responded, "We are just flying around for a bit." I huddled with several others in Air Force One's senior staff compartment, a small room with four seats not far from the president's airborne office, where we looked in horror at live news reports. We watched people jump to their deaths from the top floors of the World Trade Center. Then we watched the South Tower collapse and disappear into a plume of smoke and dust. For a number of seconds no one said a word. Then someone broke the silence by whispering, "My God."

Back at CIA, George Tenet was making a decision to evacuate the complex. In a meeting in his conference room, Tenet was reminded that years earlier, Ramzi Yousef, the mastermind of the first World Trade Center bombing in 1993, had developed a plan to crash a plane into CIA headquarters. With planes still in the air, Tenet was taking no chances.

The evacuation order, not surprisingly, did not apply to the

Counterterrorism Center. In Alec Station, supervisors told their employees that they could go if they wanted, if they felt they needed to get home to their families. No one left. Not a single person. They all stayed. Food, cots, and air mattresses began to appear.

The officers in Alec went to work on a number of questions— the most important of which were "Who exactly did this?" and "Are additional attacks coming?" The staff sent urgent priority messages to CIA stations around the globe, asking each of them to reach out to its foreign counterparts and vacuum up any shred of information that might shed light on the attacks and what might come next. And the officers began thinking about a much-expanded operational plan to go after al Qa'ida.

A few minutes following Tenet's order to evacuate, United Airlines Flight 93, a Boeing 757 carrying forty-four passengers and crew members, crashed near Shanksville, Pennsylvania. Flight 93 passengers, who had become aware of the hijackers' intentions by speaking to loved ones on cell phones, had revolted and attacked the hijackers. Their actions may have saved the lives of hundreds of others, as the hijackers were targeting the US Capitol building.

While I continued to stand in the senior staff cabin, news wires reported that a Palestinian terrorist group, the Democratic Front for the Liberation of Palestine (DFLP), had claimed responsibility for the attacks. The president called me to his airborne office and asked what I made of it. "Mr. President," I said, "DFLP is a Palestinian rejectionist group with a long history of terrorism against Israel, but they do not possess the capability to do this." (Later a senior member of the DFLP would deny the initial claim.) As I turned to leave, the president asked me to tell Tenet to let him—the president— know the instant Tenet had anything definitive on the perpetrators of the attacks. The president said, "Michael, I want to be the first to know. Got that?" He said it in a tone that meant he was deadly serious. "Yes, sir," I replied.

As I was leaving the president's office, Andy Card asked to speak with me and pulled me into the president's cabin on Air Force One. He told me that the White House had received a threat against Air Force One and that what was particularly worrying was that the caller had used Air Force One's code name—Angel. I thanked Card for sharing the information with me, but my instinct was that this was not a major concern. I figured that if a bomb had been on board, it would have already detonated, and since we now had fighter escorts and an Airborne Warning and Control System (AWACS) plane above us, we were safe from anyone trying to fly a plane into us.

I returned to my seat in the staff section of the plane and picked up one of the phones that sit beside almost every seat on the aircraft. The phone rang twice, and one of the Air Force crew members working on the upper deck of the 747 said, "Yes sir. What can I do for you?" I asked to be connected to Tenet's office in Washington and gave him the number. "Sir, we have been ordered to keep all phone lines open for the president and the military aide," he replied. I told him that the president had personally asked me to make the call. "I'll put you right through," he said, and within seconds the phone in the director's office was ringing.

Tenet's office, like much of the federal government, was in crisis mode. With Tenet's order to evacuate, he and his staff were in the process of relocating to a secure site. Tenet wasn't nearby but his secretary handed the phone to the nearest senior official, Cofer Black, the head of the Agency's Counterterrorism Center. Black was calm and collected and passed on what the Agency knew at that point, which was little beyond what the rest of the world knew. I relayed the president's request that he be informed instantly if and when information came in regarding responsibility for the attacks and asked him to get word to the director. When I hung up, I somehow knew it wasn't going to happen.

The president's military aide told me that we were heading for Barksdale Air Force Base in Louisiana. There the president would make another public statement and the aircraft would be re-provisioned—taking on additional food and water since it was unknown where it would go next or how long we would be airborne. The military aide advised me that a number of Air Force One's passengers, all those deemed not essential to national security, would be left behind in Barksdale. Shortly before landing I was told that I would not be booted off—unlike all of the White House staff working on domestic issues, a couple of members of Congress from Florida who had been on the trip, and a large portion of the traveling press pool.

On our landing at Barksdale, the president was whisked off under heavy guard. I elected to remain on the aircraft. A Secret Service agent came through the cabin and said that no one would be permitted to make cell phone calls or to give out the president's location. My heart sank. I had planned to call Mary Beth to let her know that I was safe and to make sure that she and the kids were OK as well.

Among those still on the aircraft were the two congressmen who had just been informed that they would have to find alternative means of onward travel. Together we watched the ongoing news coverage. One of them, aware that I was the president's intelligence briefer, asked me who I thought was behind the attacks. I told him I would bet every dollar I had that Usama bin Ladin's al Qa'ida was responsible.

(The next day I found on my desk a press report quoting one of the Florida congressmen, who had told reporters that a "senior national security official traveling with the President" had told him just hours after the attack that Bin Ladin was the culprit. A handwritten note on the piece, from one of my colleagues, asked, "Are you the senior official?" I hadn't planned on making news—but I guess I did.)

At 1:45 p.m. Air Force One departed with considerably fewer passengers than when we had arrived. The military aide told me that we were flying to Offutt Air Force Base near Omaha, Nebraska, home of the US Strategic Command (STRATCOM), where the president would conduct a meeting of the National Security Council over a secure video link from the STRATCOM bunker. The aide was keeping me informed of our every move, and I appreciated it.

About fifteen minutes after we left Barksdale, Andy Card walked into the staff section of the plane and said, "Michael, the president wants to see you." When I entered his airborne office I could tell the president was focused and determined. In the last couple of hours, I had seen him transformed from a peacetime president to a wartime commander in chief. He asked me point-blank, "Michael, who did this?" I said, "Sir, I haven't seen any intelligence that would point to responsibility, so what I'm going to say is simply my personal view." He told me he understood. I said that there were two terrorist states capable of conducting such a complex operation—Iraq and Iran—but that neither had much to gain and both had plenty to lose from attacking the United States. Rather, I said, the culprit was almost certainly a non-state actor, adding that I would bet my children's future that the trail would lead to the doorstep of Usama bin Ladin and al Qa'ida.

The president asked me, "When will we know?"

"I can't say for sure," I replied, and I reviewed for him how long it had taken CIA to have any certainty about responsibility for past terrorist attacks—the bombing of Khobar Towers in Saudi Arabia (which had not been an al Qa'ida operation), the bombings of the US embassies in Kenya and Tanzania, and the attack on the USS *Cole* in Yemen. With the length of time in each case varying dramatically, I concluded by saying, "It might be soon and then again it might take some time."

During my discussion with the president, I had no way of knowing that analysts at CIA headquarters had already tied the attacks to al Qa'ida. They had acquired the passenger manifest of the four flights from the Federal Aviation Administration and run the names against CIA databases of known terrorists. Hits came up on American Airlines Flight 77. Three passengers on that flight had known and definitive links to al Qa'ida (prior to 9/11 there was no national no-fly list that would have flagged the hijackers before they got on the plane). And none of this information had been passed to me to share with the president, despite the commander in chief's "tell me first" order.

A little after three p.m. Eastern Time we landed at Offutt. We were taken on buses to the entrance of the STRATCOM underground bunker. A secure videoconference call was set up in the bunker's command center. As I entered I saw the president, Andy Card, and the STRATCOM commander, Admiral Richard Mies, at a table in front of a large screen. On the screen, transmitting from three or four different locations, were senior officials in Washington. George Tenet walked the president and others through the information that tied three of the hijackers to al Qa'ida. When Tenet finished, the president turned and looked me straight in the eye. He didn't say a word, but his look told me that he felt he had been let down. He hadn't wanted to learn about this after the fact on a conference call. My look back at him was meant to convey, "I'm sorry but I don't know what happened."

I was angry that we had failed to follow through on the president's order. I went through every possibility in my mind—was I not clear when I spoke to Cofer Black, did Black not pass on my message to Tenet, did Tenet just forget in the intense activity of the day, or did Tenet knowingly hold back the information because he wanted to brief it himself? I didn't wait for the videoconference to end but rose from my seat in the back of the command center and walked out the door. I went to a nearby office and phoned the CIA Operations Center and asked to speak with Tenet's executive assistant. After expressing my frustration—in colorful language—over not having been able to meet the president's expectations, I asked that the information Tenet had just given the president be sent immediately to Air Force One, as I was certain that Tenet had not covered everything in the teleconference. The president felt he had been let down, I said, and so did I. The assistant told me that he could not send it because the information was embargoed from leaving the building. "Embargoed from the president of the United States?" I shouted. "Just send it!" I slammed the phone down. The stress of the day was starting to get to me.

When I returned to the secure videoconference there was a debate going on about whether the president should return to Washington. The director of the Secret Service, in Washington, argued, "No, we still do not know if it would be safe for you to come back, Mr. President," but it was not much of a debate because the president simply and firmly said, "I'm coming home."

Shortly thereafter we returned to Air Force One and departed for Washington. A few minutes after takeoff, a steward brought me a written communication from Tenet's executive assistant. On the cover sheet was a short note: "Michael, sorry. Here's everything we have."

I went through the material several times and highlighted several passages. Andy Card took me forward to see the president and I walked him through the material—some of which suggested that follow-up attacks were a very real possibility. We had already been sobered by the day's events, and the news brought a new jolt of concern. After reading the documents, the president simply handed them back to me and said, "Thank you, Michael."

It was early evening as we approached Andrews Air Force Base. Everyone on board was tired. Inside Air Force One, the lights had been dimmed. The military aide pointed out the window and told me to look. One hundred yards off the tip of our wing was an F-16. The military aide whispered that there was another one off our other wing as well. "They are from the D.C. Air National Guard," he said. The fighter was so close we could see the pilot's facial features. In the distance below we could see the Pentagon, smoke still rising from the crash earlier in the day, and lights flashing from emergency vehicles on the scene. It was the darkest of hours. Tears welled up in my eyes for the first but not the last time that day.

Immediately on arrival at Andrews AFB, the president flew off in Marine One back to the White House, while most of the staff piled into vans to follow him. I waited at the Andrews visitors lounge for a CIA car to take me back to headquarters. For the first time that day, I was able to call Mary Beth. I told her that I was at Andrews and waiting for a ride, adding that I would have much to tell her later. Her voice was reassuring. She simply said, "Get home soon." Eventually I made it back to the Agency, retrieved my car, and made the trek back home. As I drove off the Agency compound the weight of everything that had happened sank in and I began to cry.

I pulled into our driveway in northern Virginia, with the radio on and the president about to speak. I sat and listened for a few minutes before going into the house. I found Mary Beth on the sofa in our family room watching the president address a grieving nation. He asked for prayers for the families of the victims, said America would overcome the terrible tragedy, and promised that it would emerge even stronger. And, in a major change in policy that would become part of the Bush Doctrine, the president said the United States "would make no distinction between terrorists and nations that harbor them."

After the president finished, I went into each of my three children's rooms and found them asleep, surrounded by stuffed animals. They looked as they did on any other night, peaceful and content. I thought of the thousands of other children who would never see their parents again. I kissed my three on their foreheads and softly told them I loved them.

* * *

Back at Langley, a stunningly patriotic dynamic was playing out. Many of those who had been sent home earlier in the day fought their way back through traffic to return to our headquarters—unable and unwilling to stay away. And we had scores of recently—and not-so-recently—retired Agency officers just drive up to the even-more-heavily-defended-than-usual front gate and say, "I want to come back. I will do anything that needs to be done."

* * *

In the aftermath of 9/11, many focused on—and attempted to answer—the questions: *Where did we fail? Who was responsible for the failure—intelligence, law enforcement, policy? How could this have been prevented?* From my perspective, 9/11 was a national failure.

It is true that one can point to specific lapses by the CIA, FBI, and NSA that *might* have made a difference—the failure of FBI field offices to follow up on and report to Washington unusual flight training by young Arab men, and the failure of CIA to report to the FBI the travel of two of the 9/11 hijackers to the United States, among others. It is also true that the intelligence community did not penetrate al Qa'ida sufficiently enough to discover the threat. But the failures that ultimately led to 9/11 are much deeper than those lapses. They include not funding national security–related agencies to a level commensurate with the threat; not implementing all of the twenty sensible recommendations on aviation security made by the 1996 Gore Commission, established by President Clinton after the crash of TWA Flight 800; and not aggressively pursuing al Qa'ida following the East Africa and *Cole* bombings.

I believe that, taken together, these represent a national failure because the American people would not have supported the actions required. They would not have supported significant increases in the resources of the national security community at a time when the rest of the government was facing deep budget cuts; they would not have supported changes to aviation security that would have inconvenienced hundreds of thousands of travelers—the airline industry fought the recommendations of the Gore Commission, for example—and they would not have supported going to war in Afghanistan after the embassy bombings or the *Cole* bombing. No, it took 9/11 itself to galvanize the necessary support for these steps. One of the defining characteristics of America is that we tend to be reactive to events, not proactive. And on 9/11 we paid a significant price for this national trait.

CHAPTER 4

The Finest Hours

On most Saturday mornings, George Tenet and I would drive to Camp David on the Catoctin Mountain of Maryland, where we would meet with the president in his office complex there called Laurel Lodge. Laurel is a comfortable, homey getaway filled with leather couches, overstuffed chairs, and a big, well-used fireplace. (The first time Tenet and I went to Camp David to brief the president we flew by helicopter. When Bush heard this, he said to us, "Sounds expensive." We never traveled there by helicopter again, instead always driving.) We would typically wend our way to the president's small personal office in the right rear portion of the cabin. We would almost always be joined by National Security Advisor Rice or her deputy, Steve Hadley. The president often had one foot on his desk, cowboy-style, while I delivered that day's PDB briefing. Then we would often embark on a wide ranging *tour d'horizon*, with the president displaying a broad interest in world affairs—including many topics that would not normally arise in the briefings during the week. In the pre-9/11 days, our informal sessions would sometimes last up to two hours. When we were done we were often invited to stay for a buffet breakfast and we would sometimes find ourselves joined by world leaders who happened to be the president's guests that weekend at Camp David. One time I found myself sitting next to British Prime Minister Tony Blair as he and George Tenet bantered about the intricacies of French politics. What impressed me most that day was that, until that moment, I hadn't known my boss knew anything about French politics.

It was on one of those Saturdays in late February 2001 that the president asked to see Tenet alone after the briefing. Little did I know that in the president's office at Laurel, Bush was asking Tenet to stay on as director of central intelligence. When we got in the director's armored Suburban to head back to Washington, he told me the news. I was not surprised, as I had watched the relationship between the two men grow significantly in the previous several weeks, but I was deeply proud of my boss. Very few directors of CIA have had the honor of serving more than one president.

* * *

On Saturday, September 15, Director Tenet and I took our typical weekend drive to the presidential retreat at Camp David but this was not going to be an ordinary Saturday briefing. Bush had brought his national security team to Camp David for a discussion on how the United States should respond to the attacks on the country just four days earlier. Each department and agency was represented by both its principal—a cabinet-level official—and its deputy, and many had brought in other senior officials as well. Tenet, for example, had brought along both Deputy Director John McLaughlin and Cofer Black, the director of CIA's Counterterrorism Center.

But before the National Security Council session started, Tenet and I gave the president his daily PDB. It was the largest crowd in history to ever sit in on a briefing session—the president and vice president, Tenet, Card, Rice, and Hadley, along with Secretary of State Colin Powell and Secretary of Defense Rumsfeld. I showed the president two reports from CIA sources outlining significant terrorist plotting against US military forces in the Middle East. I noted, however, "Mr. President, we are not putting much stock in these reports as the sources do not have credible access to the information they are sharing." Rumsfeld snapped, "Then you should not be showing these to the president." Looking directly at the secretary of defense, I explained, "I was concerned that someone else, perhaps the Situation Room, might bring these to the president's attention, and I wanted him to know what we think." The president, sensing the tension, said "Don, it's OK. Let's move on." I chalked it up to everyone being on edge.

The PDB session was followed by breakfast, with the principals and deputies milling around Laurel Lodge, eating pastries and drinking coffee. I was not invited to the National Security Council session, but I decided to get something to eat before taking a car back to Washington. Near the end of breakfast, the president, Cofer Black, and I were standing to the side of the room talking. A senior State Department official walked over and expressed the opinion to the president that it was critical that America's first response to the attack be diplomatic—that we should reason with the Taliban and ask them to turn over Bin Ladin and his senior al Qa'ida leadership. As the official walked off, President Bush looked at Cofer and me and said, "Fuck diplomacy. We are going to war."

The president was speaking to Black and me in the emotion of the moment and he was playing to his audience: his CIA briefer and a tough CIA operations officer. In fact, the United States *did* give the Taliban an opportunity to turn over Bin Ladin and his top lieutenants. The Taliban refused.

* * *

At the NSC meeting, Tenet put on the table a detailed and multifaceted plan to go after Bin Ladin and al Qa'ida. It included the use of force by the United States. CIA was the only department or agency in the room that day that had a plan. Just four days after the terrible events of 9/11, CIA was prepared to respond. Our readiness was no accident. In October 2000, after the bombing of the USS *Cole* in the Port of Aden and just one month before the presidential election, Tenet had been ready to take the gloves off, and he—along with national security advisor Sandy Berger—had asked the Counterterrorism Center for a plan to aggressively go after and dismantle al Qaʿida. The CTC in December produced what it called the "Blue Sky" memo. It was remarkably detailed—for example, outlining relationships among the hundreds of different tribes in Afghanistan and how those could be used against the Taliban and al Qaʿida—and the plan it suggested was remarkably expensive, set to cost more than the entire CIA budget at the time. On 9/11, the Blue Sky memo became the centerpiece of the war plan.

CIA's plan was approved, with the president ordering Tenet to put it into action. Less than two weeks later, on September 26, the Agency had its first team of CIA officers on the ground in Afghanistan. Called the Northern Alliance Liaison Team, the eight men entered Afghanistan on a rickety old Russian helicopter that the Agency had bought the year before, and immediately began to organize local forces to rise up against the Taliban leadership that had been providing safe haven for al Qaʿida. US Special Forces joined Agency officers in Afghanistan on October 17.

The plan was to have the military forces of the Northern Alliance—a fiercely independent, but well-organized, group of Afghan tribes who had not succumbed to Taliban rule—sweep south and push the Taliban from power. They would be guided by CIA officers and the Special Forces on the ground, and they would be assisted by massive precision US air strikes. At the same time, Pashtun tribes opposed to the Taliban—and organized by CIA—would rise up in the south and east. The Taliban therefore would be facing both a conventional military threat from the Northern Alliance and an insurgent uprising from its own Pashtun ranks.

Just a few days after 9/11, Tenet brought his Counterterrorism chief, Cofer Black, to the White House to outline the plan in more detail. Black had significant charisma, confidence, and a tough-minded approach to the world. He had helped to track down the renowned terrorist Carlos the Jackal years earlier, and garnered widespread respect for it. His oversize personality was on display as we walked into the White House and sat with the president.

Black brought with him large boards with pictures of and information about the al Qa'ida leadership. He promised the president the destruction of al Qa'ida in a matter of weeks, and I eyed Tenet with a look on my face saying, "He cannot deliver on that promise. We don't have that kind of intelligence. We don't have the capability to do that." Black then methodically went through the stack of storyboards, saying, "Bin Ladin, dead," flipping the chart over his shoulder and back against the wall. "Zawahiri, dead," and on and on. I looked at Andy Card, and he looked at me. I was thinking—and I was sure Card was thinking—"This is not appropriate for a discussion with the president of the United States."

Later that day, while speaking to the press, the president said he wanted Bin Ladin "dead or alive." The next morning the president, after receiving some media criticism for his statement the day before, said to Tenet with a smile, "Cofer got me worked up yesterday. George, maybe it's best if you don't bring him to see me for a while." Card told the president that I had once been Black's deputy for a short period—a fact I had shared with the chief of staff earlier. The president looked at me with a smile and said, "That's not possible."

* * *

My briefing workload exploded. Before 9/11 I awoke at three a.m. to arrive at the Agency at four a.m., for an eight a.m. briefing of the president. After 9/11 I awoke at twelve thirty a.m. to begin work at one thirty a.m. After 9/11 there was just that much more material to go through every morning. This included the Threat Matrix, a new overnight compilation of all terrorist threats that had appeared in intelligence traffic during the previous twenty-four hours. The Matrix went on for many pages, typically covering fifty to sixty individual reported threats. I needed to know the Matrix inside and out because the president would often ask me about specific entries (he received it before I saw him in the morning). "Michael, tell me about numbers twelve and twenty-four," or "Michael, tell me about number fifty-six." One might be a report of a planned bombing of a US embassy in some part of the world; another might be a plan to assault a US oil tanker transiting the Red Sea; a third might be rumors of an attack on a nuclear power plant in Middle America.

The amount of threat reporting increased dramatically in the weeks following 9/11. Some of this reflected enhanced collection on the part of the US intelligence community and our allies, providing insights into plots we had not been aware of before. Some of it reflected plans for "copycat" attacks by a variety of extremist groups. Some of it reflected existing sources passing along speculation as well as facts and not being clear about the difference between the two. And some of it reflected individuals reporting threats that they knew not to be true—the CT version of yelling fire in a crowded theater. Bottom line: some of the increase reflected real plots, and some did not. I had to help sort all this out for the president.

Not only did I need to answer the president's questions about the threat reporting being disseminated by the intelligence community, but I also had to brief him on "imaginative" threats. After 9/11, CIA invited Hollywood screenwriters to the Agency to brainstorm possible attack methodologies—as few before 9/11 could have imagined that al Qa'ida would hijack a plane and use it as a weapon. These scenarios would be presented to the president in a special "Red Cell" format, which had a distinctive design and a disclaimer at the top to remind readers that these were not your typical reports but rather were highly speculative products that employed equal doses of intelligence and imagination. We were looking for ideas on how to keep the country safe, from wherever we could get them. The president studied every one of the Red Cell reports, but I had my doubts about how useful they were to the president.

There was an exhausting sense of urgency to everything. Rolling through stop signs and red lights, I drove aggressively to work because no one else was on the road and because I was in that much of a hurry. Once I was so tired that I missed my exit for McLean—the closest town to the Agency—and drove nearly all the way to D.C., some ten miles out of my way, before I realized what I had done. As I got back on course that morning, I thought that I was lucky to have survived driving around in such an exhausted state.

No matter how drained I was, whenever I drove down the long entranceway to CIA, I would be revived by a sense of mission, the signs of which were all around me. Access to the headquarters compound had always been tight, but in the days immediately after 9/11, security was bristling. The normal security protective officers (known as "SPOs") were even more vigilant than usual. Their numbers were augmented by officers in armored Humvees that were parked on the median strips and along the entrance road.

Once my badge was carefully scrutinized I would slowly drive onto the 258-acre compound and past a marble sign that declared it the George Bush Center for Intelligence. Congress had bestowed the name in 1999 to honor the forty-first president and the eleventh director of CIA. There are two main buildings on the complex. I worked in what is called the "Original Headquarters Building" or OHB. President Eisenhower laid the cornerstone for the place in 1959, a year after I was born. Connected to the OHB are two six-story glass-encased towers known as the "New Headquarters Building." The NHB opened in 1991. President Reagan had broken ground for the facility two years earlier. I was among those in the crowd who watched him do so.

Friends and neighbors would often ask me how many people worked at Langley. The answer I would have to give was "A lot," because the actual number is classified. But you only have to look at the traffic streaming in and out or view the overhead photos of the massive parking lots to know the Agency is a major presence. It was generally too confusing to try to explain that Langley doesn't really exist—at least in the legal sense. The actual community where the headquarters is located is called McLean. But everyone calls it Langley anyway. They do not, however, call CIA "the Company"— which seems to be popular only in old movies and novels.

In more peaceful times the headquarters compound would often be referred to as a "campus." The barbed-wire fences surround a leafy property with jogging paths and symbolic artwork competing for space with satellite dishes and old spy planes mounted on pedestals. But this was no peaceful time. So I would quickly make my way to my seventh-floor office, where I would work through the night to gather the latest intelligence to bring to the president shortly after sunrise.

I didn't work alone. A terrific group of analysts supported me. They were young, talented, and eager to learn. They did everything from finding answers to my many questions—often by waking up the analyst who had written a piece—to making copies of the briefing package. They also bailed me out of fixes on many occasions. One day I showed up for work in the middle of the night as usual. Sometime before dawn I discovered that I was wearing two differently colored shoes—one brown and one black. I did not know what I was going to do until I spotted one of the PDB support analysts and demanded to know his shoe size. Turned out it was a match and I commandeered his shoes so that I could walk into the Oval Office without looking like a disheveled mess. Some of those young analysts who supported me during my year of briefing in 2001 are today making their way to the very top of CIA. I am very proud of them.

* * *

The PDB briefings, which before 9/11 had been about intelligence analysis and reporting, now took on an added dimension. Increasingly, operational decisions were made on the spot and orders given on priorities in the war against al Qa'ida. I would provide the president with updates on exactly what was happening on the ground in Afghanistan, and Tenet would update the president on some of the latest operational developments.

Tenet was out for a few days on an overseas trip, and while he was gone, I started using a detailed table-size military map of Afghanistan to update the president. The map showed the disposition of the Northern Alliance and Pashtun forces fighting on behalf of the United States, as well as the Taliban and al Qa'ida forces defending their territory. I knew the president liked the map. When Tenet returned, he saw, during our prep session, that I was planning to use it, and he made it very clear that he did not want me to do so, arguing it was too detailed for the president.

"I'm using it," I said. "Oh, no you're not," my boss responded. "Oh, yes I am," I said. We were like a bickering married couple. I won the day, and when the president walked into the Situation Room and saw the map spread on the table, he said, "Ah, my map. I love that map!" I just looked at Tenet and smiled.

After the one-time experiment with taking Black to a briefing, Tenet started bringing one of Black's deputies, Hank Crumpton. Crumpton was the senior CIA officer with the daily job of running our war effort in Afghanistan. Crumpton, a smart, savvy, and likable officer, had been called back from a plum overseas assignment to lead the war against al Qa'ida. Crumpton's personality could not be more different from Black's. Crumpton would sit close to the president and, in a near whisper, methodically walk through the latest information. For his part, I think Black was happy to have Crumpton brief the president. Black believed that his rightful place was with his officers working the problem directly.

* * *

While all the pieces for taking on the Taliban and al Qa'ida were in place in only a few weeks, it took a while for the Northern Alliance to get going—much to the dismay of the president. For days our Afghan allies did not start the push south. They were tentative, concerned about what they would face in battle. And every day the president expressed his frustration to Tenet. "When are they going to get moving?" and "What is taking them so long?" were frequent refrains from the commander in chief. But Tenet got the message and pushed hard for action when he returned to Langley, and, in a short time, the Northern Alliance began to move. Once that happened, the collapse of the Taliban unfolded quickly. They were no match for the well-trained Northern Alliance backed by US air strikes.

Our Afghan allies took Kabul in mid-November 2001, and by the end of the year had forced the Taliban from power and significantly disrupted al Qa'ida. Looking back, it is hard to believe that in our military involvement in Afghanistan—which, at this writing, has been going on for over thirteen years—so much was achieved in the first several weeks.

This was CIA's finest hour. The paramilitary operation that Crumpton and his officers carried out, led passionately by Cofer Black, was historic. A handful of CIA officers working closely with a small number of military Special Forces operators moved mountains. At one moment they were calling in deadly accurate air strikes and guiding sophisticated bombs precisely to their targets, and the next they were calling in airdrops to receive saddles they needed to accompany their Northern Alliance counterparts in cavalry missions. Twenty-first-century military tactics merged flawlessly with methods from the seventeenth century.

CIA's post-9/11 achievement was the result of our planning and our great flexibility as an organization, but it was also the result of our knowing the turf so well. In the two years before 9/11, CIA officers had traveled multiple times to northern Afghanistan to meet with a group of tribal warlords there. One of my friends once delivered a briefcase holding a million dollars to one of the key Northern Alliance leaders ("It was heavy," he said). There were long nights of sitting around a campfire under the stars, drinking tea and discussing the history of the Afghan people, Afghan politics, and the future of a country that had been at war for decades. This is how deep and enduring relationships are built in the intelligence business— relationships that made our rapid response to 9/11 and our success possible.

* * *

In the months that followed the attacks of 9/11, despite the weight of the enormous tragedy that had befallen our nation, those of us at the Agency received a tremendous boost from the unity of purpose and determination of the American people. And it was not just Americans. CIA benefited from goodwill and good wishes from not only our traditional foreign intelligence partners but also even longtime foes like the Russians.

It didn't take long for the national sense of unity to evaporate, however. Sadly, the "we are in this together" attitude eroded in favor of "let's find someone to blame" for allowing the attacks to happen. Senator Carl Levin of Michigan said publicly, "Prior to September 11, US intelligence officials had terrorist information that if properly handled could have disrupted or possibly prevented the terrorist attacks.... This is not a matter of scapegoating. This is a matter of accountability." Senator Richard Shelby of Alabama asked, "Has anyone in CIA been held accountable for the failures of September 11 or the events leading up to it?" The officers of the Counterterrorism Center, who had been among the few in the country who recognized the threat and tried to do something about it, now felt very much alone.

A couple of years after I left the briefing job, the finger-pointing even came in my direction. I was on vacation with my family in Normandy when I returned to our hotel to find a note instructing me to call a phone number that I recognized immediately as being at CIA headquarters. I reached Jami Miscik, the deputy director of intelligence and a longtime friend. "Michael, are you sitting down?" she asked. "I am now, what's up?" I responded. "It seems Steve Biegun [the NSC staffer who had been with me in Crawford on August 6, 2001] is telling people that you told the president there was no need to worry about an al Qa'ida attack on the homeland when you briefed the August 6 PDB. They want to share this with the 9/11 Commission." "What!" I said. "That's absurd. It is wrong. The August 6 PDB made clear that there was plenty to worry about—it just didn't have the time, place, and means of attack." It became clear to me that as the political sharks circled the White House, some thought was being given to tossing me—and therefore CIA—over the side. Fortunately, with Miscik's intercession—along with that of Tenet's chief of staff, John Moseman—the idea of pinning responsibility on CIA and me did not gain traction at the more senior levels of the White House.

In fact, senior Bush administration officials later told me that they had not been aware of the idea of throwing me overboard and would have opposed it had it ever reached them. They also told me that President Bush would never have let it happen.

* * *

9/11 changed CIA more than any other single event during my time at the Agency, and probably more than any other single event in the history of the organization. Never before had CIA refocused so abruptly and dramatically as we did after 9/11. The number of officers working on terrorism—including contractors—more than tripled, and the dollars flowing to the terrorism problem jumped even more. Terrorism became the focus of nearly every overseas station and operational division in the Agency. As a result, intelligence collection on terrorism improved significantly. Terrorism analysis got better as well. For the first time, terrorism analysts became the fighter pilots of the analytic ranks. Prior to 9/11, terrorism analysts had been seen as second-class citizens by their counterparts who were working more "weighty" geopolitical issues. Terrorism analysis now attracted some of the best and the brightest of the Agency's analysts, a group who would play a very significant role in the eventual successful hunt for Bin Ladin.

9/11 would also take the Agency in some ways back to its roots—back to the paramilitary days of the Office of Strategic Services, the country's World War II intelligence service. Never before had the Agency had as much latitude to conduct paramilitary operations, and it used those authorities aggressively to protect the country. There would, of course, be a downside to the aggressive use of these authorities. CIA suffered political blowback against some of the operations and activities that were covered by these authorities, particularly our detention and enhanced interrogation program in the early years after 9/11.

Perhaps the biggest downside to our necessary focus on terrorism was the cost to the Agency's ability to be a global intelligence service—to have the access around the world to be able to warn the president in advance of developments that could undermine US national security. There is no doubt in my mind that the resource shift and focus on terrorism were in part responsible for our failure to more clearly foresee some key global developments such as Russia's renewed aggressive behavior with its neighbors.

These failures occurred because the additional personnel resources provided by multiple administrations and Congresses to fight the war against al Qaʻida never fully covered everything we needed to do that—so we had to rob Peter to pay Paul. During the 1990s, the Agency workforce had shrunk by almost 25 percent—our contribution to the "peace dividend." It was the leanest of times. And while the workforce grew significantly after 9/11, the number of employees at the Agency today is just slightly larger than it was in 1991—all trying to cover a world that in almost every respect is much more complex than it was in the immediate aftermath of the collapse of the Soviet Union. But there was no choice; the focus had to be on al Qaʻida.

* * *

So how did our initial victory in Afghanistan—in only months—turn into the longest war in American history? It happened because at some point our goal shifted from ensuring that al Qaʻida would not again be able to use Afghanistan as a launching pad for attacks against the homeland to something else. The mission changed to trying to permanently alter Afghan politics and society. It was an impossible task to turn Afghanistan's tribal society and culture into a liberal democracy. It was an impossible task to convince the Taliban that it should operate inside the Afghan political system rather than outside of it. Perhaps we should have walked away from Afghanistan after forcing al Qaʻida from the country, and we would have told all Afghans, including the Taliban, "If you let al Qaʻida return, so will we."

* * *

Being a presidential briefer is a killer job under the best of circumstances. The hours and the stress take their toll on bodies and marriages. The thought that Mary Beth and I had had early on, that the job would be good for our family life, had been a poor piece of analysis. In late October we decided to escape to Charlottesville—a two-hour drive from D.C.—for a quick romantic overnight escape to celebrate our wedding anniversary. The thing is, my day had started at twelve thirty a.m. because I'd briefed that morning. Even with a nap during the drive down, I was exhausted. We stayed at a bed-and-breakfast and booked dinner for seven p.m.—early for most but definitely late for me. During dessert I fell asleep at the table. Mary Beth saved me from going face-first into my tarte tatin. As we were walking back to our cottage, I slipped down a flight of stairs, breaking off the railing in the process. Some of the other guests looked at me, clearly thinking, "He is really drunk." I looked back, smiled, and said, "Not drunk. Just really tired." I don't think they believed me. So much for a romantic escape.

Because the job was so demanding, I had decided early on to do it for only a year. On January 4, 2002, it was time for me to move on. It was my last briefing. The president was in Crawford, and I brought with me my successor to show him the ropes and introduce him to the president. We arrived at the trailer where the president did his secure video teleconferences, a few minutes before the appointed hour. The president arrived and, before the teleconference went live, he asked me if there was any news in the briefing. I had no option other than to deliver the headline—that we had learned that Usama bin Ladin had escaped from Tora Bora, Afghanistan.

The US military had dropped more ordnance on the location than on any other area since World War II, and yet Bin Ladin had escaped. The forces that would have been necessary to box him in, to keep him from fleeing over the border into Pakistan, had simply not been there. Feeling the frustration of the moment, the president shot the messenger—me.

The president seldom raised his voice, but he did that day. He was angry. He was madder than I have ever seen him. He asked, "How the hell did you lose him? How could he possibly have eluded you? What are your plans now?" I sat there thinking, "I did not have anything to do with this," but I did not dare say a word.

You have never really been chewed out until you have had the bark stripped off of you by the most powerful man in the world. My poor successor sat there wide-eyed, no doubt wondering what he had just signed up for. When the videoconference went live and the smiling faces of Cheney, Rice, and Tenet appeared on-screen, the president wasted no time in asking, "What the hell is this? Michael just told me something about Bin Ladin getting away?"

I left the briefing without saying good-bye to the president. I thought I might never see him again, as my job as briefer was over. But I did not say anything given his understandable anger at what had just transpired in the mountains of Afghanistan. On the drive from Waco to Dallas to catch a flight back to Washington, my cell phone rang. It was the president's personal aide, who asked for my home address. Within a few days, a handwritten note arrived from the president thanking me for my service as his briefer. It was clear to me that the president also felt bad about how our last briefing together had gone.

CHAPTER 5

An Imperfect Storm

Route Irish was the US military code name for the twelve-kilometer stretch of highway that connected the Baghdad International Airport with the secure area known as the "Green Zone." The Green Zone contained the diplomatic facilities of the United States and our coalition partners, significant coalition military assets and headquarters, the Iraqi prime minister's office, the country's parliament, and several other Iraqi government buildings. By the time I first traveled on Route Irish in early 2005, this once-beautiful drive lined by large trees was a terrorist kill zone. Suicide bombers patrolled the highway looking for American or other coalition convoys to ambush.

Climbing into the back of a dusty and mud-covered black armored vehicle, I saw that the two CIA security officers in the front were armed to the teeth—knives, handguns, military assault rifles, and grenade launchers. The grenades were sitting in the open on a console between the driver's seat and the front passenger seat. Having not seen one of the cylindrical grenades for launchers such as theirs before, I innocently asked, "What are those?" The answer was immediate, direct, and sharp: "Don't touch those." And the tone said, "Don't ask any more questions." Chagrined, I turned to look out the window and saw a bullet lodged in the inches-thick glass of the armored vehicle.

I, along with another senior Agency officer, was in Baghdad at the request of Director Porter Goss. Our job was to look into an incident in which Charles Duelfer—CIA's lead man investigating Iraq's weapons of mass destruction program—and the military convoy in which he was riding had been attacked on Route Irish, resulting in the deaths of two Kansas National Guardsmen and severe injuries to a third. Before we pulled out from our parking spot, the lead security agent turned to me and said, "I just want to make something crystal clear. I will take you on one condition. If something happens along the way, you will follow my orders in full—no questions asked." I swallowed hard and said, "Yes, sir."

* * *

President Bush, after one post-9/11 briefing at the ranch in Crawford, in which we had discussed a preemptive Israeli air strike against Hamas in the Gaza Strip, told me, "Michael, my most important job is to protect the American people. I now understand why the Israelis act the way they do when it comes to terrorism." To me, nothing better captured President Bush's thinking about the war in Iraq than this statement. There is no doubt that the president's focus on Iraq was born of 9/11. There is no doubt that, while it was a war of choice, President Bush took us there because he thought it necessary to protect the American people. But there is also no doubt that the Iraq War supported the al Qa'ida narrative and helped spread the group's ideology, a consequence not well understood before the war. So, both in genesis and in effect, the war in Iraq is very much a part of the terrorism story over the past fifteen years.

* * *

President Bush—from the vantage point of his first intelligence briefer—did not come to office with any particular ax to grind with Saddam Hussein. The conventional wisdom, of course, is that Team

Bush arrived in the White House with Iraq already in its gunsights. That might have been true for a small group of Bush appointees, but it is not what I observed from the president. Periodically Iraq would come to the forefront of his attention—for example, when Saddam's forces would fire on US aircraft enforcing the no-fly zone, or when there would be signs that the international sanctions on Iraq were eroding a bit more. And there was certainly concern about whether the sanctions could be maintained over the long term and what Saddam would do when he was no longer in the box. Nonetheless, for the president, there was no early or inherent obsession with Iraq.

There was one occasion that might have conveyed a different sense, and I share it here only to set the record straight. During a session in the Oval Office in the spring of 2001, I mentioned to the president some improvement that had been made in the Iraqi air defense system and suggested to him that "if the United States were ever to engage Iraq militarily, this is something that US forces would have to deal with." The president said to me, "It is not a question of *if* but only a question of *when*, Michael." I know that some will read that comment to mean that Bush had already made his mind up about going to war with Iraq and was only looking for the provocation. But at the time—and to this day—I took him to mean only that in his estimation, at some uncertain time in the future Saddam would push us and he or some future president would have to respond.

* * *

Post 9/11, George Tenet and I continued our Saturday trips to Camp David but the routine was different—the briefings were less leisurely, more focused on terrorism and often took place in a conference room rather than the president's office. On a monitor we could see the vice president, who would be piped in via video teleconference from a "secure location." At one of these post-9/11 sessions, the president and vice president asked Tenet and me if Iraq had played any role in the attacks. Tenet and I told the president and others that there was no intelligence to suggest that Iraq had had any role in the attack—and that if any nation had supported al Qa'ida it was more likely to have been Iran, which had been responsible for the bombing of the Khobar Towers in Saudi Arabia in 1996 that killed nineteen US servicemen and wounded hundreds of others. But we quickly added that there was no evidence of an Iran–al Qa'ida connection either.

At one point after 9/11, though, it seemed as if we might have discovered an al Qa'ida–Iraq connection. The Czech intelligence service told us a source had told it that a 9/11 hijacker, Mohamed Atta, had met with an Iraqi intelligence officer named Ahmad Samir al-Ani at the Iraqi embassy in Prague on April 9, 2001, at eleven a.m., just five months before the attack. The Czechs provided a fuzzy surveillance photo of the man they thought to be Atta.

I brought this into the Oval Office. In its initial analysis of the photo, CIA gave some credibility to the report. The US legal attaché (an FBI special agent attached to American embassies overseas) in Prague met with the Czech source, and the assessment of the "LegAtt" and the Czech officers present was that they were 70 percent confident the source was sincere and believed his own story regarding the meeting. The president asked a lot of questions, but unfortunately there was much more that we did not know than that we did know.

The possibility of an Iraqi connection—particularly a connection to the man we believed to have been the lead hijacker—was explosive. The story was leaked very quickly, with the Czech interior minister confirming it publicly. In early December, Vice President Cheney was the first US official to confirm the story, on *Meet the Press*. The vice president told Tim Russert, "It's been pretty well confirmed that he [Atta] did go to Prague and he did meet with a senior official of the Iraqi intelligence service in Czechoslovakia [sic] last April." The vice president went on to note that we did not know the purpose of the meeting and that we needed to investigate more.

The bottom line of the ensuing investigation was that the Czech story did not seem to be true, and I kept the president informed throughout the process. The FBI did an exhaustive review of Atta's whereabouts during the time in question and, although we were not absolutely certain, every indication was that he had been in the United States. The Czechs did their own investigation and could not find any records of Atta's having been in the country in April 2001. In addition, Czech investigators put al-Ani seventy miles from Prague when the alleged meeting occurred.

Despite our efforts to un-ring the bell on the Iraqi–al Qa'ida Prague connection, a few in the administration—Vice President Cheney, in particular—repeatedly raised it in public comments. There was no similar obsession with the matter on the president's part, however. Once we closed the books on the issue, he never asked about it again.

After spending almost an hour every morning with the president, for four months after 9/11, I came to understand his deep concern about Iraq. To me, the president's thinking on Iraq was motivated by the soul-crushing impact of 9/11 and the legitimate fear that as bad as 9/11 had been, things could be much worse— if Saddam got it into his head to either use his weapons of mass destruction as a terrorist tool against the West, or provide those weapons to an international terrorist group. Although the intelligence community considered either of these developments unlikely, I believe the president considered both scenarios risks he could not ignore, particularly since the country had just suffered the single worst attack in our history. At the end of the day, it was the threat of Iraq's weapons of mass destruction being used against the United States that led the president to take us to war in Iraq.

* * *

When my year as intelligence briefer to the president ended, I was full of mixed emotions. I was relieved to have the burden of such a demanding job lifted from my shoulders, but I was also saddened by the thought that I might never again be an eyewitness to and occasional participant in the making of so much history.

For a short period after I left the briefing job, I kept my hand in the PDB process by leading the component within CIA that both produces the PDB and supports the briefers. (In addition to the personal briefer for the president, there are a cadre of other briefers who perform a similar mission for senior officials like the vice president, the secretary of state, the secretary of defense, and a handful of other top leaders.) It was an important job, but it lacked the adrenaline rush one got from being quizzed directly by the president of the United States six days a week.

After about nine months, in the early fall of 2002, I was selected to be one of the two deputies to the deputy director for intelligence, Jami Miscik. Miscik, the first woman ever to hold the post of CIA's top analyst, was a contemporary of mine. She had been Tenet's executive assistant when Tenet made the transition from deputy director to director, and I'd watched as she managed the nomination process—thinking of everything, leaving nothing to chance, keeping her hand on every lever of the Agency.

In my new role, Miscik asked me to focus on ensuring that the analytic directorate was making the right investments in people, programs, and processes to remain on the cutting edge of analysis—covering everything from hiring the best and brightest to guaranteeing that the analysts had the technology they needed to deal with an ever-increasing volume of information. I also, not surprisingly, helped Miscik and her principal deputy, Scott White, supervise the production of all the intelligence analysis that the Agency created.

When it came to Iraq at that time, our focus was on Iraqi links to terrorism. It was, somewhat surprisingly, not on Iraq's WMD programs.

One of the hallmarks of George Tenet's leadership style was to form strong relations with talented individuals within the Agency and select point persons on certain subjects, no matter their rank or place in the hierarchy. He referred to this as having a "belly button"—one person he could poke in the stomach (figuratively and sometimes literally) when he needed something done. The Directorate of Intelligence (DI)—my outfit—remained Tenet's go-to place for dealing with terrorism analysis on Iraq, but for matters dealing with Iraq and its weapons of mass destruction he chose a senior officer on the National Intelligence Council (NIC), Bob Walpole, to be his "belly button." The NIC is an intelligence community entity of senior analysts that, at the time, reported directly to the director of central intelligence, or DCI (today the NIC reports to the director of national intelligence, or DNI). That is not to say that the DI was not producing intelligence pieces on the subject of Iraq and WMD—in fact, it was producing the vast majority of the analysis in the community. What was different was that on Iraqi WMD, Tenet and his deputy John McLaughlin largely interacted with CIA analysts through Walpole, not through the DI front office. This left me with less of a sense of ownership on the WMD issue than on other Iraq issues. This was the downside of Tenet's belly-button approach, particularly when the chosen individual is outside the regular chain of command. This is not an excuse—it is simply an explanation that will become relevant as this story unfolds.

During the fall of 2002 and into the following winter, interest regarding Iraq grew exponentially, and Miscik asked me to get increasingly involved. I played a role in several events that in retrospect would turn out to be crucial. One occurred in October, when the White House sent the Agency a speech to vet. White House staff wanted the president to deliver remarks in Cincinnati laying out the administration's concerns about Iraq. Miscik handed me the draft and asked me to review it over a weekend. While the Agency strictly stays away from passing judgment on matters of policy, it plays an important role in making sure that the president and his top aides do not inadvertently get the facts or key analytic judgments wrong or, just as important, say something that would damage our ability to collect intelligence in the future.

Going through the draft, the group of analysts I had assembled came across the statement that Saddam had been "caught attempting to purchase up to 500 metric tons of uranium oxide from sources in Africa—an essential ingredient in the enrichment process." While there had indeed been a report to that effect provided to us by British intelligence, for a variety of reasons intelligence analysts throughout the US government did not believe it. In fact, just the day before, CIA officers had testified before a closed session of Congress that we did not believe the British report. I explained all this to the White House speechwriters in two memos—one on Saturday and one on Sunday—but found them stubbornly insisting on keeping the language in the speech. After failing to get the language pulled, I walked into Tenet's office and told him the story. He immediately punched the button on a secure phone that connected him directly with Steve Hadley, the president's deputy national security advisor. Tenet outlined our concerns with the text, and he told Hadley to take the language out of the speech. Tenet hung up the phone and said to me, "Hadley says it's gone," and indeed it was not in the Cincinnati speech. However, the British "yellowcake" assertion would mysteriously reappear in the president's State of the Union speech just months later, with disastrous political effect.

Throughout that period there were also several visits to CIA headquarters by Vice President Cheney and members of his staff to conduct "deep dives" with Agency analysts into matters involving

Iraq. When these visits became known on the outside, some observers suggested that they were an attempt to politicize intelligence, to shape CIA's analysis. I did not see them that way.

In fact, they were driven by some imprecision on our part. One of the most important aspects of the PDB briefing process was the ability of the recipients to ask questions and, for the most part, get those questions answered within twenty-four hours with a memo written by expert analysts. The National Security Council principals and deputies in the Bush administration were prolific requesters of what we called "PDB Memos." Many were requested on issues related to Iraq's weapons of mass destruction program and its ties to terrorism, and not all of the responses were well done. Different memos seemed to take the reader in different directions, particularly on the terrorism issue. For this reason, and just to understand the issues at a deeper level, the vice president made multiple trips to the Agency.

I attended at least two such sessions, and they seemed to me to be examples of good government. I felt that the senior officials who visited the Agency (Cheney was accompanied by his national security aide Scooter Libby and others) were digging down and trying to understand what we knew and thought. The vice president was *thorough* and came armed with a lot of questions, but he did not push a particular line of argument. Asking a lot of questions was his right—indeed his responsibility—and it was an analyst's job to answer the questions fully and honestly. And the analysts did so—even if on a couple of occasions it meant telling the vice president things that he might not have wanted to hear. In my experience, intelligence analysts *love* to tell policy-makers when they are wrong—and ours missed few opportunities to do so.

It was this flurry of activity in the fall of 2002—a rush to complete analytic assessments on Iraq, the Cincinnati speech, and the intense administration focus on Iraq—that led those of us at CIA to think that we could well be headed to war. There was no naïveté on our part. This realization told us that every piece of analysis we did could have enormous consequences.

* * *

In June 2002, at the direction of Miscik, CIA's Office of Terrorism Analysis, part of the Counterterrorism Center, prepared and issued a classified report called *Iraq & al Qa'ida: Interpreting a Murky Relationship*. This paper was different in scope and intention from just about any other I can recall. It was more of an intellectual exercise—an effort to see how far the analysts could push the evidence without stretching it beyond plausibility. In doing this, it demonstrated the weakness of the case as much as its plausibility. The report was forward-leaning regarding the possibility of Saddam's cooperating with al Qa'ida, and it contained a "scope note" at the top that said, "This intelligence assessment responds to senior policy maker interest in a comprehensive assessment of Iraqi regime links to al Qa'ida. Our approach is *purposefully aggressive in seeking to draw connections*, on the assumption that any indication of a relationship between these two hostile elements could carry great dangers to the United States" (emphasis added). On the issue of a relationship between Iraq and al Qa'ida, the paper left the strong impression that there might be one. Well-placed staffers in the Pentagon and the Office of the Vice President liked it.

But the scope note was not read closely enough, and some readers assumed the report represented what CIA really thought about the al Qa'ida–Iraq relationship. So Miscik now asked the analysts to write not a provocative "worst-case" paper but one on where the evidence really took them, what they really thought. The draft of this paper, also written by the analysts in the Office of Terrorism Analysis, came to very different conclusions from the first paper. It pointed out Saddam's historical and continuing support of Palestinian terrorist groups, but on the important question of the link between al Qa'ida and the Iraqi government, it concluded that while there was some contact in the past between the two, there was no evidence of any working relationship before, during, or after 9/11, and no evidence of Iraqi complicity in or foreknowledge of 9/11.

Miscik put me in charge of reviewing the second paper, titled *Iraqi Support to Terrorism*, to make sure it stood up to scrutiny and that it was supported by all the analysts as the definitive paper, not just a second view on the subject. I did what I always did in those situations—I read the paper closely several times, writing numerous questions in the margins, and then I brought all the analysts—both the authors of the new paper and the authors of the earlier analysis, as well as the terrorism and Iraq analysts—into Miscik's conference room, where we went over the new paper and its key conclusions. It took several hours. With Miscik joining us—given the importance of the issue—the authors of the latest paper were able to address all my questions and concerns, and all the analysts were able to agree on the key judgments.

With that, the paper was disseminated. It was not well received in all quarters. Scooter Libby called Miscik, saying that the paper's conclusions were wrong and that it ignored important pieces of intelligence. He said, loudly enough for White and me to hear as we stood in Miscik's office, "Withdraw the paper!" Miscik refused, saying she was standing by her analysts. Libby escalated the matter to McLaughlin, Tenet's deputy. Miscik said she would resign before withdrawing the paper. McLaughlin and Tenet both backed Miscik's principled stance—and the paper stood as CIA's view of the issue. Finally Tenet called Hadley and said, "We're done talking about the Iraq terrorism paper." That ended the matter. Libby's attempt to intimidate Miscik was the most blatant attempt to politicize intelligence that I saw in thirty-three years in the business, and it would not be the last attempt by Libby to do so.

President Bush even weighed in on the debate. Each Christmas eve, Miscik would herself do the PDB briefing for the president, giving the briefer the day off. And on the morning of December 24, 2002, she traveled to Camp David to see the president. At the end of the briefing, as Miscik was gathering her things to depart, the president told her that he was aware of the debate over the Iraq terrorism paper and that he wanted her to know that he had her back. He said that he wanted her and her analysts to continue to "call 'em like you see 'em." It was a hugely important thing for the president to say.

Despite the paper and its conclusions, there were senior administration officials, most significantly the vice president, who continued to imply publicly that there was a current connection between Iraq and al Qa'ida. This was inconsistent with the analysis, but the implications continued—all to the detriment of the American people's understanding of the truth. In a *Washington Post* poll conducted in August 2003, 70 percent of respondents believed it was likely that Saddam Hussein had been personally involved in the 9/11 attacks.

As it turns out, the overall judgments in the *Iraqi Support to Terrorism* paper were largely correct—and to the extent that they were wrong, they actually overstated the ties between Iraq and al Qa'ida. One error was the judgment that there had been, well before 9/11, contacts between Saddam's intelligence apparatus and al Qa'ida. That information had come from an al Qa'ida operative by the name of Ibn al-Shaykh al-Libi, who had provided the information under interrogation by the Egyptian intelligence service. Later, in US custody, al-Libi would recant his statements, saying that he'd only told the Egyptians what he did because he'd thought it was what they wanted to hear.

After the fall of Saddam, the United States never found anything in the files of the Iraqi intelligence service, or any other Iraqi ministry, indicating that there was ever any kind of relationship between the Iraqis and al Qa'ida.

Unfortunately, Miscik, White, and I did not apply the same kind of rigor to our analysts' assessments of Iraq's weapons of mass destruction program. Although this is something we all regret, it occurred, in part, I believe, because the National Intelligence Council had been placed in the lead by Tenet. The senior officer on the NIC responsible, Bob Walpole, was careful, experienced, knowledgeable, and well liked. It was Walpole who worked directly with the analysts and their immediate managers to draft the National Intelligence Estimate on Iraq's weapons of mass destruction that was published in the fall of 2002. An NIE represents the authoritative views of the entire intelligence community on an issue. They are carefully considered—the coordination sessions among the analysts are rigorous and NIEs are approved by the leadership of each of the agencies in the community.

This particular NIE, titled *Iraq's Continuing Programs for Weapons of Mass Destruction*, stated, "We judge that Iraq has continued its weapons of mass destruction programs in defiance of UN resolutions and restrictions." The NIE noted that Baghdad had active chemical and biological weapons programs, that Iraq was reconstituting its nuclear weapons programs, and that Iraq had missiles with ranges in excess of UN-imposed limits.

There was little controversy regarding the NIE (one agency, the State Department's intelligence shop, dissented on one aspect of the paper—the nuclear question—but agreed on all others) because almost everyone who had looked at the issue, from intelligence services around the world to think tanks and the United Nations itself, had come to the same conclusion. There were no outliers, no group with a different view, no one to force a broader debate that might have led to a more rigorous assessment on the part of the analysts. Groupthink turned out to be part of the problem. The view that hard-liners in the Bush administration forced the intelligence community into its position on WMD is just flat wrong. No one pushed. The analysts were already there and they had been there for years, long before Bush came to office.

The most significant dissent came from the Department of Energy. While DOE analysts agreed that the Iraqis were in the process of reconstituting their nuclear weapons program, they did not buy the argument that the aluminum tubes being purchased by the Iraqis overseas were for centrifuges. CIA analysts believed that these tubes were exactly the right size for the outer casings for centrifuge rotors capable of producing highly enriched uranium, and too high-end—too expensive—for use in a multiple rocket launcher system, which is what the Iraqis claimed they were building. DOE disputed the CIA view in a lengthy dissent. But, in addition to agreeing with the CIA analysts that the tubes were for centrifuges, the US Army's National Ground Intelligence Center (NGIC), the authority on conventional weapons, backed the view that they were not for rockets. Senior leaders in the intelligence community gave considerable weight to NGIC's view, given its expertise on the issue.

When I was still briefing the president, I did a show-and-tell on the aluminum tubes Iraq had been purchasing from an overseas company. CIA had clandestinely acquired one of the tubes, and one Saturday I carried it to Camp David to show to the president. The tube was about six inches in diameter and about four feet tall. The Secret Service eyed me warily as I carried it into Laurel Lodge for the briefing, but did not stop me. (Once, with prior approval from the Secret Service, I took a new terrorist assassination tool into the Oval Office. CIA will not allow me to describe it here because it remains extremely sensitive, even nearly fifteen years later.) I showed the tube to the president and explained how it worked. But that aspect of the briefing was largely a bust; the president did not seem interested, as the tube, by itself, did not prove anything. I should have known better.

The problem, of course, was not just that the briefing had fallen flat. The much bigger problem is that we were wrong. We were wrong about the tubes; they were for the rocket system, and we never figured out why the Iraqis purchased a much more technically advanced—and therefore much more expensive—tube than they had to. This highlights a problem with the analysis—mirror imaging. In this case, we knew that the US military would never use such high-end aluminum for a rocket launcher, and therefore we assumed that the Iraqis would not do so either.

We were wrong about almost everything else in the NIE, except the judgments about missiles. Saddam, for reasons we would discover later, had ended his weapons of mass destruction programs in order to try to get out from under sanctions that had strangled his economy. Once free of sanctions, he fully intended to restart the programs. But the bottom line for the intelligence community and the Agency was that we got the vast majority of the judgments on Iraq and WMD wrong.

I do not know if it would have made a difference had Miscik, White, and I devoted more time and more focus to the WMD issues, as much time as we had spent on the question of Iraq's links to al Qa'ida. Perhaps it would have. Perhaps not. But the best chance of getting to the right answer would have been for us to do so.

* * *

Perhaps my most significant involvement in the Iraq WMD story was my role in the preparation of Secretary Colin Powell's speech to the UN on Iraq.

In late 2002, John McLaughlin called Bob Walpole and me into his office. McLaughlin, Tenet's deputy, had, like me, grown up on the analytic side of the business. In addition to being an analyst, John was also a professional magician. He once did a trick for the president of Argentina wherein he took a one-dollar bill, folded it many times until it was a small square, and then slowly unfolded it, revealing a hundred-dollar bill. The Argentine president looked at John and said, "I want you to be my finance minister." After leaving government, McLaughlin came to dinner at our home and after the meal announced, to the delight of the kids, that he would be happy to perform some magic tricks. As the kids gathered around McLaughlin, each was holding a dollar bill. I had told them the story of the Argentine president, and they were looking to cash in.

McLaughlin was a magician as a leader of analysis as well, and I learned a great deal from him about that particular art. John's method, which became my method, was to ask question after question to push analysts' thinking deeper than they would go on their own. Of all the living former deputy directors of the Agency, I consider him the dean for his mastery of our profession.

In his office that day, McLaughlin told Walpole and me, "A decision has been made at the White House that we need an 'Adlai Stevenson moment' at the UN." (This was a reference to the time in August 1962 when Stevenson confronted the Soviets over the missile program in Cuba, with photographs from a U-2 reconnaissance plane.) "I need you guys to work on three papers to help inform the speechwriters for this event," McLaughlin said.

As usual, Walpole was given the task of preparing the WMD paper. I had the lead on the other two documents—one on Iraq's links to terrorism and the other on its human rights record. McLaughlin made clear that none of these papers were to be crafted out of whole cloth but that they instead should be pulled from the finished intelligence that had previously been produced. For the WMD paper, Bob relied heavily on the NIE that had been published. I relied on our controversial—at least in Scooter Libby's office—Iraq terrorism paper, as well as some other work done by our analysts on Iraq's atrocious human rights record.

The three papers bounced around in revision for a week or so before McLaughlin eventually sent them over to the White House. They were clearly read, because one afternoon White House officials, led by Hadley, came to the Agency to discuss them. They asked questions to understand exactly what we were saying, and occasionally asked why we had left a particular piece of intelligence out of our narrative. The meeting went well, and we never heard another word about the papers from the White House. Sometime thereafter we learned that Secretary Powell had been chosen to be the messenger at the UN and that his speechwriters were working on his remarks.

In late January 2003, Powell wanted to come to CIA, along with a few members of his staff, to work on the speech from inside the Agency itself. I had never heard of such a request before or since, but it was clear what he was doing. He was not going to say anything that George Tenet and John McLaughlin did not think they could stand behind, and Powell wanted it to be seen that way; preparing for the UN speech at CIA and having Tenet sit behind him when he delivered that speech were the best ways to achieve that. Tenet said yes to Powell's request and gave me the task of making sure that Powell and his aides had everything they needed.

Not everyone agreed with Tenet's decision. Miscik, Tenet's head of analysis, believed that crafting a policy speech in the halls of the Central Intelligence Agency was crossing the line between intelligence and policy—that intelligence officers should provide objective analysis of a situation and leave it to policy-makers to make policy. Miscik felt so strongly about this that she recused herself from participating in the process. I was not aware of her principled stance until much later. My own view at the time was that it was our job to fact-check the secretary's presentation but not to write it. And, while Powell's preparing for his speech at the Agency might create perception problems, I believed that what mattered was what actually happened. I felt we could do our job and meet our responsibilities to the American people at the same time.

When Powell arrived he had a working draft of his speech, and much of it contained information of unknown origin. I was sent to find out why. Both of the State Department speechwriters were former Agency employees, and I went to see them. "Where did you get the input to draft the speech?" I asked. I expected to see the three papers that Walpole and I had prepared at McLaughlin's request, but they showed me something completely different. They showed me papers produced by the vice president's office. As I flipped through the papers, I saw judgments that went well beyond CIA analysis, and facts that I had not seen before.

Not only had the vice president's staffers written their own analytic papers to get their views into the secretary's speech, they also parachuted into CIA headquarters to lobby for their point of view. John Hannah, a member of the vice president's staff, showed up at Langley, bringing with him binders filled with "intelligence" on Saddam's weapons of mass destruction program. He even took over Miscik's personal conference room.

Part of my job was to take every draft of the speech and sit with Bob Walpole and the analysts and ask, "Are all the facts correct here? Is the analysis right? Can we stand behind this?" This process took time. The analysts would ask, "Where did this come from?" Hannah joined us and would flip through his thick binder and pull out an intelligence report and say, "From here." The analysts and Hannah would then spend time debating the credibility or the meaning of the information. The analysts won every debate. The speech was slowly being stripped of what had been added by the vice president's staff.

The degree of analysis being done by political appointees was unprecedented in my career. Officials in the vice president's office were trying to be both the analysts and the policy-makers. A similar dynamic was occurring in Doug Feith's office at the Pentagon, where Feith, the most senior policy advisor to the secretary of defense, had created his own unit to conduct intelligence analysis.

My office was just ten or fifteen feet from Miscik's conference room, and at one point Hannah asked me if I had a minute to talk. I said, "Of course." He politely asked me why the British information on Iraq's trying to purchase uranium in Africa was not in the speech. "Because we don't believe it," I said. "But," he correctly pointed out, "it is referenced in the text of Walpole's NIE." "Well," I said, "I think it is caveated in the NIE, and, in any case, the analysts have some very good reasons why they do not believe the information to be true." I offered to bring the analysts up to explain it to him, and he accepted. One of our top analysts sat with him for several hours going over our thinking on the issue. Hannah never raised the issue with me again, and I did not hear anything more about the alleged attempt to purchase uranium until President Bush talked about it in the State of Union address.

After each of the various drafts went through the vetting process that I had set up with the analysts, Secretary Powell, camped out in Director Tenet's conference room, would go over it word by word, sentence by sentence. My sense was that he wanted to understand the information fully, to be able to articulate it in a way that the public would understand, and to make sure that Tenet and McLaughlin would stand behind the speech as delivered. In total, the secretary spent dozens of hours, over a weekend, in the conference room, asking question after question.

During this process, mostly with McLaughlin, Walpole, and the analysts answering questions, I began to see a trend. Point by point Powell would ask us for backup information on the assertions, and as we dug into them, many seemed to fall apart before my eyes. And the material falling apart was not the White House additions. My team had already removed those. No, what was collapsing was some of the facts used in the NIE to support the judgments there. I noticed this trend, but I did not share this with Tenet, McLaughlin, or Miscik, as I concluded that there was still plenty of solid information standing behind the judgments in the NIE. I regret not doing so, although I do not know what difference it might have made.

There was another, more significant, missed opportunity, relating to the judgment that Saddam possessed a mobile biological weapons production capability. This judgment was based on information from four sources. One of those sources was a Defense Intelligence Agency asset, and DIA had learned, after the NIE was published in 2002 (but before the sessions with Powell), that he was a "fabricator"—an intelligence source who lies for any one of multiple reasons, usually to make him- or herself appear more valuable. DIA had done the right thing and recalled the original reporting. But a reference to the source and his information made it into the draft speech, and no one—neither the DIA representative in the conference room with the secretary nor our analysts—said a word about the fabrication or the recall. I do not know why they did not speak up. When I learned about this months later, I was stunned and wrote a note to Miscik calling the episode "analytic malpractice."

One of the other sources of the mobile lab information was a German with the apt code name of "Curveball." Only after the war had started and stockpiles of WMD had failed to materialize did I hear rumblings that the Germans did not trust their own source. During the preparation of the Powell speech, and unbeknownst to me at the time, mid-level CIA operations officers did express some concerns about the credibility of Curveball—although they never said he was a fabricator—but their reasoning was not robust and not compelling to the analysts. The analysts insisted they were confident in Curveball—in large part because there were three other sources backing up his story (usually not a reason to be confident in someone's credibility)—and that an independent review from the National Labs had stated that the reporting was plausible. (The National Labs are institutions that conduct research for the US government on nuclear and other advanced weapons.) As it turned out, Curveball was a fabricator and later admitted that he had lied because of a personal agenda to get rid of Saddam.

In retrospect, this could have been a turning point. Had the analysts said to Powell, Tenet, and McLaughlin that two of the four streams of information on the mobile labs lacked credibility, it would have raised eyebrows. It would have at minimum led us to review the mobile lab issue, if not the broader issue. One of the three could well have said, "So, what else lacks credibility here?"

While the secretary's work on the WMD portion of the presentation was methodical, the discussion on the terrorism portion was short, but dramatic. The first draft of this part of the speech—which was written by Scooter Libby or one of his aides in the vice president's office, and which did not go through my vetting process— did not say directly but implied that Saddam was complicit in 9/11. It was wrong, and Secretary Powell saw the inaccuracy immediately. Several senior White House officials, including Rice, as well as Hadley, sat in on some of the sessions with the secretary, and with Libby in the room, Powell said to Tenet, "George, you don't believe this crap about Iraq and al Qa'ida, do you?" Tenet said, "No, Mr. Secretary, we do not. I do not know where that came from, but we will fix it." Tenet then turned to the deputy director of CIA's Office of Terrorism Analysis, Philip Mudd, and said, "Rewrite this."

Libby did not say a word. It had been yet another attempt to politicize the terrorism analysis. What the secretary ultimately said about Iraq and terrorism at the United Nations matched very closely what Mudd wrote in the hours after the discussion between Powell and Tenet, and was fully consistent with the second CIA paper on the topic, *Iraq Support to Terrorism*.

* * *

On a number of occasions in recent years, Secretary Powell has expressed chagrin that no one from the intelligence community has publicly come forward and apologized to him for putting his well-deserved reputation for probity at risk by arming him with bad intelligence to use as the basis of his UN speech. I am absolutely confident that no one at CIA intentionally misled him, politicized analysis, or tried to provide anything but the best information— but CIA and the broader intelligence community clearly failed him and the American public. So, as someone in the chain of command at the time the Iraq WMD analysis was provided, I would like to use this opportunity to publicly apologize to Secretary Powell.

* * *

As we approached war, the views among many Middle Eastern specialists at CIA were decidedly antiwar. Many at the Agency were concerned that bringing down Saddam would open a Pandora's box. While CIA should not put policy advice on the table, I believe we did have a responsibility prewar to produce a detailed analysis of the likely postwar scenarios—with a clear outline of the key factors that would have determined whether we ended up with stability or instability. That paper was never written (given the importance of the president's decision, it should have been a National Intelligence Estimate). No analyst initiated such a paper and no one in the chain of command, from a first-line supervisor at CIA all the way to the president, requested it.

My own feelings about the war were mixed. On the one hand, based on the views of the analysts, I believed Saddam had chemical and biological weapons, was restarting his nuclear weapons program, and was working on missiles of various ranges to deliver all these weapons. I worried less about Saddam's giving these weapons to al Qa'ida than I did about his eventually using them himself. And I worried that his acquisition of a nuclear weapon would give him the confidence to pursue a very aggressive foreign policy in the region. To top it off, Saddam had ignored nearly a dozen UN Security Council resolutions for years, and either the UN matters or it does not. On the other hand, Saddam was not an imminent threat, and I was uncomfortable with US military action—putting the lives of young Americans at risk—in the absence of imminence. And I worried about the unintended consequences of military action, which are always numerous and significant.

In retrospect it is easy to criticize the decision to go to war. But I understand why the president felt it necessary. And it is hard to say that anyone presented with the same facts and burdens would have come to a different conclusion. After all, most of Congress saw the war as necessary for the same reasons that the president did.

* * *

I was well into another assignment by the time we learned that we had been wrong in our judgments. This awareness did not happen overnight. It came on slowly, as coalition forces on the ground in Iraq could find nothing at all related to an Iraqi WMD program and as Tenet set up a survey group to thoroughly investigate the matter. When it finally became clear, we knew that this had been one of the largest intelligence failures in the history of the Agency.

Much has been written and said about what went wrong and

my intent here is not to offer excuses or to be defensive. But after spending much time analyzing why we were so wrong, I think I have some explanations of value. This is certainly not a thorough or complete analysis of this massive intelligence failure, but it highlights what I think was most important.

The first thing that should be said is that CIA's judgment about Saddam and WMD was nothing new, nor was it unique. Neither of these facts makes it OK that CIA was wrong, but they are important to consider. This analytic conclusion went back to the Clinton administration, and it was not just the US intelligence community that believed Saddam had a weapons program. All foreign intelligence services that looked at the issue thought the same, as did think tanks, distinguished university professors, and even the United Nations. If you had polled Iraqi military and intelligence officers in 2002, I am convinced you would have found a large majority saying their boss had active WMD programs.

The perception that the Bush administration pushed the intelligence community toward believing that Saddam had WMD is just wrong. No one pushed us—we were already there. The notion that we were telling the White House what it wanted to hear can easily be debunked. Look at the question of Saddam's connections to al Qa'ida. We held our ground and refused to go where the intelligence did not take us. On WMD, if we'd believed it was likely that Saddam had none, it would have been an act of madness to take the position we did. Following an invasion, a stockpile would either turn up or not. To go to war knowing you are soon going to be proven wrong would be insane.

So how could we get it so wrong? The answer is major mistakes on both the analytic and collection sides of the intelligence community— the latter being something that has not often been discussed.

First let me address the analytic question. The problems with the analysis were numerous, although a lack of resources was not one of them (Iraq was a priority focus for analysts at CIA and throughout the intelligence community). One problem was what I call "analytic creep." What had begun as assumptions about Saddam and his program became firm judgments. It took a team of our smartest analysts, looking back with twenty-twenty hindsight, to identify this analytic creep.

In addition, biases were rampant. One of these was the "hindsight bias" on the part of the intelligence community analysts who had missed Saddam's nearly acquiring a nuclear weapon in the early 1990s and did not want to make that mistake twice. Another was the "historical bias"—we knew that Saddam had chemical weapons and had used them on Iraqi Kurds and on the Iranians; and if he'd possessed this capability once, he must still have had it. The third was "review bias." In the late 1990s, Donald Rumsfeld, then a private citizen, had led a commission that assessed the intelligence community's judgments over time regarding the foreign ballistic missile threat to the United States. His critique of the analysts was blistering. He chastised them—in both his team's interviews with them and the final report—for focusing on the most likely outcome rather than on what could be the worst-case outcome. The truth is that analysts must do both, but there is no doubt in my mind that the Rumsfeld Commission created its own bias with regard to Saddam's weapons program.

Another problem was confirmation bias—the tendency to accept facts as true if they support one's view and to reject them otherwise. Some of the sources on which we relied were clearly sent our way by outside groups with an agenda, like the dissident group the Iraqi National Congress (INC), which never met a "Saddam has WMD" story it didn't like, and we accepted much of the reporting of these sources as fact. After the invasion, INC leader Ahmed Chalabi bragged about the information provided by members of his group, calling them "heroes in error." Well, he got that half right.

But by far the biggest mistake made by the analysts—and one that encompasses all the above issues—was not that they came to the wrong conclusion about Iraq's WMD program, but rather that they did not rigorously ask themselves how confident they were in their judgments. If you took all the intelligence available to the analysts when they drafted the NIE and looked at it today, you would come to the conclusion that Saddam had chemical and biological weapons programs and was on the verge of restarting his nuclear weapons program. But had the analysts at the time thoughtfully and rigorously asked themselves how confident they were in those judgments, they would most likely have said, "Not very." That would have been a very different message to the president and other policy-makers and potentially could have affected their policy decision.

Anyone who has seen the now-declassified Key Judgments from the NIE knows that a text box at the end briefly discusses confidence levels and notes that analysts had high confidence in their judgments that Saddam had chemical and biological weapons and was reconstituting his nuclear program. But the analysts did not really think about that statement before making it. It was a reflection of their gut view. It did not reflect a thorough assessment of the question of confidence levels. Such a rigorous assessment was missing. It was simply not part of an analyst's tool kit in those days.

Why do I think we would have reported low confidence if we had carefully considered the question? Because the vast majority of the information we were working with was at least four years old. It dated back to 1998, before UN weapons inspectors were kicked out of Iraq; once they'd left the country, our intelligence became more limited. And to top it off, the case in support of the notion that Saddam had active WMD programs was largely circumstantial. As noted earlier, we also relied too heavily on the knowledge that he'd once had chemical weapons, once used chemical weapons, and, at the start of the first Gulf War, been much closer to having a nuclear weapon than we had previously thought. The fact that he'd once had chemical weapons and had once pursued a nuclear weapon was actually irrelevant to whether he was doing so in 2003.

In addition to the brief sentences on confidence levels in the Key Judgments of the NIE, we created an impression that the analysts had high confidence in other ways. The text of the NIE was nuanced, but the Key Judgments were not. When we wrote pieces for the president, the analysts wrote with authority on the issue. This is why I personally never found fault with George Tenet's alleged "slam dunk" comment. The way the analysts talked and wrote about their judgments would have led anyone to think it was a slam dunk—that is, that Saddam definitely had active WMD programs. No one ever said to me, Miscik, McLaughlin, Tenet, Rice, or the president, "You know, there is a chance he might not have them." Such a statement would have gotten everyone's attention.

In the aftermath of the Iraq debacle, those of us on the analytic side of CIA spent a lot of time thinking about how we had failed. Miscik established a lessons-learned task force called the Iraq Review Group. This was an important step, as it showed the DI was willing to take ownership for the failure. The Review Group did its job with thoroughness and rigor. It identified a number of failures, and it made a number of important recommendations. Stealing an idea from the military, which periodically holds "safety stand-downs" following aviation mishaps, Miscik set aside a couple of days for the Review Group to present its findings to every analyst at the Agency. Miscik is to be commended for how she handled the aftermath. She showed leadership, integrity, and professionalism, and the Agency today is much better off for the effort.

The key recommendation made by the Review Group—which was adopted—was that in all future major intelligence products, analysts be required to include a thorough assessment and

explicit statement regarding their level of confidence in the judgments expressed. This practice is now ingrained in both analysts
and policy-makers. Confidence levels are part of the normal conversation that happens every day in the Agency, in the intelligence
community, and in the Situation Room. They were part of the discussion about whether Syrian president Bashar al-Assad was using
chemical weapons against his own people in 2012 and 2013. At first
the analysts were at low confidence, but over a period of months
they moved to high confidence. Policy-makers were fully aware
of the analysts' changing view on this, as we discussed it regularly in
Deputies Committee meetings during this time.

There was a second major factor in the intelligence community's
failure on Iraq WMD intelligence. Unlike the analytic failure, this
one has rarely been discussed in public or within government. It was
not studied in the aftermath for lessons learned. This was a failure of
intelligence collectors—CIA and the NSA—to penetrate Saddam's
inner circle, where they might have been able to learn the truth.
The leadership of the operational sides of CIA and NSA should have
requested a lessons-learned assessment, but they did not.

Of course, gaining access to the handful of people close to Saddam, who truly understood the status of Iraq's WMD programs,
was hard, in large part because Iraq was a "denied area," a place
where there is minimal or no official US government presence.
We face the same problem in other opaque regimes like Iran and
North Korea that go out of their way to make sure their actions are
shrouded in darkness. But hard can't be an excuse at the end of the
day, because the intelligence community is paid to do hard. And,
at a minimum, we should have told the president and his national
security team that we did not have good access to Saddam and his
inner circle.

I believe that one of the reasons CIA failed on the collection
front—which should be a lesson learned moving forward—was our

focus on covert action in Iraq. During the 1990s the United States had been intent on regime change in Iraq—in 1998, Congress made it the stated policy of the United States—and CIA had been in the lead. The day-to-day aim of our operations officers at that time had been to build ties to the Kurds in northern Iraq who might play a role in the overthrow of Saddam, and who were providing us with locations from which to operate against him. Our collection focus was on finding Sunnis in Saddam's military who might be willing and able to overthrow him and take control of the country (and develop a new and much different relationship with the United States in the process). With all this, collection on other issues related to Iraq—including WMD—suffered.

It is important to remember that CIA doesn't authorize covert action. That's a policy decision that requires the direction and signature of the president of the United States. Covert action has a number of unseen costs. One is that it diverts you from traditional foreign intelligence collection. When an administration gives CIA the mission of conducting a covert action, it doesn't assign additional people to perform the mission. The Congressional oversight committees are briefed on covert actions, and they sometimes provide additional funding, but they do not raise the Agency's personnel ceiling just because there is a new plan. So the folks who could have been trying to figure out how to collect intelligence from Saddam's inner circle to discover Saddam's plans, intentions, and capabilities with regard to weapons of mass destruction were diverted to trying to find generals willing to overthrow him.

We had the perfect storm of imperfect intelligence. We were not collecting the kind of information that would have saved us from inaccurate analysis, and we were not rigorously asking ourselves how confident we were in the collected information. Had we done either, the intelligence outcome would have been different—and possibly the policy outcome as well.

Charles Duelfer, who led the US WMD hunt in Iraq after the invasion, concluded that Saddam had wanted to maintain the appearance of having weapons of mass destruction in order to deter his number one enemy, Iran. But Duelfer found that Saddam had thought that US intelligence was good enough to figure out the real story and, therefore, that the United States would eventually lower the sanctions and, more important, not attack him. Even Saddam turned out to be overconfident in US intelligence capabilities.

Charles Duelfer once told me an instructive story about Saddam. In US custody, a clean-shaven Saddam became ill and needed medical attention. He was taken to a US military facility, where he proceeded to flirt with a nurse. The nurse, not surprisingly, was not responsive to the flirtations. On the way back to his cell, Saddam asked his American escort—his US debriefer, with whom Saddam had developed rapport—why the nurse had paid no attention to him. The escort, as a joke, said, "American women like men with facial hair." The next day Saddam started growing a full beard. When, a few weeks later, Saddam walked into the Iraqi courtroom that would convict him and sentence him to death, he had quite a bit of facial hair. Media commentators, including a former CIA analyst, speculated that Saddam was trying to play to the religious elements of the court by looking Islamic. The real reason—trying to make himself more attractive to a US nurse—was hidden from the public. It was a humorous example of Saddam's misjudging Americans.

Duelfer also told me that Saddam had told him that he did not believe that the United States would object to his invasion of Kuwait in 1990. Saddam, in essence, said, "Look, if you guys did not want me to go into Kuwait, why didn't you tell me you would deploy five hundred thousand troops, six carrier battle groups, fourteen hundred combat aircraft and a coalition of thirty-two countries? I am not crazy. If you had simply told me, I would not have gone into Kuwait." Again, he assumed that the United States was smart enough to know what it was doing and that we did not have a problem with his invasion of Kuwait. Another misjudgment on his part.

Together all of these stories paint a picture of Saddam misjudging us and we misjudging him. It was a recipe that took us to war and caused him to lose his rule.

* * *

The fear of al Qaʻida, and of the damage that could be done if a rogue state like Iraq ever shared weapons of mass destruction with the group, led us to war. Oddly, one of the main results of the road we went down in Iraq—like Route Irish itself—was the creation of an environment that helped spread al Qaʻida's narrative across the Muslim world. The spread of al Qaʻida's ideology, which began when some of its operatives left South Asia after the fall of the Taliban in late 2001, was given a new boost by a narrative that said that the United States was intent on bringing war to Muslim lands.

CHAPTER 6

Al Qa'ida's Nine Lives

CIA's counterterrorism analysts filed into my office in early 2013 for a prep session for a Deputies Committee, a meeting of all the number twos from the key national security departments and agencies in the government. It was a regular occurrence during my time as deputy director. During a discussion, one of the analysts handed me a single sheet of paper. He said, "This is the way we think about the threat posed by al Qa'ida to the homeland." It was a spectrum—a terrorist threat spectrum. At the left end was "No Threat." "That is a good place to be," said the analyst. At the right end was "Terrorists with Weapons of Mass Destruction." "That is not a good place to be," added another analyst. "You got that right," I answered.

Ignoring my intervention, the original analyst continued, pointing out that just to the left of the WMD point on the spectrum is where al Qa'ida was on 9/11—the ability to carry out simultaneous, catastrophic attacks that kill thousands. Slightly to the left of that is the ability to carry out single significant attacks that can kill hundreds. Further to the left on the spectrum and just to the right of "No Threat" are the lone wolves—the individuals who have no connection with an al Qa'ida group but are motivated by the group's ideology. The Boston Marathon bombing fit this category to a tee.

I took the chart to the Deputies Meeting and shared it with my colleagues. I told them, "Here is a great way to think about the threat from al Qa'ida and to measure how we are doing over time against the group and its allies." They agreed. It was clear to everyone, of course, that terrorists with WMD was the worst nightmare for all of us. But outcomes well short of that could still be horrific. We could not afford to become complacent. The lives of American citizens and the citizens of our allies depended on us.

* * *

Bin Ladin welcomed the US intervention in Iraq. He believed that US soldiers in Iraq fit perfectly into his narrative. He believed that the Soviet Union, by invading Afghanistan and by investing much money and many young men, had significantly weakened itself as a nation. And he believed that jihadists, by driving the Soviet Union out of Afghanistan, had dealt a body blow to its prestige and played a major role in its destruction. And now he wanted to do the same thing to America—draw us into Afghanistan and Iraq, watch us expend significant resources, and drive us out of the Middle East, hopefully destroying in the process the country that, in his mind, was doing more than any other to undermine and ultimately destroy Islam.

Bin Ladin himself, however, was far from Iraq. In the run-up to the Iraq War and in the initial months of the war, he was hiding in the border area between Afghanistan and Pakistan. We never figured out exactly where he was hiding in those early years. In 2005 he moved to a newly built compound in Abbottabad, Pakistan, where he would stay for the next six years. His focus during this period was on continuing al Qa'ida's attacks against the West and dealing with the rapid and significant changes his organization was undergoing. In the space of only five years, al Qaʻida moved down, then up, and back down the analysts' threat spectrum. It was a remarkable journey—one demonstrating both the group's vulnerability and its resilience.

The history of this period teaches what I believe is the most fundamental lesson of the world of counterterrorism—al Qaʻida has nine lives. When the West and its allies keep pressure on al Qaʻida, when it has to worry about its own security more than it can about its operations, al Qaʻida loses capability. When that pressure is not there, when it is free to operate, its capabilities grow. It is a pattern that has played out over and over again, wherever al Qaʻida has operated.

* * *

After being forced out of Afghanistan at the end of 2001, some of Bin Ladin's senior subordinates settled in the remote area of the Afghanistan-Pakistan border, but most took up residence in prearranged safe houses in the settled areas of Pakistan, and they regrouped quickly. At the same time, many key operatives made the decision to leave South Asia and return to their countries of origin. Both groups now posed a threat—those left in South Asia and those spread around the globe. This second group began the spread of al Qaʻida's ideology outside of South Asia. The war in Iraq did not start this spread, but it reinforced it.

By late 2001 the prestige of being the mastermind of the 9/11 attacks had propelled Khalid Sheikh Mohammed (KSM) into a new job—the role of external operations chief for al Qaʻida. Working from the safe houses in Pakistan, KSM quickly began planning new operations against the West. In a short time KSM had several plots under way, including Richard Reid's attempt to use a shoe bomb in December 2001 to bring down an American Airlines flight from Paris to Miami, and the successful assault in April 2002 against a Jewish synagogue in Tunisia, which killed nineteen. KSM was also planning to use operatives recruited in Saudi Arabia to hijack aircraft and crash them into London's Heathrow airport, employ terrorists from Southeast Asia to conduct a similar aircraft attack against skyscrapers in California, send a team of Pakistanis to smuggle explosives into New York, and use other terrorists to attack gas stations, railroad tracks, and bridges. In addition to these plots, KSM was working to carry out simultaneous attacks in Karachi, Pakistan—against the US consulate, Western travelers at the airport, and Westerners residing in the Karachi area. KSM, bursting with confidence as a result of 9/11, was being extraordinarily aggressive. We would later learn that he also personally decapitated *Wall Street Journal* reporter Daniel Pearl in a demonstration of brutality that is hard to fathom. I believe that KSM is the personification of evil.

By a coincidence, I was back in the presidential briefing seat the day after Pearl was murdered. I was filling in for my successor, who'd wanted to take a day off. When I met Tenet to conduct the final prep session for the briefing, he asked if I was going to show the president the video of Pearl's decapitation, which al Qa'ida had posted on the Internet. I said, "I have it with me, but there is no way I am going to show it to the president." Tenet and I ran into Condi Rice as we entered the West Wing and she too asked about the video. Now I was wondering if I had made the wrong call in deciding not to show it to Bush. The answer became very clear when, in the middle of the discussion about Pearl's murder, Rice told the president, "Michael has the video, if you want to see it." The president snapped, "Why in the hell would I want to watch that?" I felt vindicated, and I had not lost my sense of what to share with the president and what not to share.

Those operatives emerging from South Asia in the chaotic post-9/11 environment not only worked to support KSM's plots, they did their own plotting against local targets—some with great success. Indonesian-born Riduan bin Isomuddin—best known among his extremist colleagues as "Hambali"—left Afghanistan and became the operational leader of the terrorist group Jemaah Islamiya. He helped plan the October 2002 bombings in Bali that killed more than two hundred people, and facilitated the financing for the bombing of the Marriott hotel in Jakarta in August 2003.

'Abd al-Rahim al-Nashiri, who'd helped lead the successful attack against the USS *Cole* in the Port of Aden, Yemen, in October 2000, also fled Afghanistan after 9/11 and returned to the Gulf, this time working out of the United Arab Emirates. From there he planned a successful attack on the French tanker MV *Limburg* off the coast of Yemen in October 2002. At the time of his arrest in November 2002, he was working on a number of plots, including attacking a US housing compound in Saudi Arabia, flying a plane into a US warship in Port Rashid, UAE, and striking oil tankers in the Strait of Gibraltar.

In short, the immediate post-9/11 period saw what was probably the most significant plotting in al Qa'ida's history—despite its having lost its Afghan sanctuary. The scope of the plotting demonstrated the strength of the organization that Bin Ladin had built—in particular, the plans the group had made to resettle in the cities of Pakistan, if necessary. It was a reflection of the sense of confidence that al Qa'ida had. And it was a reflection of the additional funding flowing to al Qa'ida in the aftermath of 9/11, largely from private donors in Arab countries. Nothing boosts funding for a terrorist group like a successful attack.

What did all these operatives have in common? Three things. One, they were as committed to "the cause" and to jihad against the West, in particular the United States, as was Bin Ladin himself. Many had previously fought in Afghanistan against the Soviets and had seen many of their friends die in a fight that they eventually won. Two, they wanted to enjoy the success that KSM enjoyed. They wanted to lead a great victory against their enemy. KSM's rapid rise to the top rungs of al Qa'ida after 9/11 created strong incentives for others to mimic his career path. And three, they brought capability to the table. Not all terrorists are smart and skilled. In fact, many are not. But these operatives were. They were the best and deadliest of their generation of terrorists—battle-hardened from fighting in Afghanistan. These operatives were very dangerous.

* * *

This was one of the Agency's most active periods against al Qa'ida, a period when we put great pressure on the group. And, with new post-9/11 resources and authorities, as well as the Pakistani government's new commitment to being a partner against al Qa'ida, our work paid off. Operating largely with our intelligence, the Pakistanis began arresting senior al Qa'ida operatives—one after another. Zayn al-'Abidin Abu Zubaydah was the first to be captured, in March 2002. Abu Zubaydah, a leading al Qa'ida facilitator, had earlier helped Bin Ladin move his men from Sudan to Afghanistan in 1996. He'd assisted Ahmad Rashid's travel and attempted entry into the United States for the millennium-related attack on Los Angeles International Airport. He'd run al Qa'ida's document forgery operation as well as a number of the group's training camps in Afghanistan, including one attended by some of the 9/11 hijackers. And Abu Zubaydah had helped smuggle Abu Mus'ab al-Zarqawi and over fifty fighters out of Pakistan after 9/11 so they could make their way to Iraq. They would become the main extremist element in Iraq, killing hundreds of US and coalition soldiers during the Iraq War and later evolving to become the Islamic State of Iraq and Greater Syria (ISIS) that has gained so much ground in Syria and Iraq.

Zubaydah's arrest was followed by others—of Ramzi bin

al-Shibh, a key facilitator in the 9/11 attacks, in Karachi in September 2002, and of KSM in Rawalpindi, Pakistan, in March 2003. The Pakistanis and we were so successful that most of the remaining al Qa'ida leadership and its operatives pulled up stakes and moved a second time. Some of the most senior figures moved from Pakistan's settled areas to Iran, where they were put under house arrest. Most, however, moved to the Federally Administrated Tribal Areas (or "FATA"), an area of western Pakistan adjacent to the border with Afghanistan.

The FATA is extremely remote. It is small—roughly the size of Massachusetts—but it is extremely mountainous, with rural villages dotting the valleys. If you count the sides of the mountains as part of the area of the FATA, it grows to the size of Texas (I had a twelve-by-twenty-four-inch topographic map of the FATA hanging on the wall in my office, and the many mountain ranges stood out from the surface of the map by an inch). The FATA is semiautonomous, and its residents are fiercely independent. They barely think of themselves as part of the Pakistani state. It is a dangerous place for the Pakistani military and intelligence officers to venture, and it is exceptionally dangerous for US personnel to operate there.

Because the FATA was new to al Qa'ida, it had a hard time finding a home there, and the group's capabilities took a significant turn during this period. Without many of the group's senior operatives, without a local network of support, and without a financial pipeline, its skills and therefore the threat it posed to the United States diminished. But this would not last for long.

* * *

My year of briefing the president and my time serving as the number three in the Directorate of Intelligence's front office earned me a new assignment. In the summer of 2003 I became CIA's senior focal point for liaison with the analytic community in the United

Kingdom. The relationship was a simple one: our objective and that of the British was to share our analysis with each other to see where we agreed and where we did not, and, if we did not, to find out why. This process strengthened the analysis that both of us provided to our senior policy-makers.

I dealt largely with the UK's Cabinet Office Assessments staff. The analysts there wrote two to four assessments a week for the prime minister and other senior ministers involved in national security. In preparing the assessments, the analysts relied on information they obtained from UK government agencies, from allies such as CIA and the NSA, and from open sources. They were particularly reliant on reporting from the UK's three intelligence collection agencies—the country's internal intelligence service, the Security Service (MI5), the nation's external intelligence service, the Secret Intelligence Service (MI6), and the UK's counterpart to the NSA, the General Communications Headquarters (GCHQ).

The analysts at the Cabinet Office had to present their assessments once a week to the country's Joint Intelligence Committee (JIC). The JIC—an institution in the British government since 1936—is comprised of both senior leaders from the country's intelligence agencies and British policy-makers from the Foreign Office, the Ministry of Defence, and the Cabinet Office. The JIC could approve a paper with or without changes, send a paper back for more work, or kill it outright. The JIC was the door that the analysts had to pass through to get their assessments to the prime minister. We did not have anything like it in the United States.

My time as our representative to the British analytic community, from the summer of 2003 to early 2006, was dominated by two issues—Iraq, namely our failure to find weapons of mass destruction and the rapidly deteriorating security and political situation there, and al Qa'ida, both the immediate threat that the group posed and where it was going over the longer term.

* * *

As I began this assignment, we were still on a hair trigger regarding the threat from terrorists, because, even though al Qaʻida was now struggling in the FATA, the memories of 9/11 and of the degree of attack plotting in the immediate aftermath of 9/11 were still fresh.

While this intensity of focus is necessary for success against real threats, it can also lead to some false positives. Perhaps none was wilder than a perceived threat that arose in late 2003. A part of the intelligence community, not normally involved in analysis, believed that it had uncovered a fiendishly clever way for the al Qaʻida leadership to communicate with its operatives abroad. (I am not permitted to explain the method of communication, as it remains highly classified.)

But our terrorism analysts weren't buying it—there was very little evidence to support the existence of this communication method, it was something we had never seen before, and it seemed beyond al Qaʻida's capabilities. Many of the IC's senior leadership didn't believe it either, but this was the kind of theory that could not easily be dismissed. What if this analysis was right?

The findings were briefed to the National Security Council staff, the Department of Homeland Security, and others. Some of the information appeared to be very specific, suggesting threats to particular flights on particular days right around the Christmas holiday.

There wasn't time to investigate the claims enough to achieve complete certainty. If they were dismissed and a number of transatlantic flights were successfully attacked, the US government would rightly be vilified for ignoring the threat. So the Homeland Security Council ordered the cancellation of some transoceanic British Airways and Air France flights.

The whole matter up until that time was a closely held secret.

Several days before Christmas the number two on the analytic side of the Agency called me and walked me through the story. He wanted to make sure that if the Brits raised this with me, I would know what they were talking about. British analysts, like CIA analysts, were not at all convinced about the methodology or conclusions of the theory.

Still the administration went ahead with mitigation steps. The flight cancellations caused some serious disruptions and widespread concern beyond a few specific flights. Just after Christmas my family and our friends the Hynds were in London for the holidays. The Hynds had flown British Airways, and when it came time for them to return home they asked me if it was safe for them to fly. I was stuck in the middle of a classic ethical problem. As an intelligence officer, you cannot selectively provide warnings or advice. You cannot provide advice to friends that is different from the guidance that the government is providing to the general public. And in this case there was a big difference between what our government had to do for the sake of prudence and what most analysts, including me, believed—that the threat reporting was bogus. So in response to the question I mumbled something like, "Well, there are a lot of people working to make those flights safe."

In the end the Hynds departed as planned on British Airways. Joe, Shannon, and their four daughters were surprised to see US jet fighters escort them on their entry into US airspace and through their safe landing at Dulles Airport. When Shannon called my wife with the news, I said, "See, people were working to keep them safe."

A few months later I learned of the shaky provenance of the original warning and that the analysis had turned out to be highly questionable. In fact, this turned out to be just plain poor analysis as well as poor oversight of that analysis. But the incident amply illustrates the mind-set at the time and the fact that when it came to the terrorist threat, the attitude was "You can't be too cautious."

* * *

What was very real as my time as the representative to the British analytic community proceeded was the growth and rebuilding of al Qaʻida in the FATA region of Pakistan. Along with Iraq, the rebirth of al Qaʻida was at the top of the priority list for us and the British. Al Qaʻida had made its intentions to target Western Europe clear. In the US we tend to look at 9/11 as a singularly American event—but in fact more Brits died in the Twin Towers than in any other single terrorist attack in British history. Our British colleagues were certain that Bin Ladin was not done with them.

As al Qaʻida spent more time in the FATA, it started building close ties with local militant groups, some of which were Afghan and had crossed the border to avoid the NATO troops in Afghanistan. As al Qaʻida settled in, the group's rebuilding began.

Because of the great difficulties of working in the region—and the time it took for the US to figure out how to do so—al Qaʻida regained its footing. The pressure was off al Qaʻida during much of this period, and it took advantage of that. And by mid-2005 the group was strong enough to conduct sophisticated operations in the West, and by mid-2006 it had regained enough capability to again conduct large 9/11-style attacks against the US homeland. The rebound was surprising and quick for a group that was continuously on the move and had lost most of its senior leadership.

* * *

In my assignment as CIA's representative to British analysts, I participated in a number of conversations between Agency analysts from our Counterterrorism Center in which we shared our growing concerns with the British. Perhaps the most important such conversation happened during a fall 2003 visit from the deputy director of the analytic side of the Center, Philip Mudd. Mudd has a well-deserved reputation for being direct and pointed, with little interest in caveats. His message was profound—we were seeing the resurgence of al Qa'ida, and if steps were not taken, it would soon rebuild the capabilities it had had on 9/11. Mudd brought along analysts to walk through the details—al Qa'ida was coalescing in certain cities in the FATA, ingratiating itself with local militants, receiving ample funding again, and once more training operatives for attacks. It was a stark warning.

In March 2004, ten bombs aboard commuter trains in Madrid exploded (three other trains had bombs aboard as well, but they did not detonate). With 191 people killed and over eighteen hundred wounded, it was the worst terrorist attack in Spanish history—and it occurred just three days before Spain's general elections. Because the attacks were well coordinated and nearly simultaneous, the assumption of much of the world was that this had been the work of al Qa'ida. But the Spanish investigation and our own intelligence could turn up nothing linking the attack to Bin Ladin and his leadership in the FATA. The attackers had been a group of Moroccans, Syrians, and Algerians, whose only association with al Qa'ida was that they had been motivated by Bin Ladin's message. It was the first significant al Qa'ida–inspired attack. We, and our British friends, now had to worry about plots hatched not only by Bin Ladin and his associates but also by others who admired but had never met him.

Porter Goss, who became CIA director in the fall of 2004, was so worried that we did not have a good enough window into what was happening in the FATA that he ordered a surge of resources against al Qa'ida, the largest since 9/11. We essentially flooded the zone to maximize our chances of collecting valuable intelligence on al Qa'ida's resurgence.

* * *

In early July 2005, I was in London. It was a cool morning and I was at a meeting of UK analysts at the British Ministry of Defence. Shortly before nine a.m., someone walked into the room and simply said, "There have been multiple explosions in London." At that point everyone got up and left. The meeting was over. The traffic on the streets was horrendous as cars and people flowed away from what I would soon learn was where three suicide bombs had exploded aboard London Underground trains. A short while later a fourth bomb would explode on a double-decker bus in Tavistock Square. Altogether, fifty-two people were killed and nearly eight hundred injured.

The first thing I did was pick up the phone and call Mary Beth, who was in Florida with the kids for a summer visit with her parents. It was about five a.m. in Naples when I woke her. "Turn on the TV," I said. "I'm all right. Love you. Gotta go." Then I hung up. The rest of the day was spent discussing with the British our early assessments of the attacks.

Finally, late that night, I decided to get some sleep. I could have walked, but that evening, because I was physically and emotionally exhausted, I elected to take the bus. What struck me when I boarded was how absolutely normal all the passengers were acting. This was just twelve hours after a suicide bomber had blown up an identical vehicle fewer than two and a half miles away. Yet the bus was full, and no one seemed nervous. No one was eyeing the other passengers suspiciously. This was the legendary British "Keep Calm and Carry On" attitude at work—borne of surviving the Blitz by Hitler and hundreds of IRA bombings over the years.

A couple of days later, I made an appointment to see my main contact on the Cabinet Office Assessments Staff. He did not seem thrilled to see me. Apparently every intelligence service on the planet had lined up, trying to get briefings on what the British had discovered so far about the attacks, so that they could impress their headquarters back home. He and his colleagues were too busy analyzing intelligence to be conducting briefings. Sensing his unease, I tried to put his concerns to rest. "I'm not here for a briefing," I said. "I simply came to express my condolences." This was a small but heartfelt gesture. I remembered well George Tenet telling President Bush during the PDB briefing on September 13, 2001, that on the previous day Sir Richard Dearlove, chief of MI6, and several top British intelligence officials had flown to the United States for just an evening in order to pay their respects to the US intelligence community. That gesture had touched us all deeply and, in my own small way, I wanted to offer similar support. With that explanation the mood in the room changed dramatically, and my contact graciously gave me an hour of his time.

As I worked with British analysts in the days and weeks that followed, I was struck by the relative absence of finger-pointing in the UK. British authorities were quick to do their police and intelligence work, but British politicians and the British media did not seem to share the zeal of their American counterparts in similar circumstances to find someone (other than the terrorists) to blame. This seemed to be part of their normal makeup. From the start the Brits did an excellent job of conducting an investigation into the terrorist cells that had perpetrated the attack, but they did not rush into the second-guessing game. It wasn't until October 2010 that they initiated an independent inquiry into the attacks. Called a "coroner's inquest," it eventually made some recommendations in May 2011 for process improvement but fell well short of the finger-pointing that we saw in America after events ranging from 9/11 to the attack on US interests in Benghazi, Libya, in 2012.

The British assessment—and our own—made very clear that the 7/7 attacks in London had been the work of Bin Ladin and al

Qaʻida. This was not a Madrid situation. This was a group trained in the FATA and our concerns about al Qaʻida's growing strength had had their first manifestation on the battlefield.

* * *

While the issues on which I worked with the British most closely were very serious ones—Iraq and al Qaʻida—my time in the job did have some unique perks. The most significant was an invitation from Her Majesty Queen Elizabeth for Mary Beth and me to attend a reception at Buckingham Palace. Interestingly, there was no phone number on the invitation for an RSVP. When I inquired about how to tell the palace that we would be honored to attend, I was told that "there is no need to RSVP as no one says no to an invitation from the queen." When I relayed this to Mary Beth, she noted that this is not adequately explained in Miss Manners.

The next issue was what to wear. The invitation stated I was to wear "evening dress"—that is, a black tuxedo with tails along with a white tie and white vest. So off to the rental shop I went. The invitation also noted that Mary Beth should wear a full-length gown with gloves above the elbows for a sleeveless gown or regular gloves for a long-sleeve gown. The invite also made clear a black dress was definitely not acceptable—because black is reserved for mourning. Since black was the only color in Mary Beth's limited repertoire of long gowns, she had to improvise by also renting her dress—at a uniquely named shop in London called One Night Stand.

At the rental shop, Mary Beth was met by two lovely women who kept about eighty different gowns in a whole range of sizes. Chief gown renter Joanna welcomed Mary Beth, looked her up and down, snatched a lovely crimson beaded gown from a rack and said, "Right, dear, try this one." Mary Beth barely had it on before

Joanna was draping a faux diamond choker around her neck and wrapping a crimson shawl around her shoulders. It was an instant rental. Mary Beth asked how much the dress would cost to purchase, and she almost choked when she heard the answer. It was more than our car cost. These were high-end gowns.

Dressed to the hilt, we arrived at the appointed hour at the palace. Our taxi drove us through layers of security and we found ourselves walking up the red-carpeted Grand Entrance. Mary Beth had been on a tourist visit to the palace but this time, she said, the feeling was completely different—with bejeweled guests arriving and with the Queen's Guard standing at attention in their dress uniforms. The palace itself was opulence defined: sixty-foot ceilings, gilded molding, and master works of art seemingly everywhere (we passed a Rembrandt at one point). It was jaw-dropping.

After drinks and dinner, we were directed to the Picture Gallery, where we were told we should wait for the queen to greet us. Eventually, three of the Queen's Guard marched through the room, stomping large and dangerous-looking staffs on the floor to signify the arrival of the royals. First to appear was Sophie, the Countess of Wessex (the wife of the queen's youngest son). Sophie, the warm-up act, was lovely and outgoing and was wearing a tiara with a huge aquamarine stone as a focal point. Sophie was followed by the queen, looking appropriately regal. She was joined by her husband, Philip, the Duke of Edinburgh, and by Prince Charles and Camilla, the latter of whom stole the show. Camilla was warm, gracious, and outgoing, and she insisted on shaking everyone's hand, gushing about what a great time she had just had in America. Mary Beth instantly became a fan for life.

With that, the party—along with our fairy-tale evening—was over. It was really amazing to come out the front door of the palace and view, from inside the gates, the gold statue of the winged goddess Nike. Mary Beth said, "The queen sure has a great view from her bedroom." I started thinking about al Qa'ida again.

* * *

My time as the representative to the British analytic community served to deepen my belief, forged in the crucible of 9/11, that the fight against terrorists was the place to be. So I was thrilled in the fall of 2005 when I was offered a chance to serve as the deputy director of CIA's Counterterrorism Center. But before I could undertake that mission, the bureaucracy of Washington got in the way.

In late 2005, Philip Zelikow, counselor to Secretary of State Condi Rice, asked to meet with me. After we'd chatted for a while about the lessons learned from the Iraq intelligence failure, Zelikow said to me, "The secretary would like to have you serve as the head of INR [the State Department's Bureau of Intelligence and Research]. Are you interested?" That would be a significant move up the ladder for me—it was a presidentially appointed, Senate-confirmed position—and it would give me a seat at the table as head of one of the agencies of the intelligence community. I asked for a day or two to think it over.

After reflection, however, I picked up the phone and told Zelikow that I had already committed to a lower-level position as the deputy director of CTC and that it would be inappropriate to back out. I also told him that combating terrorism was where my heart was.

The very next afternoon, General Mike Hayden, the principal deputy director of national intelligence and a future director of CIA, phoned me. Hayden was, and is, someone I respect immensely.

"Michael," he said, "I want you to know that when you got that job offer on behalf of Secretary Rice, it was not just the secretary asking—it was John Negroponte [the DNI] and me asking you as well." I was now in a fix. The job I really wanted was in CTC, but the two most important men in the US intelligence community—technically the superiors of the director of CIA—wanted me to go to the State Department.

So I called the head of the analytic directorate at CIA—my boss in my assignment at the time—and asked what he thought I should do. "Let me get back to you," he said. Although I knew nothing about it at the time, soon CIA's deputy director, a Navy vice admiral and SEAL by the name of Bert Calland, had picked up the phone and attempted to chew out General Hayden for having the temerity to talk to a CIA officer about a job without first going to Director Goss or him.

This all happened during a period when there was enormous tension between CIA and the newly created DNI apparatus that had been placed above it. For years the head of CIA had also been the head of the entire intelligence community, and now that had changed. Outside of CIA, the view was that the Agency had appropriately been knocked down a peg. Inside CIA, the view was that DNI was demanding changes that were either duplicative of what CIA was already doing or were actually putting the country at some risk. There were many issues to be worked out, and there was a fight over almost every one of them.

But in any case, Calland's move was not a smart one bureaucratically. Hayden told the admiral that, as the DNI's number two, he could talk to me anytime he wanted about anything he wanted. For some reason, however, the CIA senior leadership decided that it was annoyed at me for what had transpired.

OK, I figured—I guess I am going to the State Department. I relayed my decision to Zelikow, who invited me to meet with Deputy Secretary of State Robert Zoellick—whom I did not know and who wanted to meet me before the nomination process began.

My interview with Zoellick went extremely well, as we discussed different parts of the globe and differing approaches to analysis. The discussions with the staff from the Office of Presidential Personnel were another matter. These were going very well until I offered up a possible problem. At one point I told the staff that I had been interviewed by Senate Select Committee on Intelligence staff regarding the flawed intelligence leading up to the invasion of Iraq. I explained that during sessions with the staff I'd said that I believed that members of the vice president's staff had overstepped their boundaries by trying to inappropriately influence the analysis on the question of al Qa'ida's relationship to Iraq. I could tell immediately that this was going to be an issue from the administration's point of view—possibly even bringing an end to the process.

A couple of days later I got a call from Zelikow, who simply said, "Michael, this isn't going to work." My career at the State Department was over before it had begun. And unfortunately, the job I really wanted in CTC had by that time been given to someone else. And I was now persona non grata at CIA. The view among Goss's aides—not of Goss himself—was that I had been disloyal in agreeing to accept the State Department job. I ended up taking another job outside CIA, at the National Counterterrorism Center (NCTC), a new organization staffed with people from across the intelligence community. With a name guaranteed to sow confusion across government, NCTC is quite distinct from CIA's CTC. I served as the head of analysis for NCTC, trying to ensure that nothing got lost in the seam between domestic intelligence and foreign intelligence with regard to terrorism. It was a good job—but nothing like the ones I had just missed out on.

* * *

After only four months at NCTC, though, I returned to CIA. Mike Hayden replaced Porter Goss in late May 2006, just weeks after

Dusty Foggo, the Agency's number three, resigned and was later indicted and arrested on fraud charges. Hayden asked me to come back to CIA and replace Foggo.

Hayden was exactly what CIA needed at that moment, and I wanted to be part of his team. Hayden is one the smartest individuals with whom I have ever worked. In grade school his football coach, the legendary owner of the Pittsburgh Steelers, Dan Rooney, made Hayden the quarterback simply because he was smarter than everyone else. Hayden was also a great briefer—one of the best I have seen. He is a master at explaining complex issues in extremely simple ways, often using sports metaphors to drive home a point. One of his common rhetorical refrains was that US law sets the boundaries of what the Agency can do and, while the country wants its premier intelligence agency to stay within those bounds, it also wants it to get chalk on its cleats—that is, to use all the space the law allows to protect the country. It was both a way to encourage proper risk-taking within the Agency and a way to be clear with the American people about what we would do and what we would not do.

An outstanding leader, Hayden focused CIA on both strategic and tactical objectives. I learned a great deal from him about how to get your arms around a big Agency by dividing what you want to accomplish into manageable chunks. He took the most important issues—substantive ones like Iran and North Korea and management challenges like leadership training and developing language skills—and ordered regular updates. These programmatic reviews held people's feet to the fire, which resulted in progress.

* * *

So in July 2006 I became a member of CIA's senior leadership team, at a time when the al Qa'ida threat from Pakistan was returning to levels not seen since 9/11. As number three in the Agency's chain of command, I was tasked largely with keeping the administrative trains running. This side of the business was new to me, and I learned a great deal about information technology, federal budgets, security, and the like. I stayed abreast of substantive developments—on both the analytic and operational sides of the Agency. I made sure I received a daily intelligence briefing—which was the first time the number three at the Agency had ever asked for one—and I attended as many of the daily CT meetings as I could.

The Agency had a serious morale problem. Goss had given his key aides—most of whom he had brought with him from the House Intelligence Committee—too much authority, and they mismanaged the place. Several senior officers were forced out and many retired, with many more contemplating it. Officers like me took rotations in other government agencies. The years between George Tenet's and Mike Hayden's tenures were the worst during my three decades of service. Goss's aides did the damage, but Goss himself bears responsibility for choosing these aides and then giving them too much authority. I'm convinced that had he chosen a different team he would have had a successful tenure in the job. Hayden moved quickly to turn the situation around and did so, using a combination of tactics—frequent written notes to the workforce, regular "all-hands" meetings in which he talked about the key issues facing the Agency and what we were doing about them, and visits to work units both in Washington and overseas.

It was an exceptionally important thing to do, particularly at a time when our biggest threat was on the rebound. Al Qa'ida's resurgence would become clearest in August 2006, when we discovered that a group of al Qa'ida operatives were plotting to blow up somewhere between ten and fifteen airliners flying between London and the United States. The plan was to smuggle different parts of an explosive on board in bottles of everyday liquids and mixed with innocent-appearing substances such as Tang. If successful, the plot might have been worse than 9/11, killing thousands. The economic impact would have been devastating.

Terrific intelligence and law enforcement work in multiple countries disrupted the plot. The British had the first lead. A British citizen of Pakistani descent had gone to the FATA for training, and the British had learned of his travel. When he returned he was put under surveillance and it soon became clear that he and more than a dozen others were plotting something of significance using liquids in bottles. We learned that another British citizen was in Pakistan working closely with the al Qa'ida leadership on the plot, and it was CIA analysts remembering the details of Khalid Sheikh Mohammed's mid-1990s plan to bring down multiple airliners over the Pacific Ocean who connected the final dots. In that plot, the terrorists also had planned to hide explosives in everyday containers. Arrests were made in Pakistan and the United Kingdom, and the plot was disrupted. The plan showed the 9/11-style ingenuity of al Qa'ida as well as its ability to place operatives in the UK ready to act. It was a close call and it spoke loudly of al Qa'ida's resurgence.

A few months later CIA's counterterrorism analysts put the work of the previous several months together in a paper that warned policy-makers that al Qa'ida in the FATA was again capable of conducting devastating attacks. The mood in the building was one of frustration that the group had rebounded. Discussions in meetings were punctuated with remarks like "They are back" and "We are going to get hit again."

In the early summer of 2007 the US intelligence community followed CIA's lead and produced a National Intelligence Estimate on the threat from al Qa'ida. Its conclusions were just as sobering as those of CIA's paper. The NIE said that the al Qa'ida leadership in Pakistan was in the process of planning high-impact attacks on the US homeland—attacks that would produce mass casualties, dramatic destruction, and significant economic fallout. The NIE added that al Qaʿida had regenerated key elements of its homeland attack capability. The group's safe haven in the FATA, the development of capable operational lieutenants, and a senior leadership now less concerned about its own security meant more time focused on planning and more capability to carry out an attack, according to the intelligence community analysts who had written the NIE.

Together the two papers were a major warning to the Bush administration and to Congress. Al Qaʿida was back and extremely dangerous. It was clear that Washington's approach up to that point—occasional CT operations against the al Qaʿida leadership—was not working and that we had to get more aggressive.

The publication of both reports led to a policy process that, while it may have taken too much time, did lead President Bush to take action in August 2008. The number of CT operations went up sharply, and the leadership of al Qaʿida was removed from the battlefield with regularity—this after the United States had failed to remove a single al Qaʿida leader from the battlefield in 2007. ("0 for 07" was how Mike Hayden had put it.) The pressure was back on—and in a very significant way.

The months that followed the president's decision were filled with events that confirmed the correctness of his new policy. Al Qaʿida attacked the Marriott hotel in Islamabad on September 20, 2008, killing more than fifty and wounding nearly three hundred people. And the Marriott attack was followed in 2009 by an attempted attack on the New York City subway system that was foiled by the excellent work of the intelligence community and the FBI.

One of the myths about the more aggressive CT operations

against the al Qaʻida leadership is that they began when President Obama came to office. This is inaccurate. President Bush started them six months before leaving office, and President Obama kept them going—both for good reason. The United States was facing the most significant threat environment since 9/11. The country was at risk.

* * *

The annual CIA holiday party—held in the lobby of our main headquarters building—is *the* party in town. Senior US government officials and ambassadors and intelligence officers from many countries attend. If you are in the national security business, it is the place to be. People arrive early and stay late. And Leon Panetta's first holiday party, in December 2009, was something special—Italian food of all kinds and the wines to go with it. The smell of garlic filled the hall. People talked about the food for weeks. It helped to cement our ties to many of our foreign partners. The party was fully consistent with the coffee cup that Panetta used every day in his office. On one side it read "C.I.A." On the other, "California Italian American."

Near the end of the party, Director Panetta's talented chief of staff, Jeremy Bash, took me aside and told me that Steve Kappes, the Agency's deputy director, was planning to step down in the spring and that I—the head of analysis—was at the top of the director's short list of potential successors. Kappes—a legend in the clandestine service and a national hero for helping to convince Muammar Qadhafi to give up his weapons of mass destruction—had served as deputy for four years and thought it was time to move on. Bash said, "I'm rooting for you." A couple of months later I found myself in Panetta's office being interviewed for the job. It was much more of a chat than an interview—about the issues, about working together, about the people we would be managing together. He told me that I was at the top of his list but that he wanted to talk with a few other people as well. Then radio silence for several weeks. I was wondering what was going on.

Panetta had gotten off to a rough start with the Agency by referring to the practice of waterboarding as torture in his confirmation hearing, leading some insiders to worry that the new administration would demonize them for doing things approved by the last administration. However, as time went on he became beloved within CIA. He was seen as having clout with the White House, using his ties to Vice President Biden and to Obama's first chief of staff, Rahm Emanuel, to win a bureaucratic turf battle with Director for National Intelligence Denny Blair over who has final approval for naming chiefs of stations overseas. Panetta was also seen as caring deeply about the men and women of CIA, having brought us through the crisis of the attack on our base in Khost in 2009, when seven Americans, one Jordanian, and one Afghan were killed in a suicide bombing perpetrated by someone we had believed was working for us.

Most of all, though, Panetta was seen as a normal guy, full of fun and with a great sense of humor. He told jokes—most of them slightly off-color—he laughed at the jokes of others, and he made fun of himself. His speeches to employees would be filled with jokes—most of them not put there by the speechwriters. He figuratively put his arms around CIA, and the Agency returned the gesture.

At one event, in front of hundreds of people, Panetta announced that he was going to tell a joke that his speechwriters had suggested he not tell. He said, "I have decided to ignore their advice." He went on: "There was a farmer that was really protective of his three daughters. In fact, he always met their boyfriends at the front door with a shotgun. At five thirty on Friday night, there was a knock at the door. The farmer answered it with his gun. The young man at the door said, 'Hello, my name is Eddie, I'm here for Betty, we're going for spaghetti. Is she ready?' The farmer paused, then said, 'OK, she's ready.' Another half hour passed and there was a second knock. The farmer answered it with his gun in hand again. The guy at the door said, 'Hello, my name is Joe, I'm here for Flo, we're going to the show. She ready to go?' The farmer paused again and said, 'Yeah, she's ready.' A half hour later there was another knock. The farmer went to the door with his shotgun. The guy at the door said, 'Hello, my name is Chuck, I'm here for Puck'—and the farmer shot him." If almost anyone else in the room had told the same story, the political correctness police would have pounced. But there is a twinkle in Leon's eye and a warmth to his spirit that causes people to instead think, "That was really cute."

Panetta and I became friends—even before I became his deputy. We shared a love of the game of golf, in particular his two-putt rule—the second putt is automatically good no matter how far from the pin the first putt ends up—a rule that keeps the score down and the game moving along. It is not a rule appreciated by purists. On those rare occasions when Panetta did not go home to his beloved Carmel Valley ranch for the weekend, he would go to noon mass, followed by golf, and then dinner at our home.

Once, when invited to watch his San Francisco 49ers in the NFC Championship Game that started at six thirty p.m., he called at three p.m. and asked, "Do you mind if I come early to watch the AFC Championship Game as well?" When I hung up and told Mary Beth, "Leon is coming early." She responded, "Let's get the place straightened up—fast—and I am so happy that he feels comfortable enough here to ask us to come early."

Panetta would not only watch sports at our home, he would share his strongly held political views with my children and their friends. The kids would gather around the table after dinner and ask Panetta questions. It was like a graduate school seminar. Mary Beth and I listened carefully as well to his candid and commonsense approach to politics, policy, and people. Panetta's main message around the dinner table was "People of different political ideologies can—indeed, have to—come together to find an agreed-upon approach to the tough problems facing our nation." He told the kids, "My time in Congress was characterized by a willingness to compromise, by a willingness to fight it out during the day and get a drink and a steak together in the evening." He said he was deeply frustrated by today's gridlock and he told the kids, "I fear for the future of the republic." I found his message sobering.

As he was leaving one Sunday evening in the early spring of 2010, he paused on my front porch as I walked him out and said, "Oh, I forgot, let's go ahead and announce tomorrow that you will succeed Steve as deputy." On May 7, 2010, I was sworn in as the twenty-fourth deputy director of the Central Intelligence Agency.

* * *

A typical day for me as deputy director started at 4:45 a.m. I would pull on my gym clothes, grab a suit and tie for the day, and jump into my armored SUV to be driven to work—just a few short miles away. There I would work out, shower, dress, and be at my desk by six a.m., catching up on any overnight e-mails from overseas.

At six fifteen a.m. my intelligence briefer would show up at my office door. This was the best meeting of my day. As I had done a decade earlier, the briefer would spend most of the night putting together a thick notebook of hundreds of pages of analytic pieces and raw intelligence to review. It was my way of keeping up with what was going on in the world and what we were saying about it. It also enabled me to press the analysts for more insights. Through conversation with my briefer and my chief of staff and executive assistants—who would join me for the briefing—I would come up with a number of questions each day that I would ask the analysts to answer, preferably within twenty-four hours.

When Leon Panetta was director, I had to finish my daily intelligence briefing by seven thirty a.m. so I could join him for *his* briefing. He liked to have me there, along with his chief of staff, Jeremy Bash, and his head of analysis, my replacement as the director of intelligence, so we could discuss the issues with him from both an analytic and an operational perspective. I often left the director's briefing with a list of to-do items.

Under both Panetta and his successor, David Petraeus, the director's intelligence briefing was followed by a morning meeting with the entire Agency leadership team. The director would brief the key issues that had come up in his meetings the day before, let us know about important meetings he was having that day, and ask any number of questions. We then went around the room with the individual senior leaders briefing us on one issue or another. It was a great way to keep the director and me informed of what was going on and a great way for the director to drive his agenda.

The rest of my day was largely broken into three pieces. The first involved attending deputies' meetings at the White House (often multiple meetings a day), being pre-briefed by Agency experts before going to those meetings, and then giving those experts a summary of what transpired at the meeting after I returned. The second involved completing all the paperwork that came into my office. I tried to finish as much of this as I could before I left for the day, but invariably I ended up taking home a good two to three hours of work each night. And the third involved internal meetings that were focused on solving immediate problems or trying to push the Agency forward in the future.

* * *

As the deputy director of CIA I found myself handling a mind-boggling array of threats and challenges daily, not to mention helping to run an Agency that is roughly the size of a large Fortune 500 company. The substantive issues on my plate included our support for the war effort in Afghanistan, the evolution of the Arab Spring, and the behavior of Iran and North Korea, just to name a few. But by far the issue that dominated my time as deputy, just as it had dominated my time as George Tenet's executive assistant fifteen years before, was international terrorism. At least half of my thick morning briefing book was filled with terrorism-related issues—every day. And at least a third of my meetings "downtown" related to terrorism.

This issue also dominated the time of my colleagues in the executive branch, whose work was guided and overseen by the Deputies Committee of the National Security Council, of which I was a member. We met frequently to deal with issues related to terrorism, led by White House counterterrorism and homeland security advisor John Brennan.

I saw my counterparts in these CT meetings more than I saw my own family. On the intelligence side, the key players besides me were Chris Inglis, the deputy director of the NSA, and Mike Leiter, the director of the National Counterterrorism Center. On the operations side, the key players were me, Sean Joyce, the deputy director of the FBI, the vice chairman of the Joint Chiefs—first James "Hoss" Cartwright and then Admiral Sandy Winnefeld—and Under Secretary of Defense for Intelligence Mike Vickers. It always struck me that CIA was the only agency that routinely found itself on both the intelligence and operational sides of the terrorism problem, underscoring the importance of CIA on the issue.

Vickers and I became close friends. Along with Brennan, Vickers and I were probably more focused on al Qa'ida than anyone else at senior levels of the US government. Earlier in his career, Vickers had served in the Special Forces and as a CIA operations officer. He had been deeply involved in CIA's support to the Afghan rebels fighting to drive the Soviet Union out of their country. In the movie *Charlie Wilson's War*, his character is the brilliant young CIA weapons analyst who plays multiple games of speed chess in the parks of Washington, D.C. My kids thought I was cool because I knew a guy Hollywood made movies about.

* * *

One of the main issues with which the deputies grappled was that of US drone operations. These operations have been the single most effective tool in the last five years for protecting the United States from terrorists. There is no doubt in my mind that these strikes have prevented another attack on the scale of 9/11. They have decimated al Qa'ida's core leadership in South Asia. Multiple al Qa'ida leaders there have been removed from the battlefield, and the group is having a hard time attracting new recruits, raising money, and plotting. The strikes have also weakened the leadership of al Qa'ida in Yemen and they have disrupted attacks against the United States by the group there.

Perhaps the best evidence of the effectiveness of the strikes are Bin Ladin's own thoughts on the subject. In documents recovered from his residence after the 2011 US raid that killed him, we learned that Bin Ladin considered drone strikes the most effective US weapon against his group. We also learned that he obsessed with discovering how drone operations worked and what countermeasures might defeat them.

Discussions about the law were always an important part of any deputies' meeting, particularly those on drones. Collateral damage is permitted under the laws of war. When done right, drone strikes are incredibly precise and collateral damage is minimal, and every effort is made to prevent such damage. Collateral damage is not zero, but it is close to zero, as these unmanned aerial vehicles (UAVs) and the missiles they carry are among the most precise weapons in the history of warfare.

What to make, then, of the claims of significant collateral damage? They are highly exaggerated. The claims flow from propaganda on the part of al Qaʿida and other groups that want the strikes to stop. They are also a result of counting as US collateral damage the women and children killed by air force strikes by the countries where the United States operates drones. And they stem from human nature—a reporter visits a mother and father of a deceased terrorist, who honestly believe that their son is innocent and would never join an extremist organization. The parents tell the reporter that, and his death gets marked as collateral damage.

When I was deputy director, a superb American reporter contacted the government to say that she was going to write a story about the significance of the collateral damage from drone strikes. She pointed out that her company, a leading US media outlet, had helped pay for a compilation of a comprehensive list of drone strikes and their outcomes. She had dates and locations of individual strikes over an extended period of time and the number of women and children killed in a number of the strikes. She said the number of innocents killed was much higher than the estimates that she was hearing from US officials and asked for a comment.

Because CIA tries to carefully monitor the truth about what damage is actually caused by US drone operations, I was tasked by my superiors in the administration to invite her to my office to talk about the data. I requested that she send her list of alleged US strikes to us ahead of time. I had each of the strikes on her list investigated.

When I sat down with her, I went through the entire list. It had three categories: (1) US strikes on her list that had occurred but had killed no women and children while her list said they had, (2) US strikes on her list that in reality were strikes by the local military, and (3) US strikes that simply had not happened and for which there was no local military action either. By far, the largest category was the first. I would tell her, "Your data says there were six people killed in this particular strike, including three children. I can tell you that there was a US strike on that day but that only two adult males were killed." The only other thing I wanted to do—but could not do—was show her the US government's video of each strike, so she could see with her own eyes the number and type of people killed. It turned out that there were no women and children killed in any of the strikes on her list.

I spent well over an hour with the reporter—going over every alleged strike on her list—and at the end she decided to walk away from the story, as she no longer believed that the study was credible. In fact, I believe she walked out of my office concerned that the data were deliberately misleading. She was a reporter who was most interested in getting the facts right, and she impressed me greatly that day.

In deciding to allow me to have this conversation with the reporter, the government recognized that we had a classic dilemma. The public hears bad things about the accuracy of these strikes. We say, "They are very accurate, trust us." The response is "Show us some proof and we will believe you." But we can't because of the sensitivities involved. It is not surprising that this argument is unconvincing. While such media interactions like the one I had can help, what we have to rely on is that the congressional oversight process works as it should. For a long time, congressional committees have played an important role in overseeing drone strikes. As the public's representatives, they must assure themselves that these activities are much more carefully administered than critics suggest, and they must say so to the American people. And they have done so on multiple occasions with regard to US drone strikes.

* * *

Collateral damage is not the only drone issue that many commentators get wrong. Another is the very nature of the weapon system itself. Some call it unique in that the individual firing the weapon is so far away from the target, which makes it impersonal, more like a computer game than a war. The often unstated implication is that because it is impersonal one is somehow more likely to use it than a traditional weapon system. But drones are far from unique. There are many such weapon systems in the US inventory. What is the difference between a drone pilot and a sniper looking through a scope and pulling a trigger a mile across the battlefield? What is the difference between a drone operator and a B-2 pilot dropping ordnance from fifty thousand feet? What is the difference between a drone pilot and an Aegis ship's weapons specialist who pushes the button that causes a cruise missile to travel hundreds of miles to a specific target on the globe? There is much hype about drones—almost none of it bearing any resemblance to reality.

Some very reasonable questions include: Don't drone strikes actually create more terrorists? Don't they radicalize the friends and relatives of those killed by drones? Don't they radicalize others who deeply believe, despite the facts, that many civilians, including women and children, are being killed in drone strikes? Don't they put on the battlefield more terrorists than they take off? Perhaps—we just don't know. What leads people to choose violence in the pursuit of their political and religious ideals is complicated. But even if the critics of drones are right and they create more terrorists than they kill, what is the alternative? You must deal with the immediate threat in front of you—the terrorist who is planning to attack the United States and kill our citizens—even as you work to deal over the longer term with the issues that created that threat in the first place.

Here is another way to think about this particular aspect of the drone issue. Counterterrorism operations using weapons fired from drones target individuals the United States believes pose a direct and imminent threat to Americans—either overseas or in the homeland. Are we better off as a country dealing with that threat by using unmanned aerial vehicles where no US servicemen or servicewomen are put in peril, or by putting US boots on the ground and therefore at risk? I think the answer is an easy one.

* * *

This chapter has been a story of al Qa'ida's vulnerability and resilience. What is the source of this seemingly inconsistent duality? There are two. First, terrorists are very easy to remove from the battlefield, but stopping the recruitment of new terrorists is a nearly impossible task. And second, terrorism is not a capital-intensive enterprise. To be successful, one needs leadership, operatives, some money, and secure operating space. Those things are very easy to take away—and also very easy to retrieve.

* * *

The digging of the tunnel began in the bathroom of a women's mosque in Yemen. Al Qa'ida operatives methodically dug toward a nearby maximum-security prison where nearly two dozen of their colleagues were being held. They dug for two months. The tunnel, roughly 150 yards in length, ended underneath a prison cell block.

On February 5, 2006, twenty-three al Qa'ida operatives escaped through the tunnel. The escapees included Nasir al-Wuhayshi, who today leads al Qa'ida's number one franchise, al Qa'ida in the Arabian Peninsula (AQAP). He is also now the number two to Ayman al-Zawahiri in the overall al Qa'ida organization; if Zawahiri were to depart the scene, Wuhayshi would be in charge. Another escapee from the prison was Jamal Badawi, who had led the al Qaʻida cell that attacked the USS *Cole*. The Yemenis were embarrassed, and the United States was furious.

Prior to the jailbreak, AQAP had been effectively defeated in Yemen. Following a flourishing after 9/11, US and Yemeni military action had ended the threat from AQAP. Now, just weeks after the jailbreak, AQAP was back in business. And just twenty-five months later, it again posed a major threat. In March 2008, AQAP fired mortars at the US embassy in Sanaa but hit a nearby girls' school instead. And then, in September 2008, AQAP militants dressed as police officers stormed the US embassy with automatic weapons and rocket-propelled grenades. Twelve people were killed, including one American. The explosive marks are still visible on the walls of the embassy.

One prison break made all the difference. It was a perfect example of the thin line between the vulnerability and the resilience of al Qaʻida.

CHAPTER 7

No Mickey Mouse Operation

In 2009, when I was serving as the third-ranking official at CIA, the Agency hosted a visit from Kevin Bacon. That's right. That Kevin Bacon. He was in DC playing in a band, and our Office of Public Affairs invited him. So I hosted him for a thirty-minute courtesy call. The discussion was wide-ranging and turned at one point to six degrees of separation. Bacon jokingly said, "I'll bet there are even six degrees of separation between Usama bin Ladin and me." Without missing a beat, our most senior operations officer, who I had invited to the meeting, replied, "Since you walked into this room, the degrees of separation between you and Bin Ladin became a lot less than six."

* * *

When he slipped away from us in Tora Bora, Bin Ladin virtually disappeared. There were lots of rumors, and occasional "sightings," but we had virtually no intelligence on where he was or what he was up to because his operational security was that good. Some observers speculated that he might be dead. Our view, based on little evidence, was that he was alive, probably living somewhere in the border region between Afghanistan and Pakistan—still the ideological leader, but not the day-to-day operational leader of al Qa'ida. We assessed that day-to-day management had passed to Bin Ladin's deputy, Ayman al-Zawahiri.

We were mostly on our own in the hunt for Bin Ladin. For their part, the Pakistanis and the Afghans pointed fingers only at each other—with the Pakistanis saying with certainty that he was in Afghanistan, not Pakistan, and with the Afghans saying he was in Pakistan. I cannot remember a single time when either country brought us a lead on Bin Ladin.

At CIA we could not afford to fixate on Bin Ladin alone— pursuing him as if he were some white whale. The evil that he'd spawned was metastasizing and causing undeniable threats to the United States and our allies around the world. But Bin Ladin remained the primary target because he was the named leader of the group and was such a powerful motivator of jihad both in South Asia and around the world. I never despaired about getting him, but it was enormously frustrating to have so little information with which to work. It was also frustrating to have to regularly answer the question "So why haven't you caught Bin Ladin?" from Congress, the White House, and the media. One of our senior operational officers came to answer that question with a sarcastic quip that was nonetheless true. He said, "Because he is HIDING!" My answer to this question was that it was hard, and I would go on to note that it had taken the FBI seventeen years to find the Unabomber and seven years to find Eric Rudolph, the bomber at the Atlanta Olympics, and that these guys had been hiding in the United States, on the FBI's own turf, not on the other side of the planet in someone else's country.

Jose Rodriguez, the now-retired former director of our Counterterrorism Center and former head of all clandestine operations at CIA, told me that he'd once gotten so tired of answering the question about why we had not yet caught Bin Ladin that he swore he would say "Fuck you!" to the very next person who asked. That evening at home, over dinner, Rodriguez's wife Patti innocently asked, "So why haven't you guys got Bin Ladin yet?" Rodriguez did not tell me how he'd answered.

We had a very systematic approach to trying to locate Bin Ladin. We devoted extensive effort to learning about and locating his far-flung family. That approach never bore fruit. Another thread was to focus on his public utterances. Periodically Bin Ladin would issue an audio statement—and on rare occasions he would release a video. Agency analysts seized on those occasions to study technical details, images, background, and the like—trying to identify anything that might suggest even a general location for Bin Ladin. We tried to reverse engineer how the messages had gotten from Bin Ladin to the media outlets that broadcast them—to see if we could backtrack to their originator. Despite the great expenditure of resources, particularly in terms of analysts' time, this approach did not produce dividends either.

The other path we pursued was figuring out how he was communicating with his immediate subordinates and then using that link to find him. We assumed that Bin Ladin was too savvy to use modern technology to communicate and instead was relying on couriers to stay in touch with his terrorist organization. Starting in 2002, we learned from detainees of a person who had worked with Bin Ladin prior to 9/11 and who had worked for Khalid Sheikh Mohammed (KSM) after 9/11. One detainee told our officers that this individual served as a courier for messages to and from Bin Ladin. Another detainee speculated that he was the sort of person who could be living with Bin Ladin. The guy's nom de guerre—his Arab nickname—was "Abu Ahmed al-Kuwaiti."

What particularly caught our interest was the reactions of the two most senior al Qa'ida detainees in our custody—KSM and Abu Faraj al-Libi. By the time we asked them about Abu Ahmed, both were typically willing to provide information about the roles of various al Qa'ida personnel. Regarding Abu Ahmed, however, KSM said he remembered him but he denied that Abu Ahmed was Bin Ladin's courier and he said that Abu Ahmed had left al Qa'ida after 9/11—statements inconsistent with what the other detainees had told us. And Abu Faraj insisted that he did not know Abu Ahmed and indeed had never even heard of him—again directly contradicting what others had told us about a close relationship between the two. The coup de grace occurred when KSM returned to his cell after the questioning and communicated to other prisoners that they should not mention anything about "the courier." Both KSM and Abu Faraj, who had given us information extremely damaging to al Qa'ida, were going out of their way to protect Abu Ahmed. Our interest in the courier was now sky-high.

It took us several years to learn Abu Ahmed's true name and several more years to find his general location—somewhere in Pakistan. We did this by employing the capabilities of CIA to recruit human sources and of the NSA to collect communications. It was a team effort. Then our challenge was to pinpoint his location, put eyes on him, and surveil him until he took us to the next lead. At that point we didn't know if he was *the* courier—the individual with direct access to Bin Ladin—or merely *a* courier who would only lead to other couriers. But we hoped that if we could find where he lived he would in some way lead us to his boss.

* * *

During one of the thrice-weekly CT sessions in August 2010, senior CTC officials told Director Panetta and me that they needed to talk privately to us after the main meeting. They had something to report. This was not an unusual event, as CTC often had something sensitive to tell us. We called it "going small." But "going small" on this particular day was the most significant such meeting I ever attended.

"We have found a guy we know as Abu Ahmed," CTC told us. They said, "He is living in the town of Abbottabad, Pakistan," and explained that his residence was within a stone's throw of the Pakistani equivalent of West Point. They told us the history of Abu Ahmed and the history behind the lead. They told us that Abu Ahmed was living in Abbottabad along with his brother, Abrar. They said they did not know for certain that Abu Ahmed was a courier for Bin Ladin, but the fact that he and his brother were practicing extraordinary operational security—for example, powering up and using their cell phones only when they were miles from Abbottabad—made them of great interest.

The CTC briefers handed out satellite photos of the place where the brothers were living. It was a compound with walls twelve to eighteen feet high and topped with barbed wire. The facility had internal walls that seemed to segment the compound, and the main house had a strange lack of windows. Most unusual was that there was an outdoor terrace off the third floor, surrounded by a privacy wall. "Who puts a privacy wall around a patio?" Panetta asked. "Isn't the whole purpose of a terrace to see out?" "Exactly," said one of the analysts.

Interestingly, no one in the meeting said what was obviously on all our minds—that there was a chance Bin Ladin might be behind the privacy wall. The hair on the back of my neck stood up. I struggled to not let my optimism get out of hand. Panetta told CTC what it already knew—that we needed to know a lot more about "AC1," the Agency's designation for Abu Ahmed's Abbottabad compound, and its occupants.

Over the next few weeks CTC briefed the director and me on additional information on the compound. CTC learned that the brothers had paid a great deal of money for the property but had no visible means of income. It learned that the compound, larger and more valuable than any other home in the area, had no telephone line or Internet connection. It learned that the two brothers were residing in Abbottabad under aliases and that their wives were lying to their own extended families about where they lived. Another piece to the puzzle was that the residents of the compound burned all their trash rather than putting it out for collection like everyone else in the neighborhood. And it was discovered that none of the multiple children living in the compound were attending school, unlike the other children in what was an upscale neighborhood of Pakistan. All of this was suspicious but did not prove anything.

We took all this information to the White House. We started with John Brennan, my friend and fellow career CIA officer. Brennan instantly grasped the significance of the intelligence and he had us give the same briefing to the national security advisor, General Jim Jones, and his deputy, Tom Donilon. They in turn asked us to brief President Obama. All the briefings were held in the wood-paneled Situation Room in the basement of the West Wing.

The briefing of the president—on September 21—walked the commander in chief through the history of our interest in couriers, from the information obtained years before from al Qa'ida detainees up to the latest intelligence on what we could observe at the compound and what we had learned about it. We told the president that there seemed to be one or two men at the compound aside from the brothers, and we highlighted the possibility that Abu Ahmed and his brother could be harboring Bin Ladin. The president gave us two orders. First, he told us that he wanted more information on the compound. And second, he told us to not brief anyone else on what we had already found. I did not hear the president order such strict security about any other issue during my time working with him.

* * *

I admired the president. He was brilliant and deeply attentive in any substantive meeting. I thought he quickly got to the heart of an issue and asked the right questions. The president, however, would sometimes take too long to make a decision (just the opposite of President Bush)—a result, I believe, of his strong desire to get all questions answered before moving forward.

At the same time, the president also had a way of making decisions that satisfied competing factions among his national security team. His decision on Libya—although unfortunately described as "leading from behind"—was an example of this. In a National Security Council meeting to discuss the issue, half of the national security team made clear that it was decidedly against any military intervention in Libya—we were already providing humanitarian support and had placed sanctions on the Libyan regime. This group argued that while Qadhafi's actions against his own people were deplorable, there was no strategic interest on the part of the United States in intervening. The other half of the team felt just as strongly, arguing that we had a moral responsibility to go all in, including by putting US troops on the ground, if necessary, to stop Qadhafi from murdering huge numbers of his own people, which was what he was doing and what he was planning to do in order to save his regime.

In NSC meetings the president would typically listen to his advisors and ask questions, but not make a decision in the room, preferring to think over the matter and discuss it with his closest aides. But the Libya decision was different. He made it on the spot. His decision to support the moderate Arab states and the Europeans in declaring a no-fly zone and ultimately in attacking from the air the Libyan regime's military units targeting civilians—but to do so only with capabilities that others did not have—satisfied everyone in the room. When he made the decision, I leaned over to Denis McDonough and whispered, "So that's why he is the president of the United States."

I also found the president personally engaging—in contrast to the media portrayal of him as aloof. I think this dichotomy exists because the president is different in large groups from how he is in small ones. He is quiet in large groups, but his personality shines through much more in smaller settings. When the president asked me to come to the Oval Office on a cold January day in 2013—to tell me that he had chosen John Brennan to be the next director of CIA—he could not have been more gracious. In a great irony, John and I had recommended each other to the president, and now, in the Oval Office, I asked the president if something like that had ever happened to him before. He said, "Not in this town, pal." He did ask me what other job I might be interested in, as he said he did not want to lose me. I jokingly said, "I always wanted to be the chairman of the Federal Reserve Board." He laughed. I felt comfortable with our forty-fourth commander in chief.

* * *

At CIA you become accustomed to handling tightly compartmented information—but no secret in my thirty-three years of work at the Agency was more tightly controlled than the knowledge that we might have found Bin Ladin. The White House made the secretary of state aware of the intelligence only several weeks before the raid, as the discussions on whether to go forward moved into full stride. The director of the National Counterterrorism Center was told just a couple of weeks before the raid, as we needed to start thinking about possible retaliation by al Qa'ida. The attorney general, the FBI director, and the secretary of homeland security learned of it only a day or two beforehand.

In the weeks and months following the initial briefing of the president there were many follow-up meetings at the White House. The security was extraordinary. Brennan scheduled the meetings and made sure that their purpose did not leak. On the official NSC calendar they were listed as "Mickey Mouse meetings." Each time we met, the security cameras inside the Situation Room were turned off. When staff entered the room to bring a beverage to the president, everyone stopped talking.

Even within CIA we kept the secret extremely close. I delegated the authority to "read in" people to the operation to the head of the Counterterrorism Center because I knew he would not abuse the authority. In fact, I knew he would be even more careful than I. When our counterterrorism analysts wanted a written briefing on everything that could be learned about the city of Abbottabad, they turned to the Open Source Center—a part of CIA that mines public sources for information important to national security. But instead of asking for research only on Abbottabad, they asked for research on a number of Pakistani cities. Like Bin Ladin himself, our analysts hunting Bin Ladin were hiding in plain sight.

Our congressional oversight committees were another story. Without the White House's knowledge, Panetta had been keeping the leadership of both the Senate Intelligence Committee and the House Intelligence Committee aware of the big picture. Panetta did not ask for permission from the White House because he knew the answer would be no. I told Panetta that I supported his decision. At one of the White House sessions, as the raid was nearing, Tom Donilon suggested that CIA might want to bring the leadership of the intelligence committees into the loop. Panetta said that he had done that from the beginning. Donilon was not pleased, but it went miles in keeping Panetta's and my relationships with our committees strong. And nothing leaked from these briefings.

* * *

Given the president's order to learn more about the compound, we ramped up our brainstorming about ways to get more information on who and what was hidden behind the walls of AC1. After a couple of weeks, Panetta was getting impatient with the lack of good ideas, and he began to drive the folks in CTC nuts with his own ideas—

and there were many of them. He asked, "Can we tap into the sewage pipes leading from the compound and do DNA testing on the outflow?" There were a few trees just outside the compound and he asked about sending assets out to climb the trees and plant surveillance cameras. (Apparently he was not the only one to think of that because a short time later Abu Ahmed and his brother were seen outside the compound chopping down the perfectly good trees.)

At a meeting in his office on November 5, Panetta pushed hard for more collection on the compound. He demanded that a list of ten proposals be delivered to him and me in just a few days. Panetta's chief of staff, Jeremy Bash, went even further, telling CTC to put everything it could think of—whether operationally feasible or not—on a piece of paper to satisfy the boss. CTC did exactly that, producing a matrix of thirty-eight ideas. The "Chart of 38," as it was called, went on for a number of pages. It worked—it satiated the director.

Some collection efforts paid off, and in the fall of 2010, we obtained two additional pieces of information, which strengthened the case that Bin Ladin might be at the compound in Abbottabad. First, we learned that a third family was living in the compound—and that the size of that family was the size we believed Bin Ladin's would be at this point in his life. We learned that no members of this third family ever left the compound and that none of the neighbors were even aware of their existence. CTC analysts thought it noteworthy that although the compound was owned by Abu Ahmed and his brother, the third family was living on the top two floors of the main house—the best quarters. This was another one of the many interesting data points our analysts weighed.

Second, we learned that Abu Ahmed was still in the game—still working for al Qa'ida. This information was a critical piece of the puzzle. It eliminated one possibility we'd feared—that Abu Ahmed was only a "former terrorist" and was no longer working for al Qa'ida. I am not at liberty to explain exactly how we obtained these two critical nuggets of information, but I can assure you it was spycraft at its best.

The new information was briefed to the president on December 10, 2010, and this time he asked us to start thinking about "finish options" or "CONOPs"—"concepts of operation"—for how the United States should go after Bin Ladin if the president decided to act. Initially he told us not to involve the military in our planning, although Panetta and I did brief the leadership of the Defense Department—Secretary of Defense Robert Gates, Chairman of the Joint Chiefs Mike Mullen, Vice Chairman Hoss Cartwright, and Under Secretary of Defense for Intelligence Mike Vickers. (The main purpose in telling our colleagues was to give them a heads up because we knew we would be coming to them for help at some point, but doing so also meant that Mike Vickers was able to help us with our initial thinking about options.) Within CTC and the Agency's Special Activities Division (SAD)—CIA's paramilitary wing—planning began for various types of action.

On January 24, 2011, the president asked that we bring the military into the discussion. On the recommendation of Panetta and me, he decided that we would turn to Vice Admiral Bill McRaven, the head of the Joint Special Operations Command (JSOC). Nearly every night in Afghanistan, military special operators carried out raids like the one we were considering.

Within days McRaven, accompanied by Mike Vickers, visited the Agency, where he was read into the operation in my office. He took the information on board, did not express any emotion—besides saying, "Great work"—and said he would send two of his best planners to the Agency to assist our folks. They were there in only two days. Soon thereafter McRaven came back to me with a request to bring in some air planners, since a heliborne ground raid would require air assets. I said yes. I also said yes to a DOD request for Air Force planners to look at an air strike option. This was all necessary, but I was getting uneasy as the circle of knowledge expanded.

Agency officers and JSOC military planners began to put together a set of options for the president to consider. They included a stealth air strike, a ground raid with troops inserted via helicopter, a ground raid with troops infiltrating the site via clandestine means, and more. Consideration was given to simply asking the Pakistanis to conduct the raid themselves, and to carrying out a "compel operation" in which we would tell the Pakistanis, "We are raiding this compound tonight, we'd like you to go with us." The Pakistanis—or any of our other allies—were not aware of our interest in the Abbottabad compound.

Each of the plans had its drawbacks. The air strike, for example, would result in the deaths of women and children at the compound, the deaths of a family in a small compound directly across the street, and (almost certainly) additional collateral damage to nearby residents because some of the weapons would undoubtedly have missed their target. (It would have been necessary to use a large number of weapons, including "bunker buster" bombs, in case the compound had underground chambers or tunnels.) Additionally, there would be no opportunity to gather intelligence from documents, material, and people found on scene or verify with absolute certainty that we'd actually gotten Bin Ladin.

A ground operation with the troops inserted clandestinely had the disadvantage of requiring that the strike team sneak into Pakistan and quite likely have to fight its way out. The probability of dead or captured Americans was high. A ground operation with the troops inserted via helicopter carried the risk of death or injury to US soldiers as well as that of detection by the Pakistani military long before the helicopters ever got to Abbottabad.

Any option that involved the Pakistanis carried the downside that the occupants of the compound might be tipped off and escape.

We were not concerned that it would have been official Pakistani policy to tip off Bin Ladin, but there would have been so many people involved on the Pakistani side that there could have been a leak, or an al Qaʻida sympathizer within the government or the military could have taken action to protect Bin Ladin—which in my view is how Bin Ladin avoided the US cruise missile strike in the aftermath of the embassy bombings in East Africa.

We began planning for a major briefing of the president. Donilon, by now promoted to national security advisor, not surprisingly wanted to be briefed first, and he set the date for March 4. Panetta and I wanted to do a dry run before we saw Donilon, so on the evening of February 25, along with our country's top military leaders, we met in Director Panetta's conference room to go over the briefing—a briefing that would cover the entire intelligence story and the options that had been developed. But this time we had something new. NGA, the National Geospatial-Intelligence Agency—those talented officers who analyze satellite imagery—had produced a scale model of the entire compound. About four feet by four feet, it was sitting on the conference table when Panetta and I walked into the room. It was incredibly accurate, even down to the placement of trees and bushes and the exact size and location of the animal pen.

The prep session went well, as did the briefing for Donilon. He started the meeting by asking how quickly we could put the various options in place, as the president was concerned that we were not moving fast enough. Donilon also gave instructions for the eventual briefing of the president, saying, "You will need to focus on why do we think this is Bin Ladin?" Donilon had some follow-up questions, which we answered in another meeting with him on March 10. He concluded that meeting by saying, "OK, let's set up a briefing for the president." The next day Donilon told us the date would be March 14.

In our discussion regarding the various finish options, Agency officers quite understandably favored an option that would place them in the middle of any operation. Having chased Bin Ladin for more than a decade, they wanted to be in on the endgame. It was understandable, but it was also crystal clear to Panetta and me that a ground operation had to be JSOC's to carry out. After one meeting on the issue in his office, Leon said to me, "Let's let the professionals do this." What he meant was that JSOC had much more experience in such matters than did CIA—but his words did not go down well within our ranks. By the time word filtered down to lower levels of CTC and SAD, it had become garbled, and the impression was that *I* had made the comment—and was somehow disrespecting our own troops. While I fully agreed with Panetta's decision, we could have done a better job of explaining it to our in-house warriors, for whom I have the utmost respect.

* * *

The session on March 14 was one of the most important meetings with a president that I ever attended. We covered two issues in depth—the intelligence picture and the options. On the intelligence, we provided the president with our bottom line that there was a "strong possibility Abu Ahmed was harboring Bin Ladin at the Abbottabad compound." We emphasized that we did not have direct proof that Bin Ladin was there—just a strong circumstantial case.

Each of the finish options was discussed in detail. The president immediately took the Pakistani options off the table because of the risk of tipping off the targets. The president also rejected the ground assault whereby the team would be clandestinely inserted into Pakistan. It was just too complicated, and getting the team out of Pakistan after the mission would be extremely difficult. The meeting ended with only two options on the table—the air strike and the ground assault with the troops inserted via helicopter—and with the president making it clear that he wanted to move sooner rather than later. Although he never said it directly, many of us left the session with the sense that he was leaning toward the air strike.

We met again with the president on March 29. Obama, largely because of concerns about collateral damage, began by taking the stealth air strike off the table. He saw the heliborne ground assault as the best option for knowing whether Bin Ladin was there or not, for getting our hands on any intelligence at the site, and for minimizing the deaths of noncombatants. He asked Bill McRaven if he thought it would work. McRaven said, "Mr. President, I can't look you in the eye and tell you yes until I exercise it. I'll get back to you in two weeks."

Because CIA had anticipated this very moment, we had built a full-scale mock-up of the Abbottabad compound. There McRaven brought together the team of Navy SEALs that he would use on the mission and they were briefed, for the first time, on the potential target. Going into the session, most of them had thought that they were going to be asked to conduct a raid to go after Muammar Qadhafi, who at the time was on the run in Libya. It was at our mock-up of the Abbottabad compound that they learned the true identity of their target. There, standing in front of the SEALs, our lead operations officer said, "This is not about Libya. We have found Usama bin Ladin, and you guys are going to go get him." Although trying not to show emotion, the SEALs were psyched. Following exercises at our facility and a full dress rehearsal at a DOD facility, the SEALs were ready to go.

Although the SEALs belonged to the US military, the president made clear that if there was going to be an operation it would be CIA's to lead. That was because the president wanted the operation to be covert. On the off chance that Bin Ladin was not there and the raid was not detected by the Pakistanis, the United States would try to keep the whole thing quiet, as if it had never happened. That meant that the chain of command for the operation went from the president of the United States to the director of CIA to the commander of JSOC. The secretary of defense was not in the chain of command for the operation. The JSOC personnel would be operationally assigned to the Agency to carry out the operation.

The pace of the meetings with the president now accelerated. Three were held in April. Mid-month, McRaven walked the president through the results of his team's exercises, concluding, "We can do this." McRaven recommended, if the raid were to be conducted, that it go down on the night of April 30. It would be pitch-black, and anyone wearing night vision goggles would have a huge advantage.

But there was a problem with the thirtieth. Someone mentioned that Saturday, April 30, was the night of the annual White House Correspondents' Association dinner—where the president was expected to speak. How would it look, they asked, if the president was at a black-tie dinner joking around with a bunch of reporters in the beautiful Hilton Hotel ballroom in Washington, D.C., while a group of Americans were dying on a failed mission in Pakistan? Secretary of State Hillary Clinton shot down that concern with a well-placed response. "Fuck the White House Correspondents' dinner," she said. "Heaven help us if we ever make an important operational decision like this based on some political event."

But there was also a new option on the table—one that the joint planning team had never looked at in any detail. This option was suggested by the vice chairman of the Joint Chiefs of Staff, Marine general Hoss Cartwright, and it had to do with someone at the compound whom we at CIA called "the Pacer." We were able to determine that there was a lone male person who regularly walked a path in an outdoor grove adjacent to the compound's main house. Everyone assumed it was Bin Ladin, but we were unable to get close enough to establish his identity or even his height. Panetta asked the experts for an estimate of the Pacer's height—Bin Ladin was well over six feet—and the answer unfortunately was "somewhere between five and seven feet." That analysis did not advance the ball.

At one meeting Cartwright took the position that the mysterious man pacing in the compound was most likely UBL, and that we could use an unmanned aerial vehicle to take him out. CIA had heard through the grapevine that Cartwright might raise this idea and we were opposed, and I took aim to shoot it down. I noted, if Bin Ladin was at the compound, then Cartwright was almost certainly right about the identity of the Pacer. But I also noted that the United States had had a great deal of experience with UAV targeting in recent years—and that the attacks were not always successful. It all depended on the physics of an explosion. If Bin Ladin was at Abbottabad, we would get only one crack at him, I argued. The chances of our missing altogether or of Bin Ladin's walking away from a strike were just too high.

Another issue was the potential response of the Pakistanis to the incursion into their territory. If the Pakistanis detected the heliborne raid early, or were able to respond to it faster than anyone anticipated, McRaven's plan was for his men to hunker down at the compound while senior officials negotiated a resolution. At the very end of one meeting, the president gave McRaven one more directive. He told McRaven that he did not like that idea of McRaven's troops rotting in a Pakistani jail for months as we tried to work out a diplomatic solution. No, the president said. "If you get put into that situation, you will fight your way out." I thought it was exactly the right decision, and by the look on his face, I know McRaven thought it was the right decision as well.

* * *

Throughout the meetings in April, one of the issues that we discussed at length was the probability that Bin Ladin was at the compound. For weeks this issue came up at meetings. The lead analyst said she was 95 percent certain that Bin Ladin was there. The senior analytic manager—the one who did the briefings for the president—said he was at 80 percent. The CTC analysts were certainly aware of CIA's failure regarding weapons of mass destruction in Iraq—where the Agency had made an enormous mistake by accepting another circumstantial case. But they kept going back over the intelligence again and again, asking themselves, "What other explanation could there be?" Taking lessons from Iraq, they outlined possible alternative explanations in their briefings. None of them were as compelling as the Bin Ladin explanation. The chief of CTC went even further. He put together a "red team"—a small group of smart Agency analysts whom he trusted but who were not involved in the operation or the analysis in any way. They were asked to review everything and tell him if we were missing something—if there were other plausible explanations for the mystery of AC1. They did so, and although not quite as convinced as the CTC analysts, they also came down on the side of saying that UBL was likely there. They were at somewhat less than 80 percent but definitely over 50 percent. I myself was at 60 percent.

With estimates all over the lot, it was no wonder that the president was perplexed, and he asked Panetta why there was such a disparity in the probabilities. Leon deftly turned to me and said, "Michael, why don't you handle that one?"

After gathering my thoughts for a few seconds, I explained to the president that the differences in the judgments about probability did not reflect any difference in what information people had; I assured him that everyone was working on the same set of data. Rather, I told him that the differences in judgments reflected individual experiences. Those at the higher end of the probability scale tended to be in CTC, and they had a confidence in their judgments borne of success over the past several years—plot after plot disrupted, senior al Qa'ida leader after senior al Qa'ida leader taken off the streets. Those at the lower end of the scale—including me—had been through intelligence failures and therefore had less confidence in analytic judgments, particularly circumstantial ones. In my case the failure of CIA's prewar intelligence on Iraq's weapons of mass destruction weighed on my mind. Indeed, I told him, "Mr. President, I believe the circumstantial case that Iraq had WMD in 2002 was stronger than the circumstantial case that Bin Ladin is in the Abbottabad compound." I added, "Even if we had a source inside the compound and that source told us that Bin Ladin was there, I would not be at 95 percent, because sources lie and get things wrong all the time."

Mike Vickers told me later that you could hear a pin drop in the room as I said that the Iraq case had been stronger. For his part, the president listened intently and clearly understood what I was saying. He followed up by asking, "So, Michael, if you are only at 60 percent, would you not do the raid?" "No, Mr. President," I said. "Even at 60 percent, I would do the raid. Given the importance of who this is, the case is strong enough." The president would later tell people that he'd personally put the odds of Bin Ladin's being there at fifty-fifty.

* * *

The question of whether to conduct a raid was hotly debated by the handful of senior officials privy to the intelligence. Some people thought that the risks were too high. The vice president was unconvinced about the intelligence and concerned about what a failed mission would do to our relations with Pakistan. And Secretary of Defense Bob Gates, a career CIA officer and former CIA director, also said that he felt the intelligence was too weak and he thought the risks to US forces going in were too high. He noted that something almost always goes wrong in this kind of military operation. He repeatedly brought up the tragedy of "Desert One," the failed

Iranian hostage rescue attempt during the Carter administration. He told us how he had sat around a conference table in that same Situation Room thirty years before as that tragedy played out. The secretary's view was that if we took action, we should go the UAV route. Hoss Cartwright was also opposed to the raid, seeing the UAV option as a better choice as well.

Beyond those three, however, the national security team came down on the side of going ahead. But even as the consensus seemed to be building to conduct a strike, there was a school of thought that advocated waiting until we had more definitive intelligence. Panetta and I responded with three points: (1) there was no guarantee that more time would deliver more intelligence; (2) the number of people who were aware of the intelligence reporting and analysis was growing and a leak could happen at any moment, thereby tipping off Bin Ladin; and (3) even without receiving some warning, there was nothing to say that Bin Ladin might not decide it was time to pull up stakes and move somewhere else, as we did not know whether this was a long-term or a short-term residence for the al Qa'ida leader. Without round-the-clock surveillance, which was simply not available, either of the latter two scenarios would force us to start all over again.

Panetta made perhaps the strongest argument—something that everyone knew but was unwilling to say. Stepping out of his role as a provider of intelligence only and not advocating policy, Panetta said at one meeting that "I've always operated by a simple test—what would the American people say?" He added, "There is no doubt in my mind that if they knew what we know—even with the range of confidence levels we have—that they would want us to go after the man responsible for all those deaths on 9/11." It was a powerful argument.

There was a final Mickey Mouse meeting in the Situation Room, where the president polled the principals on whether they would recommend going ahead with the mission. The vice president and

Bob Gates voted no; everyone else voted yes. But the next morning three of Gates's top people—Admiral Mike Mullen, Mike Vickers, and Michèle Flournoy, the under secretary of defense for policy—all came to Gates in an effort to convince him that he should support the raid. After the nearly hour-long meeting Gates called Tom Donilon and told him that he was changing his vote to yes. I have great admiration for Bob Gates for many reasons, and his willingness to be open-minded and to listen to what his subordinates are telling him is one of those reasons.

* * *

Throughout the entire process, two things were a constant—the attempt to get more intelligence and the questioning about the analysts' confidence that Bin Ladin was there. Try as we might, we were unable to get much additional intelligence to help the president decide whether to take action against the Abbottabad compound or not.

On the analytic side, there would be one more red team before the final "go" decision. In April 2011, Brennan quite appropriately wanted to consider how al Qa'ida might retaliate against us should we get Bin Ladin. To think through that problem he needed the help of the National Counterterrorism Center (NCTC). In addition to focusing on the task at hand—possible retaliation—the organization's head, Mike Leiter, suggested to Brennan that NCTC do a formal red team on the CIA analysts' conclusion that Bin Ladin was at Abbottabad.

Brennan and Leiter both asked me what I thought. I was aware of the alternative analysis that the CTC itself had done and the red teaming that the director of CTC had ordered. And while I thought it was overkill, I said, "Why not?" For a decision of this magnitude you could not be too careful. So Leiter put together a team of two NCTC analysts and two CIA analysts on assignment to his unit to review the intelligence again. Those four analysts did not reach a consensus. They had a wide range of views. One of them put the probability at 60 percent that Bin Ladin was there (which was also my level of confidence). Two others came down at around 50 percent, and one gave it only a 40 percent chance, which I took to mean that he did not think Bin Ladin was there. Each analyst did think that the Bin Ladin theory was the best explanation for what we were seeing at the compound. Still, when Leiter briefed his team's conclusions to the president, it was a replay of my earlier Iraq WMD comment—a sobering reminder of how thin the case was for Bin Ladin's presence in Abbottabad.

* * *

On April 29, just one day after the final meeting with the president, the secure phone rang in Director Panetta's office. It was National Security Advisor Tom Donilon. He informed us that the president had ordered the mission to proceed. Panetta, sensing that it was a historic moment, wrote out a memo for the record in longhand. It read:

> *Received phone call from Tom Donilon who stated that the President made a decision with regard to AC1. The decision is to proceed with the assault. The timing, operational decision making, and control are in Admiral McRaven's hands. The direction is to go in and get Bin Ladin and if he is not there, to get out. These instructions were conveyed to Admiral McRaven at 10:45 a.m.*

It is impossible to fully convey the size of the knot you feel in your stomach when you are among the few people on the planet who know that such a major event is about to occur, and when the outcome is so uncertain. Just an hour or so before the raid, as we two were alone in his office, Panetta asked me what I thought in my heart of hearts: "Is he there?" "Sir," I said, "I will not be surprised if we find him there—and I will not be surprised if we don't." Panetta simply answered, "Me too." It was a roll of the dice.

After the raid was conducted, media commentators talked about the president's "gutsy decision." My view was that the decision to take action had not been the tough part. The case was strong enough to take action; in fact, the case was strong enough that the president had to take action. Had he not, and had it later become known that CIA had thought Bin Ladin was there, it would have been extraordinarily damaging to his presidency and to US credibility. No, to me, the gutsy part was the president's decision about what kind of action to take. By putting US boots on the ground and placing American lives at risk, he made a difficult, but ultimately correct, decision. The easy way out would have been to obliterate the compound with munitions from a couple of B-2 bombers. As a result of his decision, we limited the collateral damage significantly, knew for certain that we had gotten Bin Ladin, and obtained a treasure trove of intelligence from the compound.

As it turned out, the debate about launching a raid on the night of the correspondents' dinner was moot—the weather was bad in Pakistan and McRaven elected to postpone the operation for one day.

* * *

The CIA director's wood-paneled conference room, across a narrow hallway from my office and that of Leon Panetta, had been turned into a makeshift command center. The long, polished table was stacked with computer terminals manned by CIA and JSOC personnel in constant touch with Admiral McRaven's headquarters in Jalalabad, Afghanistan, and monitoring various sensors around the region. A handful of senior CIA officials were there, but nowhere near all of them.

Many senior CIA personnel, all with the highest security clearances possible, were still unaware that we thought we had found Bin Ladin, unaware of the history that was about to be made. In keeping the information from Agency officials, cabinet officers and the like, we were not signaling any measure of distrust. It is simply that in a mission of this magnitude, every additional person briefed on the operation increases the possibility of an unintentional leak that might scuttle the operation. In the days that followed the raid, I would have to explain (if not apologize) to a lot of people who wished they had been clued into the operation in advance.

The extraordinary operational security had also given me some trouble much closer to home. A friend of mine had offered tickets to the Washington Capitals hockey play-off game against the Tampa Bay Lightning on May 1. And since the raid was called off on April 30, I thought there was a chance that bad weather would postpone it again the next day and that I would be able to go to the game. So I accepted the tickets.

By midmorning D.C. time on May 1, however, it was clear that the weather in Pakistan was cooperating and the mission would be a go. Not wanting the tickets to go to waste, I called Mary Beth and asked her to pick them up so someone else could put them to use. As the wife of the deputy director, Mary Beth had her own CIA pass and could normally drive onto the compound and come into the headquarters building without an escort. But if she came to my office on May 1 she would have seen the extraordinary beehive of activity in the adjoining conference room and would have figured out that something was up. She too was among the many who did not have a "need to know." So I told my security detail to meet her "downstairs" and "under no circumstances should she be allowed upstairs." But they went a step further than that and decided to meet her at the Agency's front gate a quarter mile away from the main entrance to the building. They simply said, "Ma'am, here are the tickets," with a tone and look that said, "This is as far as you go." She already hadn't been too happy with my working schedule over the past several months, and now the frosty reception from the security detail was a big push toward the edge.

But what really angered her was something else. She called me later that morning and said that clearly I should be able to stop working for a short while and dash to Georgetown Visitation Preparatory School, where our daughter Sarah was about to have her last high school choral performance. "It will just take an hour," she said. "Whatever you are doing can't be that important." She was quite insistent. "I'm sorry," was all I could muster. "I can't. I can't. Gotta go." Mary Beth subsequently told me that she spent the rest of the afternoon and early evening furious with me. By about eight p.m.— after I had been "radio silent" for nearly eight hours—she sat on the couch and asked herself, "So, how does this divorce thing work?" It was only after the president made the decision to inform the American people about the raid that I was able to call her. I still did not tell her what we had done, but I said the president would be talking to the nation in a bit and that she would understand and hopefully forgive me. She asked, "Did something terrible happen?" I said, "No, it will be good news." "You got him?" she asked. Mary Beth had been on the fringes of the al Qa'ida story long enough to correctly decipher what "good news" meant. I only responded, "Love you, gotta go." At least my marriage was saved.

* * *

A little bit earlier in the day, Director Panetta and I had monitored the raid from the outfitted CIA director's conference room. We were sitting in the middle of the large conference table, connected by secure video teleconference to both Admiral McRaven in Afghanistan and the White House. The director was technically in charge, but in reality he and I had little to do with the actual operation. We were spectators, not participants. And it felt like it. The next day the director held an all-hands meeting in the CIA auditorium to talk about the raid and at one point mentioned to the workforce that, since this had been a covert action, he had been in command of the operation. He paused for a few seconds and said, "OK, that is total bullshit. I was not in charge of anything." He and the entire audience exploded in laughter.

But there was no laughing going on when the raid was taking place. Our hearts were in our throats when one of the raid helicopters crashed while hovering a short distance over the grounds of the compound during the raid. My first thought was for the safety of the SEALs on board. This was quickly followed by my second thought: "Shit, Bob Gates might have been right to warn as much as he did about bad things happening on a mission like this." I also thought, "So much for operational security." That was sure to wake up everyone in Abbottabad. Agency officers noted that nearby residents were starting to stir, but thankfully there was not an immediate security response that might have doomed the raid.

During the helicopter crash, I did note that Admiral McRaven remained completely composed and collected. He calmed me down by his demeanor. I have great admiration for McRaven. I think he is one of the greatest warriors ever produced by the US military. I have been impressed with him on many occasions, but never more so than when that helicopter went down. Only moments after the crash, McRaven would announce that no one was hurt, that the mission would continue, and that a backup helicopter was being brought up to replace the damaged helo. The extra helicopter was in place in part because of the president's earlier insistence on supplying a backup in case the team needed to fight its way out.

The actual attack has been more than adequately depicted by both reporters and participants, so I will not attempt to do a play-by-play here. Among the things not fully understood by the public, however, is that even in the immediate aftermath of the raid we were not certain that we had gotten Bin Ladin.

After the departing mission helicopters cleared Pakistani airspace, Panetta and I went to the White House to meet with the president and his senior national security team to discuss next steps. The last thing anyone wanted was for the president to come out and declare Bin Ladin dead only to have him pop up very much alive sometime later. The SEALs on scene said they *thought* the man they'd killed on the third floor looked like Bin Ladin, and that when they'd questioned some of the women and children in the house one of them had said the dead man was "Sheikh Usama." Still, that was hardly enough evidence. Once the body was back in Afghanistan, McRaven had it laid out on a hangar floor while one of his taller troops lay down alongside it to estimate the height of the dead man to see how it compared to Bin Ladin's known six-feet-four-inch frame; the height looked right. CIA's Science and Technology experts employed facial recognition technology and told us they were 90 to 95 percent sure we had our man, and I briefed this analysis to the president. But still he was not sure he should inform the American public if there was any uncertainty. There was discussion of possibly waiting till the next day, when we would have preliminary DNA analysis, or even the day after, when the final DNA analysis would be completed. That all changed when Admiral Mike Mullen, the chairman of the Joint Chiefs, called his counterpart in Pakistan, General Ashfaq Kayani. Before Mullen could say anything, Kayani told Mullen that we had gotten Bin Ladin. With this, and with the certainty that news would start getting out, the president felt it safe to make his announcement to the world.

(The next morning we received preliminary DNA tests from a US military lab in Afghanistan, and the results were positive. Later that day we got the final DNA results from a lab in the United States. The lab said that there was only a one in one trillion chance that it was not Bin Ladin. That was good enough for even the most skeptical of analysts.)

At 11:35 p.m. the president addressed the nation. I watched his remarks from a chair in the Situation Room, where so much planning for the mission had taken place. It turned out that my job was not done for the day, however. Media interest in the events of the raid was, to say the least, enormous. So the White House press office had set up a "press backgrounder." This is a session with the media, usually led by senior officials, in which the media are able to use whatever the officials say; however, for reasons of sensitivity, such as talking about intelligence matters, they cannot quote the senior officials by name. Instead the ground rules are set ahead of time regarding how the media are permitted to refer to the senior officials—"senior administration official," "senior military official," etc.

I was there to explain to the media the intelligence that had led us to conclude that Bin Ladin was probably at the compound. I did so carefully, without giving away any classified information. I was followed by Mike Vickers from the Defense Department, who provided a briefing on the raid itself.

It was probably close to one a.m. when Director Panetta and I walked out of the West Wing and onto West Executive Avenue, where our security details were waiting to take us home. We heard partygoers in nearby Lafayette Square chanting, "USA, USA, USA, CIA, CIA, CIA." It was surreal, and I said to myself, "I'll never hear that again." Panetta and I hugged. It was the second time we'd done so that day—the first being during the raid, when the SEAL commander on the ground in Pakistan—just nineteen minutes after the SEALs' boots had hit the ground—announced, "For God and country, Geronimo EKIA," the code words indicating that the SEALs thought they had gotten their man.

In the days that followed, there was a tremendous sense of pride, satisfaction, and relief. I have never had such a mix of emotions.

CIA headquarters from the air. The Original Headquarters Building (OHB in CIA parlance) is in the foreground. The New Headquarters Building (NHB) is to the rear. (© 2011 Greg E. Mathieson Sr./MAI Photos)

The iconic seal of the CIA, in the main lobby of the Original Headquarters Building. (CIA photo)

IN HONOR OF THOSE MEMBERS
OF THE CENTRAL INTELLIGENCE AGENCY
WHO GAVE THEIR LIVES IN THE SERVICE OF THEIR COUNTRY

The Memorial Wall at the CIA's headquarters, which had forty-three stars honoring Agency officers killed in the line of duty when I first arrived in 1980. As of early 2015 that number had reached 111. (CIA photo)

The 258 acres of the CIA's headquarters, named in honor of the eleventh director of central intelligence, who went on to be the forty-first president of the United States. *(CIA photo)*

Former president George H. W. Bush at the ceremony to name our headquarters compound after him, April 26, 1999. *(CIA photo)*

With my dad on my front lawn in Cuyahoga Falls, Ohio, May 1966. *(Author's personal photo)*

My mom and me, 1963. *(Author's personal photo)*

Graduating from the University of Akron, May 1980. *(Author's personal photo)*

CIA director Tenet and his staff in 1999. From left to right, Tenet, Counselor Buzzy Krongard, Special Counsel Ken Levit, Chief of Staff John Nelson, and me. *(CIA photo)*

Director of Central Intelligence Tenet presenting me with the Director's Award, one of the most prestigious awards at CIA, 1999. *(CIA photo)*

The cover of the President's Daily Brief, within which resides the most sensitive secrets collected by our nation. *(CIA photo)*

On the morning of September 11, 2001, at Booker Elementary School. The president is on the secure telephone and White House officials point to television coverage of the attack on the World Trade Center. I am on the left. *(Photo by Eric Draper, courtesy of the George W. Bush Presidential Library and Museum)*

At President Bush's ranch in Crawford, Texas, with Barney and Spot, January 2002. *(Official White House photo)*

With CIA director General Mike Hayden and his deputy Steve Kappes in 2008. The three of us were a team running the Agency from 2006 to 2008. *(CIA photo)*

With President Obama in the Oval Office on May 2, 2011, the day following the operations in which Usama bin Ladin was killed. *(Official White House photo)*

Briefing the president and his senior aides on a particularly sensitive intelligence issue, July 2012. *(Official White House photo)*

An Oval Office briefing for President Obama, about an operational breakthrough against a key intelligence target, July 2012. *(Official White House photo)*

With Senator Dianne Feinstein, chair of the Senate Select Committee on Intelligence, 2013. *(Courtesy of Senate Select Committee on Intelligence staff)*

During one of my many trips to Iraq, a visit to Saddam's former palace, which at the time (2009) was the headquarters of coalition forces in Iraq. *(Personal photo taken by Agency officer)*

On one of my many trips to Afghanistan as deputy director. A meeting with General John Allen, ISAF commander, September 2011. *(International Security Assistance Force photo)*

On one of my many visits to one of our country's most important allies. A meeting with His Majesty King Abdullah II of Jordan in Amman, spring 2012. *(Courtesy of the Royal Hashemite Court)*

The scale model of Bin Ladin's compound in Abbottabad, Pakistan, built by the National Geospatial-Intelligence Agency and used to brief senior officials. A copy of the model is now on display in a museum in CIA's headquarters. The original is at NGA. *(CIA photo)*

The moment we heard we'd gotten Bin Ladin, in the CIA director's conference room, May 1, 2011. *(CIA photo)*

Obama and his national security team discussing when to publicly announce the Bin Ladin operation, May 1, 2011. *(Official White House photo)*

The night Bin Ladin was killed, crowds outside the White House were chanting "USA, USA, USA" and "CIA, CIA, CIA." I never experienced anything like it. *(© 2011 Greg E. Mathieson Sr./MAI Photos)*

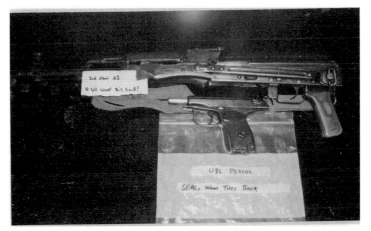

Weapons found in Bin Ladin's bedroom in Abbottabad. *(CIA photo)*

A brick from Bin Ladin's home in Abbottabad. *(Photo by author)*

A charity basketball game Director Panetta and I played in on behalf of the Combined Federal Campaign. *(CIA photo)*

The CIA departure ceremony for Leon Panetta as he leaves to become secretary of defense, June 2011. The emotion was heartfelt. *(CIA photo)*

The announcement that John Brennan would be the next CIA director, January 7, 2013. (*Official White House photo*)

Walking with President Obama along the West Wing colonnade following the announcement of John Brennan as the next CIA director, January 2013. (*Official White House photo*)

A farewell gift to me from my security staff, a Washington Nationals jersey with my security call sign, August 2013. The 33 signifies the years I spent at the Agency. *(CIA photo)*

At my going-away ceremony, August 2013. Director John Brennan displays the photo used for my first CIA badge in 1980. *(CIA photo)*

A book of letters from employees, provided as a gift upon my retirement. The book has hundreds of pages, each containing four or five letters. *(Photo by author)*

My most precious retirement gift: personal notes, framed together, from the two presidents I served most closely. Nothing better demonstrates the nonpartisanship of our country's intelligence officers. *(Photo by author)*

Brandon Leach, on his visit to CIA, preparing to conduct a mock raid against terrorists. *(CIA photo)*

A sign outside the CIA's Counterterrorism Center reminding everyone of the need to be vigilant. *(CIA photo)*

Welcome to the ⬜ Today's date is: September 12th, 2001

One of the stars etched on the Memorial Wall in the lobby of CIA's headquarters. I kept this photo above my desk for the last eight years of my career to remind me of the sacrifices made by Agency officers. *(CIA photo)*

When I arrived at work the morning after the raid, there was a letter sitting on my desk. It was from a close colleague and friend in a foreign intelligence service, with whom CIA and I had worked closely against al Qa'ida. It was the first of many such letters, but none was more beautifully written. It read:

Dear Michael,

May I be one of the many who offer you and the Agency my most profound congratulations and deep professional admiration for this outstanding success. Brilliantly developed, conceived, planned, and executed. Exemplary stuff—the CIA at its best. Our world is one where contemporary history is carved in stark events and dates. Today is one on the side of justice and will be remembered for generations. Many successes have come before and many are yet to come before the end of the al Qa'ida menace, but today the United States has written a new chapter and shown that none may escape. Outstanding. My congratulations to all.

* * *

But despite our success, there was still a lot of work to be done. One major issue was the state of US–Pakistan relations and particularly the relations between CIA and Pakistan's intelligence service, the Directorate for Inter-Services Intelligence (ISI). The ties between our two nations and their intelligence services had long been strained. But in recent months, just before the Bin Ladin raid, they had gotten much worse. In January 2011, Raymond Davis, a United States citizen assigned to the consulate in Lahore, killed two armed men in Lahore, Pakistan, who were trying to rob him. A car from the US consulate coming to the aid of Davis accidentally struck and killed a third Pakistani. Davis was held for almost two months in a Pakistani prison and was released only after intense diplomatic pressure and payment of $2.4 million in compensation to the families of the dead Pakistanis. Feelings among Pakistanis were more than a little raw over the Davis incident and grew worse with the Bin Ladin raid.

So a few weeks after the raid, the president sent his South Asian special envoy, Marc Grossman, and me to Pakistan to start repairing ties. My job was to meet with the head of the Pakistani ISI, Lieutenant General Ahmad Pasha, one of the most powerful men in a country where civilian institutions are largely subservient to the military. After flying all night to Pakistan I was taken to General Pasha's home in a military garrison outside of Islamabad. It reminded me of the kind of home one would see on any US military base. I was ushered into a small sitting area where only the two of us were present. No aides, no note takers. A waiter arrived with juice and appetizers. After exchanging greetings and questions about our families, the two of us just sat there looking at each other. The silence went on for a minute or more. We both then laughed because it was so uncomfortable. But the subjects at hand were no laughing matter.

Pasha explained to me that the United States and particularly CIA had deeply embarrassed Pakistan. I clearly understood this. He explained that the embarrassment was twofold: one, embarrassment for his service because it had not found Bin Ladin, and two, embarrassment for the Pakistani military because it could do nothing to stop such a raid deep in its country. Pasha said that if one of the United States's allies conducted a military raid in the United States, killing a fugitive and hauling his body away, we would be livid—and rightly so.

But I hoped that Pasha understood our position. I explained that we had found the most wanted man in the world living less than a mile away from their military academy—a place where he had apparently resided for years, despite years of Pakistani officials' arguing that Bin Ladin was not in Pakistan. I reminded Pasha that the United States—including President Obama—had said publicly that if we found Bin Ladin we would come and get him. There had been ample warning. Finally, I told Pasha that while I knew that neither he nor the most senior officials in Pakistan had been aware of Bin Ladin's presence in Abbottabad, it was impossible to dismiss the notion that some Pakistani security officials at some level might have been aware of his presence. I said, "Americans find it hard to believe that no one in your Abbottabad detachment or in the Abbottabad police ever questioned what was going in that compound."

We were in a standoff over the Bin Ladin raid, but we moved on to "Where do we go from here?" We eventually had a fruitful discussion. It was so fruitful that Pasha suddenly decided that we should immediately visit his boss, General Ashfaq Kayani, and continue the conversation with him. Kayani was the chief of the army staff at the time and the most powerful man in Pakistan. It was by now late in the evening, but Pasha was insistent. "Come with me! I will drive us." I assumed that Kayani lived in the same military cantonment, but it turned out he lived across town. With me in the passenger seat without a cell phone, Pasha sped off for God knew where. As we were driving off, my security detail caught a glimpse of what they thought might be their boss—the guy they were supposed to be protecting—being driven off in the night. They jumped in their cars and started off in hot pursuit. Pasha too had a security detail and they were following their boss, but they had the huge advantage of knowing where they were going. In retrospect the scene was comical—although it certainly did not seem so at the time to my security team, which was racing through the dense traffic to make sure I wasn't being kidnapped. Nor was it humorous to one of my agents, who bravely pushed his way through Pasha's security at the entrance to Kayani's cantonment to make sure I was OK. The head of my detail—who had held his position for over a decade—told me later that it was his worst moment on the job.

* * *

After the Bin Ladin raid, I had one more related mission to complete, one that was considerably more comfortable to perform. President Obama, knowing that I was with President Bush on 9/11, personally asked me to fly down to Dallas, Texas, a few days after the raid and give his predecessor a complete briefing on the operation. It was an incredibly generous gesture on the part of President Obama.

President Bush was gracious as always. But on that day, he was like a kid in a candy shop. He wanted to know every detail. I had taken the senior CIA analyst with me, as well as a senior JSOC officer. We walked the former president through the intelligence picture and the raid itself. At the end the president said, "You know, Laura and I were supposed to go to the movies tonight, but this is better than any movie I will ever see. I think we will stay home." There was also a personal moment between me and the person I used to brief. He gave me a challenge coin, a highly prized medallion that military commands and some senior officials hand out. It was his commander in chief coin. When he handed it to me and we shook hands, I felt closure for the first time since 9/11.

* * *

When I was serving as deputy director, my staff would put together a reading package every Friday for the weekend. Dozens of highly classified multi-page documents would be sent home with me when I left Langley on a Friday evening. I stored these documents in a safe in what we call a Sensitive Compartmented Information Facility, or SCIF for short. The SCIF itself, sort of like a small bank vault, was in my attic and was protected by multiple alarm systems and security cameras. And my security agents were never far from my home.

In August 2011, when I was serving as acting director for the first time, I poured myself a cup of coffee, pulled the weekend reading material from the safe, put the pile on my lap, put my feet up, and started to read. About halfway through the pile was a paper produced by our counterterrorism analysts outlining their take on the information derived from a treasure trove of documents scooped up during the Bin Ladin raid. I had been waiting for this paper, so I settled in for a thorough, word-by-word read.

I was not surprised by most of what I read. One of the many takeaways from the DOCEX (document exploitation) from Bin Ladin's office at Abbottabad was that al Qa'ida was still very much intent on attacking the West. The documents showed that Bin Ladin, in the months before his death, had been engaged in ongoing discussions with his key operatives about pursuing mass casualty attacks in the United States and against the infrastructure that operates the global oil industry—oil pipelines, terminals, and tankers. The oil industry has long been a target of al Qa'ida (in February 2006, al Qa'ida attacked Saudi Arabia's Abqaiq facility, the largest oil processing facility in the world, responsible for half of Saudi oil exports). And, as expected, Bin Ladin had underscored the group's enduring interest in attacking commercial airlines.

As I read on, I became more engrossed in the paper. The captured documents also made clear that the United States was still by far the primary target of al Qa'ida. Bin Ladin considered us enemy number one, calling us "the leader of the nonbelievers." And although the United States and its partners had done great damage to the terrorist group's central leadership operating out of the tribal areas of Pakistan, al Qa'ida, and similar groups inspired by it, was still intent on attacking us and still capable of inflicting significant damage. When I finished reading, I just sat there. The paper had reinforced all my instincts about the group.

The one thing that surprised me was that the analysts made

clear that our pre-raid understanding of Bin Ladin's role in the organization had been wrong. Before the raid we'd thought that Bin Ladin's deputy, Ayman al-Zawahiri, was running the organization on a day-to-day basis, essentially the CEO of al Qa'ida, while Bin Ladin was the group's ideological leader, its chairman of the board. But the DOCEX showed something quite different. It showed that Bin Ladin himself had not only been managing the organization from Abbottabad, he had been micromanaging it. He had been approving personnel appointments, approving how money was spent, and intimately involved in attack planning. He had still been very much involved in day-to-day terrorist operations, and he had still been very much involved with al Qa'ida's growing offshoots around the world, particularly al Qa'ida in the Arabian Peninsula (AQAP) in Yemen. This, of course, magnified the value of removing Bin Ladin from the battlefield.

CHAPTER 8

Al Qa'ida Spring

As a result of having to work through the aftermath of the Bin Ladin raid with him, I became better acquainted with General Pasha. We had many frank conversations—about the counterterrorism work we did together, but also about our countries and their futures. I found him to be a proud and patriotic Pakistani whose thinking was sometimes clouded by his nationalism (Pasha was the most nationalistic Pakistani leader I met). A few months after the Abbottabad raid, we were in my office in Virginia discussing the future of Pakistan and its priorities. Pasha emphasized the absolute importance of Pakistan's staying focused on India, as, he said, "the Indians have been, are, and will remain an existential threat to the state of Pakistan." I could not disagree with him more. I told Pasha that India was focused on growing its economy and improving the standard of living of its people. India had moved on long ago from a singular focus on Pakistan. I added that Pasha and his government were stuck in a time warp and that while they worried about India, other much more serious threats were emerging around them. "What is an existential threat to Pakistan is the state of your economy and the growing militancy inside your borders. Look at what is happening across the Arab world," I said. Pasha did not respond.

* * *

Early in 2012, while I was having this conversation with my Pakistani counterpart, there was a revolution under way in parts of North Africa and the Middle East—one that would bring the most significant change to the region since the Arab revolt against the Ottoman Empire at the end of World War I. And, importantly for the threat posed by terrorists, this revolution would end up feeding al Qa'ida in a way that few people expected.

* * *

Forecasting revolutions is an inexact science. At CIA we were very good about providing strategic warnings but not as good on the tactical front. That is like a meteorologist telling you, "Winter is coming and it looks like a bad one." Good to know, but what you really want to find out is whether it will snow on Thursday and how bad the storm will be.

For a number of years CIA analysts had been warning about powerful pressures in the Arab world. In one piece after another they told policy-makers that, without significant policy change in the Arab world, the status quo would not stand. They offered a wealth of analysis—citing political, demographic, economic, and societal trends that all pointed to trouble for the authoritarian regimes in the region, as these governments were not meeting the expectations of their people. There were two fundamental problems—one we saw and one we did not. The one we saw was that fairly well-educated people could not find jobs and were concerned that they and their children would not find a better life. The one we missed was that social media were helping to quickly spread these people's views in a profound way.

What we failed to do was provide a tactical warning—either "Something bad could well happen in Tunisia in the next few months" or "The pressures that we have been discussing for years are now building to a dangerous level across the entire region." While some criticized us for not providing that first warning, it would have been nearly impossible to do so. The fuse of the Arab uprising was lit on December 17, 2010, in Tunisia, when Mohamed Bouazizi, a street vendor, set himself on fire out of frustration over the way the oppressive government of President Zine El Abidine Ben Ali was treating him and his fellow citizens. Bouazizi was the catalyst for demonstrations that brought Ben Ali's twenty-three-year reign to an end in just under four weeks. No intelligence agency could have predicted this chain of events—although we did point out in the early days of the Tunisia crisis that the end of Ben Ali's reign was one possible outcome, and once Tunisia fell we did begin to warn about spillover to the rest of the region. One paper we produced at the time carried the title *Jasmine Revolution Resonating in Tunisia's Neighborhood*.

But there is no good explanation for our not being able to see the pressures growing to dangerous levels across the region. Why didn't we? It was not a resource issue—the Middle East and the Arab world always attracted substantial Agency resources. We failed because to a large extent we were relying on a handful of strong leaders in the countries of concern to help us understand what was going on in the Arab street. We were lax in creating our own windows into what was happening, and the leadership we were relying on was isolated and unaware of the tidal wave that was about to hit them.

Another problem at the time was that the intelligence community was not doing enough to mine the wealth of information available through social media. Not only was social media spreading ideas, it was becoming a means of organization for those opposed to the current regimes. The surprise of the Arab Spring in general and social media–inspired demonstrations in particular caused us to redouble our efforts to monitor the enormous amount of information available on social media platforms as indicators of political change and political movements. We had become too accustomed to stealing secrets and were not paying enough attention to important information that was streaming on Twitter for the world to see.

To be fair, it certainly was not—and is not—clear to me what difference our failure to "call" the Arab Spring had at the end of the day. I do not believe that the events would have turned out any differently if we had told policy-makers exactly what to expect.

But for all the analytic missteps we made during the run-up to what became known as the Arab Spring, the one that seems the most important to me—because it gave people false hope—and the one most important to this story was a misjudgment that was made after the street erupted. We thought and told policy-makers that this outburst of popular revolt would damage al Qa'ida by undermining the group's narrative. Our analysts figured that the protests would send a signal throughout the region that political change was possible without al Qa'ida's leading the way and without the violence that al Qa'ida said was necessary. Instead, with a few exceptions, the development of people's gaining the right of self-determination had the unforeseen effect of key countries suddenly losing the will or the capability to deal with al Qa'ida and other militant groups.

In short, the Arab Spring was a boon to Islamic extremists across both the Middle East and North Africa. Egypt and Libya illustrate this point well, and they just happened to be places where I again found myself at the center of things.

* * *

Inspired by the events in Tunisia, where President Ben Ali had just fallen, enormous public protests erupted in Egypt in January 2011. Tens of thousands of protesters hit the streets of Cairo and other major cities demanding an end to Hosni Mubarak's three decades of rule. Many of the protesters' grievances were legitimate, as conditions for the masses in Egypt were appallingly bad. The inequality was striking. While westerners were used to seeing pictures of stunning pyramids and beautiful Red Sea beach resorts, abject poverty affected millions of people. It was a difficult moment for US policy-makers because Mubarak had been a faithful ally of the United States. Egypt, a focal point of Arab culture, with the largest population in the Arab world, plays an enormously pivotal role in the region, and US officials could not ignore the fact that Egypt's peace agreement with our closest Middle East ally, Israel, rested on a narrow pedestal of just a few leaders—like Mubarak.

The demonstrations grew in size day after day, with periodic outbursts of violence, mostly on the part of the government, which was trying to put down the protests. The White House held daily Deputies Committee meetings to discuss what, if anything, the United States could do to ensure a peaceful resolution and a stable outcome. I was CIA's representative to those meetings. There was no clear answer. The participants agreed on a couple of things, however. First, you cannot throw yourself in front of the speeding freight train that is a people's revolution. It was clear that the outcome would be decided in Egypt, not in the United States. Second, as much as the United States appreciated Mubarak's support over the years on issues ranging from Middle East peace to counterterrorism, his domestic situation appeared too far gone to save. It seemed his days were numbered. Still, it was viewed as possible that he could play a role in a peaceful transition to a new type of government in Egypt. The representatives from the NSC and the State and Defense Departments agreed that there was no way the US government could directly support either Mubarak or those who sought to overthrow him. The best we could do was publicly say that the United States was for a peaceful resolution, and then work

diplomatically behind the scenes with Mubarak to engineer an outcome that would not include a bloodbath and that would ensure a
transition to a stable new government.

I was asked to get involved in making that happen. Going back
over a decade, I had had many experiences with Omar Suleiman, the
head of the Egyptian General Intelligence Service. A tall, reserved,
and well-spoken man, Suleiman was an army general who always
wore business suits. He was very wise about security issues in his
region and we would often seek out his views on complex matters.
You could ask Suleiman a single question about any regional issue
and then sit back for what might turn out to be a half-hour lecture
packed with insights. His remarks would be interrupted only by a
quirky habitual clearing of his throat every few minutes as he gathered his thoughts to further expand on the topic.

With the situation in Egypt rapidly spiraling out of control, the
United States kept pushing Mubarak to resolve the crisis through
compromise, but the Egyptian president was proving stubbornly
resistant. Four days after the demonstrations started, Mubarak surprised the world by naming Suleiman vice president, a position that
had been unfilled for almost thirty years. Outside of his immediate
family, Suleiman was Mubarak's closest advisor. This decision was
received poorly by the protesters—because they saw it as another
step by Mubarak to hold on to power by promoting his most powerful ally.

At the same time, I was approached by the intermediary for an
international businessman. (I cannot provide more information
about him or the intermediary.) This businessman was a friend of
Suleiman's and he wanted to relay messages from Suleiman to the
US government through me. The intermediary's credentials were
impeccable and several conversations with the businessman convinced me of two things—he was talking directly with Suleiman
and he had the best interests of Egypt and the United States in

mind. I sought and received the approval of Director Panetta and my fellow deputies to talk to Suleiman through the businessman. A number of conversations then occurred over a period of days. The main message Suleiman wanted to deliver to the White House was that he was deeply concerned about the stability of his country, he wanted to help resolve the crisis, and he was asking what the US government thought Cairo should do with that goal in mind.

Although this was never clearly stated, it was our assumption that Suleiman (who could have picked up the phone and contacted Director Panetta or me directly) was looking for some deniability. If seen talking with me, he would be viewed by the inner circle as working against Mubarak—which, in fact, was exactly what he was suggesting—and he was unwilling to openly go against his boss. Secrecy was required because even the head of the Egyptian spy service could expect to be spied upon. It was also clear that he was looking for a way to survive this ordeal—and perhaps even come out of it in a more senior position, possibly as the new leader of Egypt. I never lost sight of the fact that Suleiman was in this for Suleiman.

I took Suleiman's message to the deputies, and it was decided that I would send a message back to the Egyptian spy boss detailing exactly what the United States recommended he do. At the time Mubarak was preparing to deliver a major speech that was anticipated as a key moment in the crisis. I sat down with Denis McDonough, the deputy national security advisor, in his West Wing office—about the size of a walk-in closet but a few steps from the Oval Office—and we drafted a list of things the US government would like to hear Mubarak say. These things, we thought, might help defuse the crisis. McDonough typed faster than I could think and printed the talking points. The basic message was, *I have heard the views of the people and I am going to step down from the presidency immediately. I am turning power over to a transitional council with representation across Egyptian society, and this council will run the country and put into place the mechanisms for elections that will determine the leadership of Egypt going forward. And all this will occur in a way that is orderly and secure.* Denis and I returned to the deputies, who were still in the Situation Room, and he shared the points with everyone to make sure each was on board. When everyone signed off on the message, McDonough handed me the paper and said, "Go to it, brother."

I found a private room in the Situation Room and called my business contact. I told him that I had a message for Suleiman and that it came from the highest levels of the United States government. I went through the points carefully. It was clear my contact was writing them down word by word, as he asked me to slow down at a couple of points and to repeat a phrase or two. He said he would pass the message to Suleiman immediately. Later my contact phoned me back and told me that Suleiman had not only gotten the message but that he had convinced Mubarak to make those points in his remarks.

The next principals meeting on Egypt happened to coincide with Mubarak's big speech on February 1. We were all watching the multiple video screens in the Situation Room with great anticipation, but it quickly became clear that Mubarak was heading in a different direction from the Suleiman talking points. Mubarak talked about the peaceful protests of noble youth and about citizens being exploited by those bent on confrontation and violence. He made it clear that it was his sacred duty to protect the country and that he would continue to do so until the end of his term. The closest he would go in the direction of the protesters was to say that he would not run for the presidency again. The Egyptian street reacted quickly and violently. Mubarak's forces subsequently engaged in a brutal crackdown. (After leaving office Mubarak was tried on charges of murder for the deaths of some of the demonstrators.)

I felt horrible—mostly for Egypt but also because my personal diplomacy had failed so miserably. It was clear to me that Suleiman's influence was no match for that of Mubarak's wife and children, in particular his son Gamal, whom Mubarak had been grooming as his successor.

Mubarak's speech was a turning point for the US government. The president took a first step toward distancing himself from our long-term ally by saying publicly the next morning that the transition in Egypt "must be meaningful, it must be peaceful, and it must begin now."

As the violence grew, so did the debate at the White House. Giving up publicly on a longtime ally was difficult for many to accept, but others thought the time had come. A crystallizing moment came in an NSC meeting when UN ambassador Susan Rice asked President Obama how he wanted history to judge him— as on the side of Mubarak or as on the side of the Egyptian people. The president made his decision to take a significant step away from Mubarak. He put out a statement, saying, "The voices of the Egyptian people must be heard. The Egyptian people have made it clear that there is no going back to the way things were: Egypt has changed and its future is in the hands of the people." The president had sided fully with the protesters. He walked away from Mubarak, who resigned soon thereafter, and Suleiman announced that control of the government was being turned over to the Egyptian military.

There was joy in the streets of Cairo and great angst in the corridors of power elsewhere in the Middle East. The blowback was huge. I felt it myself on a trip to the region shortly thereafter, when I visited Egypt, Israel, Saudi Arabia, and the UAE. Our friends in the region asked how we could so quickly abandon a longtime ally like Mubarak. The unspoken but ever-present question was how quickly we would abandon them if similar circumstances arose. The truth is that we had no other options in the case of Egypt. There was no way we could have saved Mubarak—even if it had made the most sense for US policy, which it did not.

As interesting as the developments throughout the Middle East in early 2011 might be, I would not be including them in this book were it not for the unintended impact they had on the war against terrorism. As positive as the development of greater democratic rule might be over the long term, one of the biggest winners in the Arab Spring—at least in the short-to-medium term—was al Qa'ida.

In Egypt, Mubarak was replaced by Mohamed Morsi, a prominent member of the Muslim Brotherhood who quickly started granting himself extraordinary powers. Morsi turned out to be a horrible leader, making bad decisions on both political and economic matters. Whatever the benefits of having a popularly elected leader, they were more than offset by poor governance. This was all to the dismay of many—both inside Egypt and out—who had hoped he would lead efforts to reenergize the Egyptian economy and transition the country to democracy. One of the ways this poor governance played out was that, while the mechanisms for combating terrorism in Egypt remained largely intact, there was no political will to use them. The military, intelligence, and law enforcement communities in Egypt essentially stopped fighting al Qa'ida because they felt they had no political support to continue to do their job. In a remarkably short time, al Qa'ida, which had been defeated in Egypt for almost two decades, made a comeback, establishing new footholds in the Sinai and other parts of Egypt. From these locations al Qa'ida could now strike Israel, energy pipelines important to Israel and Jordan, and tourist sites popular with westerners within Egypt. The Sinai went from being a prime location for scuba divers and beach goers to a war zone.

Morsi's government was essentially doing nothing. Eventually the White House sent counterterrorism czar John Brennan to tell Morsi that al Qa'ida was on a rapid road to recovery in Egypt and that its overarching goal was to kill Morsi and overthrow his government. While Brennan got Morsi's attention—Egyptian CT operations against al Qa'ida partially resumed—the Egyptian military several months later decided that it had had enough and replaced Morsi after little more than a year in office.

But the damage had been done. Al Qa'ida had gained enormous ground in the largest and most important Arab country in the region. We are still paying for the Egyptians' lack of focus today, with al Qa'ida fully entrenched in the Sinai, where it regularly conducts attacks against Egyptian military and police units, and in Egypt's most important cities, where it still poses a threat. The Arab Spring, that flowering of self-determination and public expression, had turned into a catalyst for the worst kind of violence and oppression. From a counterterrorism perspective, the Arab Spring had turned to winter.

* * *

We experienced a different kind of setback in another major country in the region, Libya, where the problem was not a lack of willingness to deal with al Qa'ida but rather a lack of capability to do so.

On the surface Libya would not seem to be of much interest to the intelligence community. The country, while large in size, is primarily desert. In terms of population, Libya is not even in the top one hundred among the nations on the planet. But mere numbers can be deceiving. Throughout my thirty-three years at the Agency, Libya demanded a disproportionately large share of our attention. Most of that focus can be attributed to just one of the country's six million people: Muammar Qadhafi. Qadhafi made himself an international pariah with the course he chose for his nation—the pursuit of weapons of mass destruction, including nuclear weapons, and the practice of terrorism as a tool of statecraft, including the bombing of Pan Am 103 flying over Lockerbie, Scotland, in 1988, an act of terrorism that killed 259 people on board and eleven on the ground. Qadhafi was also behind the 1986 bombing of a Berlin discotheque frequented by US servicemen, which killed two.

Then, in early 2003, just as the United States and its allies were beginning the invasion of Iraq, representatives of the Libyan government reached out to our British counterparts suggesting that Qadhafi might be willing to discuss voluntarily ridding his country of its weapons of mass destruction. CIA and British intelligence officials met secretly with Qadhafi and his senior leadership, eventually brokering a deal designed to remove Libyan weapons of mass destruction without firing a shot.

Once that deal was negotiated, the United States and its allies engaged in an awkward resumption of relations with Libya—ties that had been strained since Qadhafi seized control of the country in 1969. By 2006 the United States had reestablished diplomatic relations and sent an ambassador to Tripoli for the first time in twenty-seven years.

While we had no illusions about the harsh, authoritarian nature of the regime led by the "Brother Leader," as Qadhafi liked to be called, in the aftermath of 9/11 we were more than prepared to work with his regime if it would help in our efforts to prevent attacks and defeat al Qaʻida and similar organizations. And help it did. For very different reasons, the most important being that al Qaʻida wanted to overthrow secular Arab regimes, Qadhafi hated and feared al Qaʻida as much as we did. Since a number of top leaders of Bin Ladin's organization were Libyans, his assistance proved quite useful.

The world of intelligence is packed with strange bedfellows—and few stranger than the Libyans. But due to this "the enemy of my enemy is my friend" mind-set, we found ourselves working with them. I made a trip to Libya in late 2010, just weeks before their revolution began. As deputy director of CIA, I was visiting to ensure that the Libyans continued to work with us against al Qaʻida.

My principal point of contact in Libya—and my host for the visit—was Abdullah Senussi, Qadhafi's domestic intelligence chief. Senussi was known for being ruthless. He had been implicated in bombing airplanes, massacring prisoners, and possibly trying to assassinate foreign leaders. I did not know what to expect when I walked into his office, but what I found was a strangely personable interlocutor.

While it was clear to me that Senussi was a tough guy (he was also Qadhafi's brother-in-law), I was able to see another side of him. I found Senussi to be smart, straightforward, and funny. We had an intense meeting in his office, where protocol—that is, his boss—demanded that he lecture me on his view that the United States was moving too slowly to restore full diplomatic relations with Libya. Once we got over that box-checking, we settled into a detailed discussion on al Qa'ida and what we could do together against the group. It was almost as if Senussi flipped a light switch to go from the first topic to the second.

Near the end of the meeting, we found common ground in talking about our families. We told each other about our children, and it was clear to me that the light of his life was his daughter, Anoud, who was in her late teens. He was enormously proud of her—and I could relate on a human level by telling him about my own kids, who were not far from her age. By the end of the meeting, I had to remind myself of the horrible deeds Senussi had undertaken for the sake of the "Leader."

My next stop was a three-hour lunch with the head of Libya's external spy agency, Abuzed Omar Dorda. Set next to a Roman ruin, the restaurant was one of Tripoli's finest. We had a large table in the middle of the restaurant, with Dorda sitting across from me. Security agents—mine and his—filled the tables around us. Dorda smoked nonstop before, during, and after lunch. It was like a scene from *The Sopranos*.

During the meal I learned that lecturing was part of the personality of senior Libyan officials. The intelligence chief used most of the lunch to tell me that everyone in the world was a Muslim but not everyone knew it yet. He said, "Michael, you are a Muslim. You have just not yet acceded to Allah's will." But he pleasantly suggested that I would someday. When I mentioned that this was not what I'd learned in eight years of Catholic school, he proceeded to tell me about the great significance of Jesus in Islam. To me his lecture was not just rhetoric. Dorda actually believed deeply what he was telling me, and I found his sincerity and his interest in my personal relationship with God endearing.

Intelligence cooperation between any two countries is based largely on personal relationships and trust. And from that perspective, my visit to Libya paid off. Within a day Senussi and I had developed a relationship. On a very basic level, there was trust established between us. I departed Libya with the relationship between our two services stronger and with the knowledge that I could at minimum pick up the phone and call him if I needed. This was important because Libya had a very effective intelligence service.

Very soon I had to do just that. Early in 2011, protests and clashes with security forces broke out across wide swaths of Libya. The bloodiest clashes occurred in the country's second-largest city, Benghazi. In late February a decision was made at the State Department that the US embassy in Tripoli should be temporarily closed and its employees—as well as any other American citizens who wanted out—evacuated. The only way to get all of them out quickly was to charter a ferry to Malta. The State Department set up the ferry—as well as a follow-on air flight to take out the last few Americans—but there was still concern about the safety of Americans as they moved from the embassy to the Port of Tripoli, where the ferry was docked.

White House officials, aware that I had established a relationship with Senussi, asked me to reach out to him and seek his assistance in ensuring that the State Department employees were allowed to safely withdraw. I called Senussi on February 24 and asked him to provide security for our diplomats as they moved to the dock. He promised me that he would ensure their safety, and he was as good as his word. Nearly two hundred Americans managed to depart without incident.

Whenever I talked to Senussi during this period he would go out of his way to try to convince me that the people rising up against Qadhafi were not freedom seekers but wholly owned agents of al Qa'ida. There was no doubt that mixed among the various rebel factions were some extremists loyal to Bin Ladin's ideology, but the vast majority had no agenda other than to rid their country of the oppression imposed over four decades by their "Brother Leader."

It was the policy of the US government at the time to be supportive of the goals of the rebels, and we gave them considerable assistance—short of lethal arms. Eventually military support was provided to the resistance through NATO and other allies.

A second opportunity to employ my back channel to Senussi came in March 2011 when four *New York Times* employees were captured by Qadhafi's forces outside the town of Ajdabiya. The group included a Pulitzer Prize–winning reporter, a videographer, and two still photographers (one of whom was a woman). We later learned that they had been badly beaten by their captors and were convinced they would likely not survive captivity.

As is often the case with media operating in a war zone, low-level soldiers holding the journalists thought they might be spies. Again the White House asked me to help, and I picked up the phone and called Senussi. After another lecture about how the rebels were really al Qa'ida operatives and how we should be working with the Libyan government against them, I was able to turn the conversation to the reporters. I told Senussi that the four were exactly what they said they were—reporters, not spies—and that they should be released. Two days after my call, they were let go. I am not sure that the leadership of the *Times* was ever told of the role CIA played in making the release possible.

Senussi's cooperation was not the result of our personal relationship. That got me in the door. No, the cooperation resulted from Senussi's belief that if he assisted me on these tactical matters, it would make it easier for him to convince me that Libya was indeed under assault from al Qa'ida and we would see the error in our ways. His was a strategic play.

My third encounter with Senussi was designed to be a wake-up call. It was May, and the NATO and Arab coalition had been active for a number of weeks under the banner of protecting the Libyan people from their own government. No senior official in Washington had yet publicly demanded Qadhafi's departure. The White House thought that needed to change and asked me to speak with Senussi again—this time to make it clear that there was only one solution to the ongoing violence: Qadhafi had to go. Once I passed on the message, Senussi said over and over again, "This is a very important message. This is a very big deal."

My final encounter with Senussi was the most dramatic. The conflict had been dragging on for months and there had been considerable bloodshed on both sides. It was apparent that the Qadhafi regime's days were numbered and that its end would be violent and perhaps protracted. In an effort to speed up the inevitable collapse of the dictator's rule, my fellow participants in the Deputies Committee asked me if I could convince Senussi to do the right thing, to join the future of Libya, not remain in its past. The thinking was that if someone of Senussi's stature in the regime changed sides it could lead others to do the same, perhaps resulting in a rapid collapse of the regime and the saving of thousands of Libyan lives.

The last thing I wanted to do was discuss this with him over the phone, however. There was a high probability that a call such as mine would be intercepted and my suggestion alone might be sufficient to get Senussi killed. So I reached out to him and offered a personal meeting in either Egypt or Tunisia. He agreed, and we set the Tunisian island of Jerba as the meeting place. But just two days later, he sent word that the meeting had to take place at a border crossing on the Libyan-Tunisian border. I thought perhaps the Leader did not want Senussi venturing too far from home. So I said OK and dispatched a security team to Tunisia to quietly assess the proposed meeting location. The team reported back that in order to reach the proposed meeting site it had had to pass through more than a hundred thousand Libyan refugees who had swarmed across the border to avoid the fighting. Still I insisted that the planning for the trip continue.

But a week before the proposed meeting I received word that Senussi would not attend. I later learned that Qadhafi had refused to let him travel to the border—perhaps correctly guessing my intent, fearing that his intelligence chief was looking for a way out of the crisis.

Of course, I never lost sight of the fact that Senussi was far from a good guy. That's not a surprise when you're dealing with the intelligence chief of a totalitarian dictatorship. My interest in talking with him at this point was to speed the demise of a brutal regime and minimize the loss of life in the process.

Since I'd failed to lure him to a face-to-face meeting, my next-best option was to have my discussion with him over an open phone line and hope for the best. "Abdullah," I said, "you must know that the Leader's days are numbered. You must know that it is just a matter of time now. The most important thing now is to think about your country and what will be best for you and your family." He knew exactly what I was saying, and he said, "No, Michael, I could never leave the Leader's side in difficult times like these." He was holding firm, so I played my trump card.

"Abdullah, my friend," I said, "think about your daughter. Think about her future. By choosing the right side, you can save her, she can have a future in Libya." What he said next sent chills down my spine. "Michael," he said, "the Leader is more important to me than my family." From the tone of his voice I could tell that this was not something meant for anyone listening in—he was deadly serious. The discussion was over. Senussi wasn't going to change. It was the last time I ever spoke with him.

Qadhafi's regime collapsed in August 2011, and Senussi went on the run. He was arrested in Mauritania in March 2012. The International Criminal Court in The Hague sought custody so that he could be tried for crimes against humanity. But on September 5, 2012, he was returned to Libya instead. Subsequently his daughter Anoud was also arrested—later released, and then kidnapped by gunmen just as she stepped outside of the prison gates after a visit to see her father. She was eventually freed by her captors. In December 2013 she publicly called for her father to be tried by the ICC in The Hague—not because she knew him to be guilty, she said, but because he faced a show trial and almost certain death if he was tried in Libya. Nonetheless, Senussi and thirty-six other former Libyan officials were placed on trial in Tripoli in the spring of 2014. (As of this writing there has been no verdict.)

* * *

The aftermath of the fall of Qadhafi was chaotic. The institutions of the state withered away—most important, the security services responsible for dealing with terrorists. A power vacuum swept the country, and it was filled by militias that could not agree on anything beyond getting rid of Qadhafi. Some of those militias had extremist views of the world—giving al Qaʻida an opportunity. The defeat of the Libyan military also resulted in the spread of a huge number of conventional weapons not only in Libya but also around the region, strengthening al Qaʻida affiliates from Mali to Egypt.

With our concerns about al Qaʻida growing, the White House sent me to Libya in January 2012 (I took with me Mike Vickers, the under secretary of defense for intelligence; Vickers was a frequent traveling companion of mine due to the critically important collaboration between CIA and DOD). My objective was to convince the new Libyan prime minister of the urgent need for him to build an intelligence service capable of dealing with the al Qaʻida problem (the previous Qadhafi-era service had collapsed and no longer existed). I was only in the country from nine a.m. to five p.m. For safety reasons my security detail would not allow me to spend the night.

With the ambassador and Vickers at my side, I made my argument, pointing out that al Qaʻida had its sights set on Libya and that an intelligence service was an absolute must for dealing with it. I explained to the prime minister that a leader of al Qaʻida in the Islamic Maghreb (AQIM) was at that very moment in Tripoli purchasing as many weapons as he could get his hands on. The prime minister pushed back—saying that he was only leading an interim government, that he had a lot to do, and that it would take time to figure out how to build a service the "right way." I told him that if he was referring to the excesses of Qadhafi's former service, he needed to know that there were many democracies in the world with intelligence services that operated within the law and upheld human rights and that this could certainly be the case in Libya.

Still nothing. In frustration I emphasized to the prime minister that I was certain al Qaʻida's growing strength in Libya would result in attacks against Libyan interests, European interests, and American interests. The meeting ended—with only the vaguest of commitments to building a service. I knew it was not going to happen.

My warning would become a tragic reality in less than a year.

* * *

In both Libya and Egypt there were important lessons to be learned.

The day that the Egyptian military moved against President Morsi, I received a call from a senior Arab ambassador to the United States. He simply said, "Michael, what do you think about Egypt?" I said, "This is a good thing. Morsi was leading the country to ruin, to instability, and to extremism. Now Egypt has a chance again." I knew that I was being inconsistent with US policy, but I had been trained all my life to speak the truth as I saw it. The ambassador said to me, "I have made similar phone calls all morning. You are the first to say that this is a good thing. You are right."

Not every country is ready for democracy, and democracy—to work effectively—is much more than free and fair elections. It certainly includes those—along with the freedom to form political parties, compete for political support, and vote—but it also includes freedom of expression, the availability of multiple sources of information, and institutions that make and carry out the preferences of the electorate as expressed in elections. And to force democracy on countries that do not have these characteristics, and cannot develop them quickly, is almost always a recipe for instability and a set of outcomes that are inimical to US national security interests. The poster child is Gaza, where, in 2006, voters elected a terrorist group to lead them. And Hamas has led its fellow Gazans exactly where you would think a terrorist group would—to ruin.

9/11/2012

Eight months after my hurried visit to Tripoli to warn the Libyan government about the dangers within its borders, tragedy struck in the country's second-largest city. I want to stress that much of what transpired in Benghazi became fully known to us only some time later—with some things still not known with certainty. As is so often the case in crisis situations, it was only after the smoke cleared—literally, in this case—that one could understand what had happened. And while Benghazi would ultimately unleash a political firestorm, the most important context for understanding the incident has largely been missed—it was the first manifestation of the Arab Spring–induced spread of al Qa'ida's ideology and franchise.

* * *

Muammar Qadhafi's departure from the scene in Libya in 2011 was a good thing in that it prevented the slaughter of thousands of his own citizens. But what followed was a failed state that provided room for extremist groups to flourish. At the end of the day, are the Libyan people better off after their revolution than before? I'm not so sure. Certainly what occurred in Libya was a boon to al Qa'ida all across North Africa and deep in the Sahel, which includes parts of Mauritania, Mali, and Niger. The fledgling government that replaced Qadhafi's lacked even a rudimentary ability to govern, militias with various ideologies reigned in large parts of the country, and much of Qadhafi's stockpiles of conventional weapons were openly available throughout the country and, because of poor or nonexistent border security, the region.

Because of this lack of governance, during the spring and summer of 2012, the security situation across Libya, particularly in the eastern part of the country, was deteriorating and extremism was on the rise. CIA analysts accurately captured this situation, writing scores of intelligence pieces describing in detail how the situation in Libya was becoming more and more dangerous. One of them from July was titled *Libya: Al Qa'ida Establishing Sanctuary*. These pieces were shared broadly across the executive branch and with the members and staff of the intelligence committees in Congress. This was not welcome news to some of those senators who had supported the overthrow of Qadhafi. A senior DOD official told me that at one closed-door hearing of the Senate Armed Services Committee, he was taken to task for being too pessimistic about developments in eastern Libya.

Normally I would not be able to confirm the existence of a CIA base overseas, let alone describe its mission. But because of the tragic events in Benghazi on September 11, 2012—and the controversial aftermath—the Agency's role there has since become declassified, which allows me to discuss it here.

The city of Benghazi was vitally important in Libya. It had been the center of much of the opposition to Qadhafi for years, and it remained a key outpost used by the United States to understand developments during the revolution and to influence key players in eastern Libya after Qadhafi. CIA had established a presence there with the mission of collecting intelligence in eastern Libya, to include on terrorists there, which had long been a hotbed of extremism as well as the birthplace of many key Libyans in the leadership of al Qa'ida. The CIA base in Benghazi performed this mission well. Contrary to some press reporting, the CIA base in Benghazi did not play any role in moving weapons from Libya to the opposition in Syria—and neither did any other CIA officer or facility in Libya.

The State Department facility in Benghazi has been widely mis-characterized as a US consulate. In fact it was a Temporary Mission Facility (TMF)—a presence that was not continuously staffed by senior personnel and that was never given formal diplomatic status by the Libyan government. The TMF included a large plot of land that housed numerous buildings. The CIA base—because it was physically separate from the TMF—was simply called "the Annex."

In the months leading up to the September 11 attacks, many assaults and incidents directed at US and other allied facilities occurred in Benghazi—roughly twenty at the TMF alone—and CIA analysts reported on every significant one, including an impro-vised explosive device (IED) that was thrown over the wall of the TMF, an attack on the convoy of the UN special envoy to Libya, and an assassination attempt against the British ambassador to Libya.

As a result of the deterioration in security, we at CIA at least two times reevaluated our security posture in Benghazi and made a num-ber of significant enhancements. It was only later—after the tragedy of 9/11/12—that we learned that only a few security enhancements had been made at the TMF. CIA does not provide physical secu-rity for State Department operations. Why so few improvements were made at the TMF, why so few State Department security offi-cers were protecting the US ambassador, Chris Stevens, why they allowed him to travel there on the anniversary of 9/11, and why they allowed him to spend the night in Benghazi are unclear (I would like to know the conversations that took place between Stevens and his security team when the ambassador decided to go visit Benghazi on 9/11/12). These were all critical errors. The reader will remember from the previous chapter that my security detail would not even allow me to spend the night in Tripoli, and the leader of my security team brought what seemed to me like a small army to Libya to protect me.

With the anniversary of 9/11 on the horizon and the security situation throughout much of the Arab world in flux, in early September CIA sent out to all its stations and bases worldwide a cable warning about possible attacks. I don't want to imply that there was any particular intelligence regarding planned attacks. There was not. We routinely sent such cables each year on the anniversary of 9/11—but we did want our people and their US government colleagues to be extra vigilant.

We also sent an additional cable to Cairo because we had picked up specific intelligence from social media that there might be a violent demonstration there in reaction to an obscure film made in the United States that many Muslims believed insulted the Prophet Muhammad. The social media posting encouraged demonstrators to storm our embassy and kill Americans. It turned out that our embassy in Cairo had independently picked up the same social media report and had already taken precautions. The ambassador and most of her staff were not at the Cairo embassy on 9/11/12 when a mob breached the walls of the compound, setting fires, taking down American flags, and hoisting black Islamic banners. Eventually Egyptian security forces restored order, although the news of what the protesters had accomplished in Cairo spread quickly through Arab media, including to Benghazi.

On September 11, 2012, I was in Amman, Jordan, in the middle of meetings with intelligence counterparts in the region. I had already been to Israel and was due the next day to depart for Saudi Arabia. Earlier in the day I had seen reports about the incident in

Cairo that, although troubling, seemed to have ended without too much damage and with no injuries. I had dinner with the head of the Jordanian military and the head of Jordanian intelligence, and upon returning to the hotel I checked in with Washington and caught up on e-mail before going to bed. I was woken from a sound sleep by a knock on the door from one of my assistants, who told me that another incident had taken place, this one at the State Department facility in Benghazi, and that CIA security officers had responded in order to assist. My assistant told me that one State Department officer had been killed and the ambassador's whereabouts were unknown. She said that everyone else had relocated to the CIA base in Benghazi and was believed safe, adding that our chief of station (COS) in Tripoli was sending security officers as reinforcements from Tripoli to Benghazi.

Early the next morning, my assistant banged on my door again to tell me that the CIA base was now under heavy attack. I threw on some sweats and made my way to my command post, just down the hall from my room. In the command post was a security tent that covered two tables holding secure phone lines and computers capable of accessing CIA's top secret network.

At CIA we make use of an instant messaging program called Sametime for informal quick communications among our personnel worldwide. I "sametimed" the Agency's chief of station in Tripoli to ask him for an update and to see if I could help him in any way. But I did not want to be a pest. On my mind was the thought that the last thing our senior officer in country needed was to be micromanaged by the Agency's deputy director.

During our back-and-forth messaging over Sametime, the chief recounted what he knew about the attack on the Annex, which had by that time just concluded. He told me two officers had been killed in a mortar attack on the Annex—I simply typed, "I am sorry"— bringing the total number of Americans killed to four, including

Ambassador Stevens, who had been reported dead at a Benghazi hospital. Stevens was a legend in the diplomatic corps for his understanding of Arab culture and for his ability to work effectively in it. The others were Sean Smith, a State Department communications officer, killed at the TMF, and Glen Doherty and Tyrone Woods, two security officers, both killed at the Annex.

Over our nearly two-hour on-again, off-again instant messaging conversation, the COS said that he had decided to pull his people out of Benghazi and was working on getting transportation for them and the State Department personnel back to Tripoli. I asked him several times if he needed anything, if I could help in any way. He said he thought he had everything he needed at the moment. I told him that I wanted "to know when everyone is safe," adding that I was heading to the embassy in Amman and that he could reach me there. I signed off by typing, "Hang in there. I am praying for you." When I stepped away from the computer, I told my staff that I was very impressed with how the COS was handling a very difficult situation and that I was proud of him. He was calm and determined—and was making all the right decisions.

From the embassy in Jordan, I called Director Petraeus and told him that I thought I should cut my trip short. He agreed. I hung up the phone and told my staff, "We are going home."

* * *

Dave Petraeus is one of those larger-than-life figures, with a reputation borne of real and significant success on the battlefield as well as a multitude of media stories about him. But to know him—to be his deputy—was a real lesson in leadership. He taught me a great deal. He was effective at driving an organization in the direction he wanted it to go—concerning himself with everything from a large strategic initiative like leadership training to a specific type of weapon he wanted to provide our allies overseas. He accomplished this through sheer force of personality—he would not stop pressing, he would not stop asking about the follow-through on a directive until it was done.

Like almost all directors, Petraeus came to love CIA. He walked into my office on a Friday afternoon in the fall of 2011, just two or three months after arriving. He shut the door and sat down. He said, "Michael, I've been the commander of CENTCOM and the commander of coalition forces in Iraq and Afghanistan, and I can tell you that this is the best job that I've ever had. Bar none. The mission here is critically important, and the capabilities of this place are unique. And the people here are the best I have I worked with anywhere. I am very lucky." I know he meant every word.

Unfortunately, the organization did not feel the same way about him. He did not connect with most of the people of the organization the way Panetta did. Part of it was that he created the impression through the tone of his voice and his body language that he did not want people to disagree with him (which was not true in my own interactions with him). And part of it was that his expectations of what a staff would do for him—borne of being a four-star general—were inconsistent with the Agency culture. This all improved over time, and he was missed after he departed.

Petraeus was very good to me. He allowed me to manage the Deputies Committee process and the day-to-day operations of the Agency—keeping him fully informed along the way. He also consciously made an effort to mentor me, to make me a better officer. I was sorry that circumstances required his early departure from the Agency, and I know that no one feels more than he does that he let the organization down.

I first learned about his extramarital affair on November 8, 2012, the night before he resigned, just two days after the 2012 presidential election. He had not come to work during the day or communicated with me—despite visiting with the president in the afternoon and asking, through staff, that I attend an NSC meeting on his behalf. At about nine p.m., he finally called. His tone was decisive, as always. He walked me through the entire story of the affair. He told me, "Michael, I am going to resign," saying that he had made a terrible mistake and his resignation was a first step toward redemption. He added that his focus now was to save his marriage and his family and that "I cannot accomplish that and run the Agency at the same time." He read me the note to the workforce that he had drafted. I did not know how to respond, so I kept repeating the phrase "I understand."

The next afternoon I took a phone call from the president of the United States. He shared with me that Petraeus's resignation was unfortunate but understandable and he asked me if I would again serve as his acting director of the Central Intelligence Agency, saying, "We need now, more than ever, stability at the top." I of course said yes immediately. I owed it to both the Agency and to General Petraeus.

* * *

My return to Washington on the morning of September 13 coincided with the beginning of a long process of piecing together what had happened in Benghazi. It took weeks before most of the details were known. My understanding of what happened was shaped in large part by an intelligence community analysis—led by the National Counterterrorism Center and coordinated fully with CIA analysts. This was the best information available to us at the time and was completed a number of weeks after the attacks and shared with the two congressional intelligence committees. This analysis was based on all available sources, most important the video feeds from both the TMF and the Annex.

* * *

There are a number of myths about what happened during the night-time and early-morning hours of the Benghazi attacks. One mis-conception is that there was a single four-hour-long battle. Another myth is that the attacks were well organized, planned weeks or even months in advance. In fact, there were three separate attacks that night, none of them showing evidence of significant planning, but each of them carried out by Islamic extremists, some with connec-tions to al Qa'ida, and each attack more potent than the one before. Since the definition of terrorism is violence perpetrated against persons or property for political purposes, each attack in Benghazi was most definitely an act of terrorism—no matter the affiliation of the perpetrators, no matter the degree of planning, and no matter whether the attack on the TMF was preceded by a protest or not (an issue that would take on enormous political importance in the weeks and months ahead).

The first attack was on the State Department's Temporary Mis-sion Facility. We know from having monitored social media and other communications in advance that the demonstration and vio-lence in Cairo were sparked by people upset over a YouTube video that portrayed the Prophet Muhammad negatively. We believe that in Benghazi—over six hundred miles away—extremists heard about the successful assault on our embassy in Egypt and decided to make some trouble of their own, although we still do not know their motivations with certainty. Most likely they were inspired by the prospect of doing in Benghazi what their "brothers" had done in Cairo. Some may have been inspired by a call Ayman al-Zawahiri—the leader of al Qa'ida in Pakistan—had made just the day before for Libyans to take revenge for the death of a senior al Qa'ida leader of Libyan origin in Pakistan. Still others might have been motivated by the video—although I should note that our analysts never said the video was a factor in the Benghazi attacks. Abu Khattala, a terrorist leader and possibly one of the ring leaders of the attacks, said that he was in fact motivated by the video. Khattala is now in US custody and under indictment for the role he played in the assault.

I believe that, with little or no advance planning, extremists in Benghazi made some phone calls, gathering a group of like-minded individuals to go to the TMF. When they attacked, at about 9:40 p.m. local time, the assault was not well organized—they seemed to be more of a mob that had come to the TMF with the intent of breaching the compound and seeing what damage they could do. This was my interpretation of what I saw on the video feed from the cameras at the TMF and the Annex. And it was also the interpretation of the intelligence community analysts who watched the video.

When you assess the information from the video, there are few signs of a well-thought-out plan, few signs of command and control, few signs of organization, few signs of coordination, few signs of even the most basic military tactics in the attack on the TMF. Some of the attackers were armed with small arms; many were not armed at all. No heavy weapons were seen on the videotape. Many of the attackers, after entering through the front gate, ran past buildings to the other end of the compound, behaving as if they were thrilled just to have overrun the compound. They did not appear to be looking for Americans to harm. They appeared intent on looting and conducting vandalism. They successfully broke down some doors but failed to do so with others, often in what would appear to be a farcical fashion, if you did not know that tragedy was about to take place. When they did enter buildings, they quickly exited with stolen items. One young man carried an Xbox, another had a suit bag stolen from an American's quarters. The rioters started to set fires, but there was no indication that they were targeting anyone. They entered one building with Americans hiding inside, did not find them, and quickly departed. Through it all, none of the Department of State security officers at the TMF fired a weapon.

Clearly, this was a mob looting and vandalizing the place—with tragic results. It was a mob, however, made up of a range of individuals, some of whom were hardened Islamic extremists. And it was a mob that killed two Americans by setting fires to several buildings. After reviewing the information in the video, I was in favor of releasing it publicly. Doing so would have helped Americans better understand the nature of the attack. I do not know why the White House did not release the information—this despite urgings to do so from Jim Clapper, the director of national intelligence, and from other senior intelligence officials, including me. The videos, at this writing, still have not been declassified.

The ambassador and Sean Smith were in the main building when a fire was set there, and the thick black smoke that quickly enveloped the building suffocated them. There is no evidence that the attackers were targeting the ambassador specifically or US officials generally when they set that fire or any of the other fires that night.

About an hour after the mob stormed the compound, officers from the CIA base came to the aid of their State Department colleagues. The Agency security team fired the first American shots of the night, exchanging gunfire with the attackers, pushing them back, and then helping the State Department security officers search (unsuccessfully) for the ambassador. They recovered the body of Sean Smith, and unable to find the ambassador, organized a retreat to the Annex. The State Department officers had to fight their way to the CIA base, speeding past a roadblock just down the street from the TMF. Our officers took a different route and returned to the CIA base without incident.

The second attack of the evening was on the CIA base. This

attack occurred just after midnight and within minutes of the CIA team's arrival back from the TMF. My assessment is that some of those who had conducted the assault on the TMF—the best-armed and most highly motivated of the group—followed the State Department officers back to the Annex after they ran the roadblock. The attackers on the Annex were armed with light weapons and rocket-propelled grenades and CIA and State Department security officers drove them off in what was a short firefight. But, unlike at the TMF, this was a more organized attack with the clear goal of killing Americans.

Three and a half hours after the start of the assault on the TMF, reinforcements arrived in Benghazi in the form of CIA and military personnel who had managed to charter an aircraft from Tripoli and fly to Benghazi to assist their colleagues. After being delayed at the airport in Benghazi for some time, they arrived at the Annex at five a.m. Some of them took up fighting positions on the roof of the main building on the Agency base. They arrived with virtually no time to spare, as the third attack of the night was about to begin. There is no evidence that the final group of attackers followed our officers from the airport to the Annex, as has been alleged in the press.

It was at approximately five fifteen a.m. that the third, final, and most sophisticated attack of the night occurred. My subsequent analysis is that after the extremists were driven from the CIA Annex the first time, they regrouped, acquiring even heavier weapons and most likely additional fighters. Most important, they returned with mortars. Five mortar rounds were fired and three made direct hits on the roof of the main building, killing Glen Doherty and Tyrone Woods and seriously injuring others.

Long after the attack, I asked myself, "Why did the attackers use only five mortar rounds?" They had time and space to fire additional rounds as they had driven our security officers from their positions.

The logical answer to me is clear—they had only five mortars. If this had been an assault with days, weeks, or months of planning, the terrorists would have been much better armed and they would have brought those weapons to the first assault at the TMF as well as the first assault on the CIA base. And they would have had more than just five mortar rounds for the second assault on the Annex. Libya, after all, is a country awash in weapons, including mortars. Instead all three were opportunistic attacks that escalated in sophistication during the night as the extremists had more time to organize.

As awful as it was, the events of the evening could have been much worse without the incredible heroism of a handful of CIA officers and military personnel. Had CIA officers not responded to the TMF, there undoubtedly would have been more fatalities there. During the fight at the CIA base, the actions of two Special Forces officers stood out. In Tripoli, when the first attacks began, they responded as you would expect our country's most elite soldiers to respond. They volunteered to go to Benghazi and stand shoulder to shoulder with our officers in a firefight with terrorists. While they were not technically in the chain of command, their training and experience, their excellent judgment, and their calm demeanor under fire effectively resulted in their taking charge at the Annex. Everyone looked to them for leadership, and they provided it. And they were the ones who recovered the dead and wounded officers from the rooftop immediately after the mortar attack.

One of our injured officers on the roof where Glen Doherty and Tyrone Woods were killed was nearly unconscious and unable to move. Fearing that the mortar fire could resume at any moment, the two Special Forces operatives improvised a maneuver in which one of them strapped the six-foot-three, 240-pound man to the other's back. In a supreme test of strength, focus, and determination, the soldier bearing our wounded officer scaled a wall at the edge of the roof and then worked his way down a rickety ladder—all under the constant threat of enemy fire. Both Special Forces officers received awards for their bravery and heroic actions in response to the tragedy in Benghazi.

CHAPTER 10

Stalking Points

April 2, 2014, House Permanent Select Committee on Intelligence, US Congress. Open hearing on "The Benghazi Talking Points and Michael J. Morell's Role in Shaping the Administration's Narrative." Selected quotes:

MR. DEVIN NUNES, CONGRESSMAN FROM CALIFORNIA'S TWENTY-SECOND CONGRESSIONAL DISTRICT: Mr. Morell...I read your testimony and you have an excuse for everything, right? For everything.

MS. MICHELE BACHMANN, CONGRESSWOMAN FROM MINNESOTA'S SIXTH CONGRESSIONAL DISTRICT: Mr. Morell, they [the White House] didn't have to change, because you made the changes for them. That is the point. That is why you are in front of this committee today. You made significant substantive changes for the White House.

MR. LYNN WESTMORELAND, CONGRESSMAN FROM GEORGIA'S THIRD CONGRESSIONAL DISTRICT: You know, it just seems—I mean if you look at the whole picture that I think the majority of people look at, when those talking points were edited, they were edited in favor of the administration's philosophy of how they wanted to be portrayed in Libya, you know.

Mr. Peter King, congressman from New York's Second Congressional District: Mr. Morell, there are so many questions from beginning to end on this whole issue of the talking points. And to believe your version would require almost absolute faith in your word.

* * *

I had many unforgettable experiences as a result of my time at CIA, and it's odd that one of them came months after I left the organization. It was April 2014 and I was called to appear in open session before the House Permanent Select Committee on Intelligence and testify about Benghazi.

Appearing before Congress was not a new experience for me. I had done so hundreds of times before—but doing so in public, and on live TV, was new (all but one of my past sessions with Congress had been behind closed doors). But this did not faze me. What did shock me, after standing and swearing an oath to tell the truth, was to hear at that session a handful of members of Congress essentially accuse me of lying. As someone who had always thought of himself as honest to a fault, I was stunned to hear respected political leaders question my integrity. Here is how that came about.

* * *

Politics in America should end at the nation's shores—that is, national security policy should be off-limits for playing politics. Both parties should respect this, as statesmen in both know that making national security policy is difficult enough and should not be made more so by the bare-knuckle brawls of politics and as both know that to be strong in the world the country needs to be united at home—in principle, purpose, and practice. Unfortunately, as our political system has evolved to become more partisan and as almost every issue has become politicized, so has national security and so has the most important issue within that arena—terrorism and our nation's response to it. Both parties are to blame.

Benghazi is a poster child for this new dynamic. It is the poster child of the intrusion of politics into national security. It was not the first time, but it was the most significant time that I can remember. This chapter is a detailed look at the politics of the Benghazi issue—from the point of view of someone who found himself in the gunsights of one of the two sides in the debate. I believe Benghazi is an example of what is wrong with American politics—politicians focused on scoring political points rather than working together to advance the interests of our country. I took the time in this book to go through this event largely because I hope it becomes a shining example of how not to respond to a national security crisis.

I should mention to readers that most of the rest of this chapter is detailed—in fact, very detailed. If you are an "inside the Beltway" kind of person and want to know all the facts, read on. Otherwise, jump to the end of this chapter, where I draw some broader lessons that I believe our nation should learn from the Benghazi tragedy.

* * *

While those on the ground in Benghazi during that fateful night did what they do so well—carrying out their mission, protecting each other, watching each other's backs—the political wheels in Washington started to turn. Benghazi emerged as a major issue in the 2012 presidential campaign, and will probably remain an issue until the 2016 presidential campaign is completed. The essential question in the 2012 debate was whether the Obama administration had deliberately downplayed the terrorism aspect of the attack to keep intact its campaign claim that Obama had made great progress in the war against al Qa'ida. And an essential question in the 2016 debate will undoubtedly be what responsibility Secretary Clinton should shoulder for what happened that night in Benghazi.

In pursuing the first question, a few in the media and a small group of politicians have mounted an assault on me personally. Their narrative is that I "cooked the books" regarding how CIA thought and wrote about the tragedy in Benghazi—particularly with reference to the now-famous talking points that CIA produced at the request of the House Intelligence Committee—and that I did so in conspiracy with senior White House and State Department officials or that I did so on my own with politics in mind. It has been alleged that I did all this with the intent of assisting in President Obama's reelection in 2012 and protecting Secretary Clinton. It has also been alleged that I lied about all of this to Congress in order to cover up what I had done.

I thought I had put this narrative to bed before I left government. I testified before Congress three times in closed session—twice before the House Intelligence Committee and once before the Senate Intelligence Committee—and, at the request of the White House, I briefed the media in detail on the unclassified talking points after the White House decided to publicly release internal government e-mails related to the talking points in the spring of 2014.

The issue reemerged in early 2014 after the Senate Intelligence Committee publicly released a report on Benghazi. One media outlet used one reference in the bipartisan portion of the report to argue that I'd known the talking points were wrong when I edited them (the bipartisan Senate report did not say this) and a second reference in the Republicans' "Additional Views" section of the report to argue that I'd lied to the committee when I answered a specific question about the talking points (the Senate report did not say this). Interestingly, very few news outlets picked up on the story. In fact, beyond the lead reporter working on the story, no other reporter even called me to ask about the allegations.

But then a handful of senators joined the scrum, with Senator Lindsey Graham of South Carolina calling me a liar and Senator John McCain of Arizona questioning why I would violate my oath of office. These public comments got my attention, as I have always respected both senators' care for and attention to the national security of the United States—and as there was not a single shred of evidence for the allegations being made against me.

And then the big blow. Two of the senators whom I respected the most spoke out against me. Both Senator Saxby Chambliss of Georgia, vice chairman of the Senate Intelligence Committee, and Senator Richard Burr of North Carolina, a leading member of the committee, publicly questioned my integrity. Senator Chambliss said, "It is really strange. I always thought Mike was a straight up guy."

The allegations made by all of these senators were serious ones. The fundamental tenet of an intelligence officer is to call it like you see it—no matter what your audience wants to hear, no matter the implications for policy, no matter the impact on politics, and no matter what the implications for yourself. Intelligence officers must be totally nonpartisan and objective. I was being accused of violating that fundamental tenet. I was also being accused of lying to Congress—a serious accusation against anyone in the executive branch, because misleading Congress undermines the central pillar of our constitutional democracy—Congress's role in overseeing executive branch activities.

In response to these allegations, I sat down to write my side of the story. I wrote it as a letter to my children—to explain why what they were hearing in the media and from a handful of senators about me was not true. I wanted them to know the truth. And that is what I am going to do in this chapter. In fact, this chapter began as that letter to my children. Some will not like what they read here, but I am only doing what I was trained to do—put the facts and analysis on the table and let the chips fall where they may.

As I was finishing the letter to my children in late February, I met with Representative Mike Rogers of Michigan, the chairman of the House Intelligence Committee. Rogers and I had seen each other one recent Sunday on the set of CBS's *Face the Nation* and decided to get together and catch up.

Rogers is smart, tough, and interested in doing what is right for national security—an interest that was drilled into him when he served our country in a different way, as an FBI agent. His retirement from Congress was a loss for the country, and it speaks volumes about the dysfunction on Capitol Hill when Congress loses it best people.

I asked Chairman Rogers what he thought I should do about the small but vocal chorus about Benghazi and me. "What would you do if I asked you to testify again?" he asked. I responded immediately, "If you want me to testify in the open, before the American public, I would jump at the opportunity." He said, "I will get back to you," and two days later we agreed that I would testify on April 2, 2014.

It was not lost on me that I was doing the chairman a favor by testifying (even though he never asked me for the favor). I knew from friends on the Hill that Rogers had been under pressure for months from his leadership to be "tougher on Benghazi." But Rogers was trying to stick to the facts. He even told me, "Michael, I have looked at Benghazi from every possible angle, looking for something, anything that would demonstrate political influence on the intelligence process, but it's just not there." Still, bringing me before his committee to testify in open session would certainly help the chairman with certain members of his caucus.

During my testimony I explained in detail the views of CIA's analysts about what had happened in Benghazi and how those views had evolved, I explained in detail the process by which the talking points had been produced, including my own role, and I took on directly the allegations that had been made against me. The session lasted for three and a half hours, with many questions being asked, some multiple times. The hearing got testy at times—perhaps in part because Speaker of the House John Boehner before the hearing had told one of the members of the committee to, in short, "Go after Morell"—but when the dust settled there was not a shred of evidence that politics, in any way, had influenced the production of CIA's classified analysis or the unclassified talking points. Not a shred. No such evidence exists because it simply never happened.

* * *

Those arguing against me believed that by saying there had been a protest, CIA and I—in conspiracy with the White House—were trying to hide the hand of al Qaʻida in the attack and thereby protect President Obama's campaign theme that he was tough on terrorism. Here is what actually happened.

The initial intelligence reporting on what had transpired in Benghazi was understandably limited. The analysts' job was to tell the president and his national security team what they thought based on the information they had at that moment. Intelligence analysts do not have the luxury of waiting for all-knowing clarity. That is just not how the process works.

While I was flying home from Amman (I was on a trip to see our partners in the Middle East and not involved in any way with the initial production of the Benghazi analysis), the analysts were completing their first full report on what had happened, a piece that would be published and shown to senior policy-makers and to Congress on the morning of September 13.

A short item was published in the early-morning hours of September 12, but it was largely a summary of the few facts we had in the immediate aftermath of the attacks. That update contained a crucial error that would come back to haunt us. In a single sentence, the September 12 item characterized the attack as an organized military assault. When this characterization was not included in the piece the next day (the thirteenth), many critics saw the change as evidence that the intelligence community was politicizing the analysis. Nothing could be further from the truth.

The real story behind the September 12 report involves nothing nearly as nefarious as changing analysis for political purposes. What really happened is that the critical sentence was not written by the analysts. It was added after the analysts had finished their work and gone home for the night. It was written by a senior CIA editor with expertise in military matters but no expertise in Libya or what had just happened in Benghazi. This editor added the sentence because she thought the early-morning update on the twelfth needed a bottom line. She never showed the sentence to the analysts; had she done so, they would have removed it. When the analysts came in the next morning, they complained vehemently about the edit. This is how a simple bureaucratic screw-up became fodder for allegations of a political cover-up.

The September 13 piece—the first piece to go beyond a simple factual update—said four things. First, that the assault on the TMF had been a spontaneous event that evolved from a protest outside the TMF. Second, that the protest and subsequent attack had been motivated by what had happened in Cairo earlier in the day (there was no mention in the piece of the YouTube video defaming the Prophet Muhammad). Third, that there was evidence of extremist involvement in the attack, and by "extremists" the analysts absolutely meant terrorist involvement, because *extremist* and *terrorist* are synonyms to terrorism analysts. Indeed, the piece reported that people with ties to al Qa'ida had been involved in the attack. The bottom line here is important: the analysts thought Benghazi was terrorism from the beginning. And whether or not the assault evolved from a protest, it was still very much a terrorist attack. Fourth and finally, the September 13 piece said that there was no evidence of significant planning on the part of those responsible— not days, weeks, or months ahead of time. Hours perhaps—but no longer than that.

The analysts came to these conclusions on their own—with no interference from the White House, the State Department, or the CIA leadership, including me. In fact, all of these judgments were coordinated across the intelligence community, making them IC judgments, not just CIA ones (so if there was a conspiracy, it was a big one, involving multiple analysts and agencies). Contrary to statements by the media and a few senators, I played no role in the judgment that there had been a protest.

It is important to note that the analysts' view was fully sup-ported by my boss, Director Petraeus. At an NSC principals meet-ing the day after the attack, Petraeus outlined the analysts' view that the attack had evolved spontaneously from a protest. Some of the principals, including Defense Secretary Panetta, pushed back, arguing that demonstrators do not show up at a protest with weap-ons. Petraeus defended the analysts' work, arguing that there were so many weapons in Libya that the analysts' judgment was indeed quite plausible.

It is true that, after all the relevant information became avail-able, the protest judgment turned out to be inaccurate. It turned out that there had been no protest immediately outside the TMF— although some in the intelligence community believe that there was a protest nearby, and others believe that the gathering of the attackers outside the TMF just before the assault could have been interpreted by some on the scene as a protest. But the other initial judgments of the analysts have held up over time.

And the analysts did not just make up the judgment about the protest. Two things led them to that conclusion. First, a dozen or so reports—both intelligence reporting and press reporting—said there had been a protest ongoing at the time of the attack. And second, not a single piece of information in the analysts' *possession* at the time they wrote the piece that was published on September 13 said there had *not* been a protest.

CIA's analysts have been criticized for not reaching out to the officers who were on the ground that night at the TMF and asking them what happened, asking them if there had been a protest. But that is simply not how intelligence analysts operate. They are analysts, not investigators. They wait for information to come to them; they do not go out and gather it. Additionally, the FBI had just opened an investigation into the deaths of the four Americans, and the Bureau would have been extremely concerned if CIA officers had interviewed the witnesses to a crime before the Bureau did.

I do think that the analysts can be criticized—and therefore the Agency and I can be criticized—for not pushing those in the field harder for more and better information faster. For example, it took the FBI a number of days to write and disseminate intelligence reports from its interviews of the eyewitnesses. We should have pushed hard to get those reports much earlier.

On Friday morning, September 14, my boss David Petraeus led a team to Capitol Hill to brief the House Permanent Select Committee on Intelligence (HPSCI). He had done a similar briefing the day before at the Senate Intelligence Committee. The talking points that had been prepared for him for these two briefings paralleled what the analysts had written on the thirteenth.

I didn't accompany the director to the HPSCI, and learned what had transpired only late that afternoon. As I was standing in the director's conference room between two regular but important meetings—the director's thrice-weekly update on counterterrorism and his weekly update on Syria—Director Petraeus's chief of staff handed me a copy of talking points on Benghazi.

He said he was concerned that I was not yet aware of an important issue and that I needed to be brought into the loop—that at the morning HPSCI briefing, the ranking member of the committee, Representative C. A. "Dutch" Ruppersberger, had asked for unclassified talking points that he and others might use that coming weekend should they be asked by the media about the attacks in Benghazi. He added that Director Petraeus had agreed to the request and that a draft of the points was already circulating both inside and outside CIA. He said, "These are the talking points as they now stand."

I learned later that the talking points had been drafted by the head of the Counterterrorism Center's Office of Terrorism Analysis (D/OTA), who had been with Petraeus on the Hill. She had produced a draft quickly after returning to headquarters. She had coordinated this draft with substantive experts on both the analytic and operational sides of the Agency and, because of the issues associated with speaking publicly about an ongoing FBI investigation, with attorneys from our Office of General Counsel.

After she made changes that were suggested by substantive experts and by the Office of General Counsel, the D/OTA sent the draft of the talking points to CIA's Office of Congressional Affairs (OCA), which then took the unusual step of holding a coordination session with officers from CIA's Office of Public Affairs (OPA). No substantive experts were involved in this process.

This was a significant mistake. The OCA and OPA staffers went well beyond their expertise and responsibilities in editing the points. The officers in these two staffs made a number of changes to the draft, including changing *attacks* to *demonstrations* in the first sentence of the D/OTA draft, which had originally read "The attacks in Benghazi were spontaneously inspired by the protests at the U.S. Embassy in Cairo and evolved into a direct assault against the U.S. Consulate...." Participants in the editing session say they do not have a clear recollection as to why they made this change, but some have said that they believed the sentence to be illogical as written: saying that "attacks" evolved into an "assault" does not make sense, because *attack* and *assault* are synonymous. In my view, the most important point here is that the concept of an attack/assault still existed in the first sentence even after this change. Again, contrary to some media and Congressional allegations, I did not make this change. In fact, it occurred before I was even aware that the talking points had been requested.

The group of Public Affairs and Congressional Affairs officials also deleted the phrase "with ties to al Qa'ida." They say they did so to ensure that they would not compromise the FBI investigation by prematurely attributing responsibility for the attacks to any one person or group. They had reason to be concerned about this. One of the internal CIA e-mails sent that day came from our general counsel, Stephen Preston. It said, "Folks, I know there is a hurry to get this out but we need to hold it long enough to ascertain whether providing it conflicts with express instructions from NSS/DOJ/FBI that, in light of the criminal investigation, we are not to generate statements as to who did this etc., even internally not to mention for public release." Again, this change took place before I was aware that the talking points had been requested, which, of course, undercuts yet another of the claims about me—that I was the one to remove the reference to al Qa'ida from the talking points. I did not do so.

I do believe that the removal of the "with ties to al Qa'ida" language was a mistake. It did not attribute responsibility to a particular group or particular individuals in a way that would have put the FBI investigation at risk. Those words would have made the talking points better.

The OCA/OPA version was then shown to Director Petraeus, who asked for a significant addition. The director asked that language be added regarding CIA's assessments starting months earlier regarding the deteriorating security situation in eastern Libya, as well as the warnings sent out just days before the 9/11 anniversary. Having made these changes, the Office of Public Affairs circulated the draft talking points to its counterparts around government—the State Department, NSC, FBI, National Counterterrorism Center, and others. More changes were suggested.

This was another mistake on the part of the OCA and OPA. They had no business taking the lead in coordinating the points with the rest of the government. The substantive experts in the Office of Terrorism Analysis should have been the lead. Those experts did not even realize their points were circulating among the other national security agencies.

One of the most significant changes suggested at this point was proposed by the FBI, which requested that the phrase "We do know Islamic extremists participated in the violent demonstrations" be amended to "there are indications that Islamic extremists participated in the violent demonstrations." The FBI did not want the talking points to be so definitive in describing the perpetrators, since the investigation was just getting under way. Finally, the State Department wanted to remove an entire sentence that linked the Islamic extremist group Ansar al-Sharia to the attack—because, it reasoned, the only unclassified evidence we had that they were involved was an initial public claim by Ansar al-Sharia taking credit for the attack that had been quickly retracted by the group. All our other evidence indicating the group's involvement was still classified at that time.

All of this occurred before I first learned of and read a draft of the talking points on that Friday afternoon standing in the director's conference room. As I skimmed the talking points, with the director's chief of staff standing there, one thing leaped out at me—the inclusion of the prior-warning language. While they were factually accurate, I thought that including those sentences was ill-advised and I made my views clear to the chief of staff. To begin with, the request had been to give members of Congress language they could use to describe what had happened on September 11, 2012. What CIA had done in the months, weeks, and days leading up to the attack was simply not relevant to the request. More important, I saw the language as an attempt by the Agency to thump its chest, to say, "We did our job," and to deflect any blame from CIA to elsewhere. I thought we would pay a price for this in the relationships that make up the interagency process in Washington. Contrary to what some of the critics have said, I did not take this position to protect the State Department. I did so to protect the Central Intelligence Agency. And I made this decision well before I even knew that the State Department did not like the warning language—in direct contradiction to what several members of the House Intelligence Committee have implied in questioning my integrity in an "Additional Views" section of its report, released in late 2014.

While he never said a word as I vented about the warning language, the chief of staff's body language suggested to me that he agreed. In fact, I believe that this is why he'd brought the talking points to my attention in the first place. I believe he thought that I would react exactly the way I did.

In addition to protecting the Agency, I also believed it was unfair to the State Department for us to say that we had warned them, without giving the department an opportunity to say what it had or had not done with those warnings. There would be plenty of time for that discussion to take place. Months later it would become clear that the State Department had not taken adequate steps to protect itself in light of our warnings in the months and weeks leading up to the 9/11 anniversary, but during that second week of September

CIA had no way to know that, and I believed it would be unfair to suggest it simply to protect ourselves.

Again, a few members of the House Intelligence Committee have argued that I acted outside my purview when I removed the warning language. Since these were "CIA talking points," such an argument is absurd. But it is particularly silly given that the primary reason I excised the material was to protect the Central Intelligence Agency.

What I didn't know at the time was that the warning language had been inserted at the suggestion of my boss, David Petracus. The director's chief of staff did not tell me that. Had I known it, I would have walked into the director's office and discussed it with him that evening. Even though I made it clear that I did not like the warning language, I made no changes to the talking points on Friday evening—this is an inaccuracy in the Senate Intelligence Committee report on Benghazi, which said I did make a change on Friday—as I told my staff I would look at the talking points after they had been fully coordinated in the interagency review process.

The next morning, Saturday, started with my executive assistant's informing me of two things. First, the State Department, at the working level, had informed us that it objected to the inclusion of the warning language and, because of this, the talking points were in limbo (this was the first time I became aware that the department did not like the talking points). And second, Denis McDonough, Obama's deputy national security advisor, wanted to discuss the talking points at the deputies meeting scheduled for that morning, which suggested to me that he had been made aware of State's concern about the warning language. I mentioned all of this to Director Petraeus and his chief of staff on Saturday morning, telling them that I agreed with the State Department's position and explaining why. Petraeus didn't argue the point and didn't tell me he was the one who'd asked for the language to be inserted in the first place.

By the very end of the deputies meeting, McDonough had not raised the talking point issue, so I did. I told my colleagues that I had some concerns about the talking points and that I knew other agencies did as well. I did not say what my concerns were. I concluded by saying I would edit the talking points myself and share them with the relevant deputies before sending them to the Hill. McDonough simply said, "Thank you, Michael."

That Saturday was "Family Day" at CIA—an annual event at which the kin of Agency employees are invited to tour our headquarters complex. Because of the nature of intelligence work, the close relatives of CIA officers are rarely allowed to visit Langley. But once per year, on Family Day, employees can bring loved ones in to view exhibits, try on disguises, look at spy gear, take a polygraph test, and tour the director's and deputy director's offices. So while hundreds of folks trooped through my office to say hello, I was thinking about the talking points that were waiting for me on my assistant's desk. I finally sat down with them late that morning. While I did some significant editorial work, my main substantive contribution was to remove the warning language.

I also took out the word "Islamic" in front of "extremists," an action for which I have also been criticized (for allegedly trying to downplay the role of al Qa'ida in the attacks). I removed the word "Islamic" for risk mitigation. Demonstrations were occurring in many countries throughout the Muslim world because of the YouTube video defaming the Prophet Muhammad, and the last thing I wanted was to encourage any American to say anything that could make the situation worse. And I thought, incorrectly, that "extremists" would carry the same message as "Islamic extremists"—that this had been a terrorist attack.

When I coordinated the talking points with my deputies colleagues, no significant changes were made. Throughout the entire process, the White House suggested only three changes and all of them were editorial—not a single one involved an analytic judgment—undercutting the conspiracy theory that the White House played a large role in editing the talking points. Finally, before having our Office of Congressional Affairs send the talking points to the Hill, I asked that the substantive experts and Director Petraeus review and sign off on them. All did so.

One of the narratives in the media has been that I "overruled" my boss on the question of whether or not to include the warning language. Believe me, there was no overruling Director Petraeus on anything. I had a conversation with the director about the warning language, in which he did not oppose my decision to remove it, and he had the opportunity at the end of the process to ask that the warning language be added back in. He did not do so.

While I am the first to admit that the talking points could have been better—they could have been more clearly written and they could have been more robust—the analytic judgments in them were fully consistent with what CIA had written for policy-makers on the morning of the thirteenth. This included the language about the assault on the TMF having evolved from a spontaneous protest. In short, what we were allowing HPSCI members to say publicly was exactly what we had said in our classified publications. Also, and importantly, CIA did not know that the talking points would be used publicly the next day by a senior administration official. We did not know that Susan Rice was going to use them on the Sunday-morning news shows.

It was only much later—in the spring of 2014—that it became clear to me how UN ambassador Susan Rice had come to receive our talking points. They were embedded in a much longer set of White House–produced talking points designed to prepare Ambassador Rice to appear on the Sunday shows the next day. Again, nothing in the CIA talking points was markedly different from the finished intelligence that Rice and other senior officials had been seeing over the previous four days.

But there was something different in the White House–produced points sent to Rice's staff. There was a phrase in the "Goals" section: "To underscore that these protests are rooted in an Internet video, and not a broader failure of policy." The White House has argued that its talking points were not about Benghazi but about the broader protests taking place in the region. But that explanation does not hold water—because just one bullet point later in the "Goals" section of the White House talking points is the following: "To show that we will be resolute in bringing people who harm Americans to justice"—and the only place Americans had been harmed during that period was in Benghazi. My reading of the White House talking points is that they were blaming the Benghazi attack on the video—which is not something CIA did in its talking points or in its classified analysis.

The White House view that its talking points were not about Benghazi had an important consequence. That view meant that the White House talking points did not need to be publicly released in the spring of 2013 along with the other materials related to the executive branch's public narrative on the Benghazi attacks. This put the entire focus on the CIA talking points.

I had another reaction to the White House talking points as well. I have always believed that there should be a bright red line in any White House between the individuals responsible for national security and those responsible for politics. And the line about how Benghazi was not a failure rooted in broader policy seemed to me to be a political statement, not a national security one.

The reaction to what Ambassador Rice said on those Sunday shows became a slow-moving tidal wave that eventually sank the president's intention to nominate her as secretary of state. A good bit of what she said was consistent with the CIA points, but she also said that the video had led to the protests in Benghazi. Why she said this I do not know. It is a question that only she can answer. Perhaps she was following the White House talking points. Perhaps she had her own views; policy-makers are permitted to do so. In this regard, perhaps she was "connecting the dots." After all, the analysts did believe that the incident in Cairo had been caused by the video and that at least one of the motivations for the protest in Benghazi had been the "success" of those who had gotten over the embassy fence in Cairo. The harder statement to explain is why Rice said that there was a "substantial security presence" in Benghazi, as that point was not in either the CIA or the White House talking points.

That Saturday morning, a day before Ambassador Rice went on the Sunday shows and before I edited the talking points, another set of conversations took place that some would come to see as evidence of politicization on the part of the Agency and me. One media outlet accused me of knowing that there had not been a protest when I edited the talking points—because the CIA chief of station in Tripoli had written me a note telling me so on the morning that I edited them. Here is the real story.

Each CIA station chief in the Muslim countries affected by the regional violence had been asked to send in daily situation reports. In the situation report, or SITREP, from Tripoli filed on Saturday, September 15, our chief there noted that the attacks in Benghazi "were not/not an escalation of protests." The word *not* was repeated for emphasis. That claim immediately jumped out at me—because I recognized that it was inconsistent with what the analysts thought.

What also jumped out at me, however, was that neither of the chief's two explanations in the e-mail was compelling. He noted that some press reports said there had been no protest—but that was not convincing because there were also press reports saying just the opposite. And he explained that his officers in Benghazi, when they reached the TMF that night, had not seen a protest. That was also not compelling because his officers had arrived at the TMF almost an hour after the attack started, and a protest, if there had been one, could easily have dissipated by then. Finally, I was struck by the fact that on the previous day the chief's own station had sent in a report from a CIA source saying there had been a protest at the TMF. Given all of this, I immediately requested that the chief send a more detailed note, with "supporting evidence and logic" for his view.

I took another step that morning. During the Deputies Committee meeting, I told my colleagues about our chief of station's view regarding the protest; I pointed out that it differed from what the analysts thought and that we would work to resolve this difference, and get back to everyone. This was not the action of someone who was trying to hide the chief's view—a charge made against me by some in the media and some in Congress.

The chief responded quickly to my tasking and his follow-on note arrived early on the morning of Sunday, September 16. I did two things. First, I tasked the analysts to read it and to tell me in writing by five p.m. that same day whether the chief's argument changed their judgment in any way regarding the protest question. Second, I forwarded the chief's e-mail to Director Petraeus, telling him, "Sir—The bottom line is that I do not know what to make of this. We need to have the analysts look at this and see if there is anything here that changes their view. I have asked them to do so." The director responded to my note, saying, "Look forward to what the analysts have to say."

That same Sunday afternoon, the analysts responded with a memo to both the director and me. They stuck with their original view, although they indicated that they were keeping an open mind on the question.

I handled this situation exactly the way I should have. Despite the claims of some members of Congress and some media commentators, at CIA our operations officers collect intelligence and our analysts produce the assessments. Period. That is the way it has been for the entire history of the organization. Operations officers are the eyes and ears of CIA; analysts are the voice of the organization. Analysts have access to all the available information; our officers in the field do not.

Some have said that I "sided with the analysts" in this debate and that I made a decision that the Agency was going to "go with the analysts' view rather than our station chief's view." At CIA, directors and deputy directors do not tell the analysts what to think and they do not determine the analytic line of the Agency. The analysts do.

While the analysts establish the official line of the Agency, CIA chiefs of station are free—indeed, they are encouraged—to put on record their own view, particularly if it differs from that of the analysts. Our chiefs can, and do quite frequently, disseminate across the intelligence community and within the policy community assessments that capture their own views on a situation (these assessments are called "aardwolfs"—named after an African mammal that has a keen understanding of its environment). Our chief in Tripoli did not produce such an assessment on the protest issue.

Seven days after the CIA talking points were produced—on September 22—the analysts changed their judgment based on new information they had received in the days since their initial assessment, explaining that armed assailants had been present from the incident's outset and that this suggested it had been an intentional assault and not the escalation of a peaceful protest. The analysts changed their judgment after the Libyan government recovered the security surveillance footage from the TMF's multiple video cameras, watched it, saw no protest, informed our station of that on September 18, and turned over the footage a few days later.

* * *

In the days, weeks, and months that followed, Benghazi became a constant stream of controversy. Take for example a media story at the time—and recently replayed in a book—that alleged that CIA senior leaders had ordered their officers at our Benghazi base to "stand down" and not come to the aid of their State Department colleagues. Here is what really happened. Within minutes of the attack, the TMF called our base and asked for immediate assistance. The Agency officers sprang into action, breaking out their weapons, armor, and vehicles. These are the kind of men who instinctively run toward danger rather than from it, to help those in harm's way. And that is exactly the kind of response I'd expected from them. It took about fifteen minutes for them to assemble their gear and be ready to deploy. I expected a different kind of response from the chief of base, and he delivered on that expectation. He had to ensure that he was not sending his officers needlessly to their deaths. So he tried to round up assistance from local Libyan militias. In a few minutes it became clear that there would be no assistance from the locals. While these calls were being made, the response team was frustrated that it was not moving out. Although the delay was no more than five to eight minutes, I am sure that to those involved it must have seemed like forever. The delay was in no way ordered by anyone further up in the chain of command. It was totally justified under the circumstances, and it was exactly the right decision by our chief on the ground.

The allegation that there had been some intentional delay gained media traction, however, and Director Petraeus asked me to call in members of the media and conduct press backgrounder. During this session, I carefully recounted—minute by minute—the time between the Annex's getting the first call for help from the TMF and when the CIA team arrived at the ambassador's compound, about an hour in total, as the team first stopped short of the TMF and tried to enlist the support of a militia group. I then spent another thirty minutes or so answering questions. Many media outlets ran stories the next day outlining what had really happened, and the stand-down allegation was relegated to the fringe press.

I actually did two media backgrounders that day. The second was with a group of a dozen or so national security reporters, while the first was a one-on-one session with David Ignatius from the *Washington Post*. I have the greatest respect for Ignatius's commentary on national security. I have always found it fair and insightful, and therefore I wanted Ignatius to have the opportunity to ask as many questions as he wished and I wanted his questions to help prepare me for the larger group of reporters. We also committed a faux pas when our public affairs office failed to invite Andrea Mitchell from NBC News to the group session. They just forgot. Mitchell was angry and so was I. Mitchell in many ways is the dean of national security reporters and to leave her out was a huge mistake. I ran into her several weeks later and apologized, which she accepted in good humor. Years earlier, when I was George Tenet's executive assistant and Mitchell was doing a story on the Agency, she asked me, "Is it true that George dribbles a basketball in the halls of CIA?" I responded, "Andrea, I will tell you the answer to that question if you tell me what your husband [Alan Greenspan, then the chairman of the Federal Reserve Board] is going to do with interest rates!"

There was also a controversy over how I answered two questions at a closed hearing before the Senate Intelligence Committee. It is over these answers that Senators Chambliss and Burr questioned my integrity. The first question, from Senator Burr, was directed to all the witnesses testifying that day: "Who took 'al Qa'ida' out of the talking points?" Because I did not know the answer at the time, I said I did not know. While this was truthful, Senator Burr told me later in a private meeting before I left government that he would have expected me to say, "I do not know, Senator, but you should know that I myself edited the talking points at one stage in the process." I agreed with Senator Burr, and I told him so at the time. I wish that the "Minority Views" section of the SSCI report on Benghazi had captured this conversation. It did not.

The second question was "Were the talking points provided to the White House for coordination or for awareness?" I said awareness. That was clearly not right, as the White House had suggested changes—albeit editorial ones—that we accepted. The important thing is that my answer to this question was not meant to mislead. I was careless with my words. What I meant to convey in my answer was that there was no way we would have allowed the White House—or anyone else for that matter—to make a substantive change with which CIA did not agree. Was there a lack of clarity in my response to the question? Yes. Should I have been clearer? Yes. Deliberately misleading Congress? No way.

There was additional uproar over how I sat next to DNI Jim Clapper at a closed House Intelligence hearing the very next day and did not speak when Chairman Rogers asked the DNI, "Who did take out...the al Qa'ida–linked information in the talking points as they were being formed up?" I did not say anything, again because I did not know who had taken out the reference to al Qa'ida. Later, Representative Peter King would try to reframe the chairman's question, saying the DNI had been asked, "Who changed the talking points?"—suggesting the question "How could Morell sit there and not answer when he'd made extensive changes to the talking points?" But King was wrong; the question had been much narrower. But again, I would have served the committee better had I followed the DNI's answer by saying, "I don't know who took al Qa'ida out, but you should know that I took some other stuff out."

The argument of my critics with regard to the HPSCI testimony—and the earlier SSCI testimony—was that I was trying to hide the fact that I had made changes to the talking points. Nonsense. The strongest evidence that this was not the case was that just days before the two testimonies, I met with a large number of senior Congressional leaders, and in those meetings I told them that I had made changes to the talking points, I told them that I had taken out the warning language, I told them that I had removed the word *Islamic*. I was fully transparent. I was not hiding anything.

The biggest controversy on Benghazi was the one that arose over Ambassador Rice's use of the talking points in her public statement. She became a lightning rod, and it was clear that her potential nomination for secretary of state was in jeopardy. In an attempt to end the attacks on her, she wanted to face her accusers directly. A meeting with Senators John McCain, Lindsey Graham, and Kelly Ayotte was arranged for November 27. I was asked by Denis McDonough, still deputy national security advisor at the time, to accompany Ambassador Rice to the Hill. He made clear that my job was to show that the talking points were fully consistent with the classified analysis produced by the intelligence community. I said yes to the request.

In retrospect, attending the meeting was a mistake. The meeting was inherently political, and by attending, I inserted myself into a political issue. I'm sure that McCain, Graham, and Ayotte saw it that way. I'm sure they saw me as taking sides in a political fight. That is not where an intelligence officer should be. I was politically naïve to have attended, and I have paid a price for it.

The meeting went forward in a secure Senate conference room. The news media had the hallways leading to the room staked out, and photographers snapped photos of me while reporters yelled questions. A friend e-mailed me later that evening, saying that I'd looked as if I were going to my own execution, and urging me to force a smile in such situations. But once we got started there was nothing to smile about.

Senators McCain, Graham, and Ayotte were on one side of a

table, Ambassador Rice and I on the other. McCain and Graham wasted no time in launching an attack against Ambassador Rice. They repeatedly called Rice a "political hack," and they sometimes would not let her finish a thought before interrupting her with a new question. Senator Ayotte did not contribute to the vitriol and seemed genuinely interested in getting to the truth.

I was a silent witness, until Rice asked me to explain the consistency between the talking points and the classified intelligence analysis. Then it was my turn to be attacked. I had brought along copies of the talking points and the classified analysis from September 13, and I tried to show the senators that every sentence in the talking points had a virtual match in the classified analysis. McCain and Graham turned on me, attacking my analysts' capabilities, judgment, and integrity, interrupting me mid-sentence as they had Rice. "Why did it take you so long to admit there was no demonstration?" they asked. "Why didn't you immediately interview the people on the ground?" "Why didn't you call this a terrorist attack?"

At one point, while being battered with questions, I made an error. One of the senators asked me who had removed the reference to al Qa'ida from the talking points—and I, incorrectly, said it had been the FBI. I was thinking about the one change that the FBI had made—when it asked for a change in the talking points so that they would not be too definitive in describing who might have conducted the attack, because the Bureau was just beginning its investigation. I got the two changes mixed up. I made a mistake. In the car on my way back to headquarters, our director of congressional affairs, who had joined me in the meeting, told me that he thought I had made a mistake. I immediately responded, "If I made a mistake, let's fix it." Upon returning to CIA headquarters and looking at the facts, I quickly realized that I had misspoken. The decision to remove al Qa'ida from the draft talking points had been an internal CIA decision—made long before I knew that the talking points existed.

I immediately directed our Office of Congressional Affairs to notify the senators' staff of my mistake. It did so within a couple of hours. In response to my clarification, the senators issued a press release citing my mistake and using it to blast the administration about unanswered questions on Benghazi.

Even worse, months later, Senator Graham publicly insisted that he'd asked me, "Who changed the talking points?" In fact, I was asked, "Who took al Qa'ida out of the talking points?" By providing an inaccurate account of what he had asked me, Graham left the impression that there was no way I could have made an honest mistake in answering such a broad question. Graham also insisted that it had taken me twenty-four hours to correct the record and that I'd done so only after receiving an angry call from the FBI for saying that it had made all the changes to the talking points. The facts, as with much about what many people have said about Benghazi, could not be more different. The senators had asked a much more specific question that it was indeed possible to make a mistake in answering: "Who took al Qa'ida out of the talking points?"—a fact that Graham, McCain, and Ayotte's own press release issued the day of the meeting with Ambassador Rice makes clear.

Here is what that press release stated: "Around 10:00 this morning in a meeting requested by Ambassador Rice, accompanied by acting CIA Director Mike Morell, we asked Mr. Morell who changed the unclassified talking points to remove references to al-Qaeda. In response, Mr. Morell said the FBI removed the references and did so to prevent compromising an ongoing criminal investigation. We were surprised by this revelation and the reasoning behind it. However, at approximately 4:00 this afternoon, CIA officials contacted us and indicated that Acting Director Morell misspoke in our earlier meeting. The CIA now says that it deleted the al-Qaeda references, not the FBI. They were unable to give a reason as to why."

In addition, the FBI never called me to complain about the mistake

I'd made while briefing the three senators. Moreover, as the timing of their own press release makes clear, I corrected the record within a couple of hours, not twenty-four.

* * *

At the end of the day, I find three significant ironies in the views of those who were attacking CIA and me. The first is the striking difference between the record of CIA in assessing what happened in Benghazi and the record of those making allegations about the executive branch.

The judgments of analysts, operating with only twenty-four hours of information, have held up over time. Only one of their main judgments regarding what had happened in Benghazi that night— that a protest immediately outside the TMF had evolved into the attack—has been shown to be wrong. They still believe their other judgments.

Contrast that with the conclusions at others:

• *The US military was ordered to stand down and not come to the aid of the State Department and CIA officers in Benghazi.* Wrong. The House Armed Services Committee report on Benghazi, the House Intelligence Committee report on the issue, and the Senate Intelligence Committee report on Benghazi all specifically concluded that this assertion was false.

• *The CIA officers in Benghazi were ordered to stand down and not come to the rescue of their comrades at the TMF.* Wrong, as I have already explained. Again, the Senate Intelligence Committee and the House Intelligence Committee said there was no evidence to support this allegation.

• *There was a conspiracy between CIA and the White House to spin the Benghazi story in a way that would protect the political inter-ests of the president and Secretary Clinton.* Again, wrong. There was no such conspiracy, as I have already explained, and there is no evidence to support such a theory. No committee of Congress that has studied Benghazi has come to this conclusion.

The second irony is that some believe the CIA leadership, including me, should have forced the analysts to accept COS Tripoli's view that there had not been a protest outside the TMF, while at the same time they firmly reject another view of the COS, who wrote that one of the possible motivations for the attack on the TMF had been the YouTube video. These critics cannot have it both ways—accepting from a source, our COS, what fits their narrative and rejecting from the same source what does not.

Finally, the third and most important irony: my critics have alleged that I misled the American people about what happened in Benghazi, while the truth is that they are the ones misleading the public—in almost everything they say about the issue. For example, in multiple commentaries after my open testimony before the House Intelligence Committee, a small number of members of Congress and a small segment of the media got many facts wrong in talking about me and my role in Benghazi. As Daniel Patrick Moynihan once said, "Everyone is entitled to his own opinion, but not to his own facts."

The best example of this is an op-ed written in the days after my testimony by Michael Mukasey, who was an attorney general in the Bush administration, and who was writing in support of my critics. In only a dozen paragraphs, Mukasey, a former US district judge as well as a former US attorney, made seven factual errors. Here are a handful:

- Mr. Mukasey wrote, "Mr. Morell changed 'terrorist' to 'extremist'" in the talking points. No, I did not. As is clear from the e-mails released by the White House in the spring of 2013, no one changed "terrorist" to "extremist." The original draft of the talking points, written by our most senior terrorism analyst, said "extremist."

- Mr. Mukasey wrote, "He [meaning me] substituted 'demonstration' for 'attack'" in the talking points. No, I did not. As my sworn testimony and the e-mails make clear, this change was made by others at the Agency and before I ever saw the talking points.

- Mr. Mukasey wrote, "Yet the CIA was asked soon after the attack by the White House to help draft 'talking points,' which should have tipped him [again meaning me] off that some extramural talking was planned." Not even close. No one has ever claimed that the White House asked for the talking points. Again, as all the evidence makes clear, the House Intelligence Committee asked Director Petraeus for the talking points.

Even Representative Trey Gowdy, the leader of the House Select Committee on Benghazi, got his facts wrong in the days immediately following his appointment as chairman of the committee. Gowdy, before being elected to Congress, was a career federal and state prosecutor and a very good one. He rightfully prides himself on uncovering the facts and letting them take him to a conclusion. But even he made mistakes.

In media appearances after his appointment as chairman, Gowdy said that I had changed "attacks" to "demonstrations" in the CIA talking points. This is untrue. He said that I had changed "terrorist" to "extremist" in the talking points. This is untrue. And he said that the initial draft of the talking points had included the warnings that CIA had provided to the State Department. Again, this is untrue. Later drafts included the warning language, but not the initial draft and not the final one. Even the Congress's best and brightest was getting things wrong about Benghazi.

In a press conference after my testimony, Senators McCain and Graham made a similar number of factual errors in attempting to argue that my appearance had raised more questions than it answered. Senator McCain said that the Tripoli station chief had reported "immediately" after the attack that there had been no protest. This report was not immediate; it came over three days after the attacks. The senator also said I had been the acting director at the time of the attacks. Wrong again. I was deputy director. Dave Petraeus was the director. For his part, Senator Graham said that he knew I had not removed the reference to al Qa'ida from the talking points, "but he [meaning me] did everything else." False. Many others within and outside CIA made changes to the talking points.

I do not know why my critics have gotten the details so wrong. Perhaps it was poor staff work. Perhaps it was the inaccurate facts repeated over and over again by some in the media. Some of Gowdy's inaccurate statements, for example, mirrored those of Michael Mukasey. In any case, such inaccuracies have serious consequences because inaccurate facts lead to inaccurate narratives and inaccurate conclusions—which lead to inaccurate understandings on the part of the American people. The administration's critics were doing exactly what they accused the administration of doing.

* * *

I was acting director for four months of the Benghazi controversy—from early November 2012 until March—and I directed that two studies be undertaken—one on why our analysis had been wrong with regard to the protest and another on how we could have done a better job on the talking points. Both studies found fault inside the Agency, and both studies offered extensive lessons learned. I sent the first study—on the analysis—to Congress in January 2013. But for months the White House would not allow me to send the second study—on the talking points—to the Hill, citing executive privilege. I finally did so without asking—after the White House had released publicly all the e-mails related to the talking points. But that did not happen until a few weeks before I left government. It should have happened much sooner.

In my opinion two broad lessons can be learned from all this.

First, CIA should stay out of the talking point business—especially on issues that are being seized upon for political purposes. Those who want to speak publicly on a national security issue should write their own talking points, and then CIA can advise them on what is accurate and unclassified—but holding the pen in the first instance is fraught with peril. CIA officers are not trained to communicate with the American people, and sometimes we do not do it well. The best example is that to us, "extremists" was synonymous with "terrorists." That was clearly not the case for many in the public.

Second, when an administration finds itself in a mess like this, the best remedy is transparency, as early and as fully as possible. I know that sounds odd coming from someone who has spent his life at a secretive agency—but we would have been much better off if the administration had released the full surveillance video of the attacks of 9/11/12, had released its own talking points on the issue, and had released the chain of e-mails on the evolution of the CIA talking points as soon as Benghazi started to become politically controversial. And it was a mistake on the part of the administration to withhold materials from Congress on any aspect of Benghazi.

* * *

What is most frustrating to me is that all the hubbub over the talking points and politics has meant that much of the public has missed the key question—in the years ahead, how are we going to keep American diplomats as safe as possible overseas? Benghazi will not be the last US diplomatic post to be attacked by terrorists. There will be many other attempts, and some will be successful. We need to do a better job of protecting those who serve our nation overseas.

I see three keys to mitigating this threat. One: At some spots in the world, the United States will need tactical warning, the same kind of tactical warning we have on a battlefield to protect our soldiers. If we'd had that in Benghazi, we almost certainly would have heard the chatter as the extremists were preparing to attack both the TMF and the Annex. Any advance warning—even one just minutes ahead—could have been the difference between life and death. Two: We must provide the best and latest security for Americans serving overseas. They are putting their lives on the line for their country, and they deserve the very best security. That did not happen in the case of Benghazi. And three: We and our allies must oppose and combat terrorists wherever they pose a threat to us—or they will come after us. All three of these responses cost money, of course—a lot of money. The bottom line is that protecting Americans abroad cannot be done on the cheap.

* * *

My final point has to do with the raw nature of America's current political system. Politicians are so fixated on scoring points and thinking in terms of partisan advantage that they project these same attitudes and behaviors on public servants. They have a hard time understanding that intelligence professionals are trained to be objective, not political. They have a hard time remembering that we serve Democrats and Republicans with the same professionalism and dedication. Accusing CIA of playing politics with talking points comes naturally to those who think and work only in a political environment and who survive by shaping talking points (or thirty-second spots) regardless of the facts.

* * *

April 14, 2014, House Intelligence Committee hearing on Benghazi. Selected excerpt:

THE CHAIRMAN (MR. MIKE ROGERS, CONGRESSMAN FROM MICHIGAN'S EIGHTH CONGRESSIONAL DISTRICT): Mr. Morell. . . . At any time did you have any verbal conversations with anybody at the White House about what the nature of those talking points were and what they needed to look like?

Mr. Morell: No, sir.

The chairman: At any time did you have any conversation with anybody at the White House, and I mean anybody, that had anything to do with preparing Susan Rice for going out and being the face for America on that September 16?

Mr. Morell: No, sir. In fact, I didn't even know she was going to be on the Sunday shows.

* * *

April 14, 2014, House Intelligence Committee hearing on Benghazi. Selected quotes:

Ms. Jan Schakowsky, congresswoman from Illinois's Ninth Congressional District: Thank you, Mr. Morell. I really appreciate your testimony and, given your three decades of service to our nation and always looking to protecting our security and never in a partisan role or spirit, I believe what you are telling us today.

Mr. James Langevin, congressman from Rhode Island's Second Congressional District: You have always put the country first and, in my opinion, have always done your duty and been very candid and forthcoming in your testimony before the committee whenever you've appeared before me when I was there, since I've been on this committee. And the fact that you are here, voluntarily here, today reinforces how seriously you believe in the truth.

CHAPTER 11

Tortured Logic

Every new job has its obstacles. In the case of the position I started on July 5, 2006, as the number three official in CIA, the doorway to my new office had recently been blocked by crime scene tape. No kidding. As I mentioned earlier, the previous occupant of the office, Dusty Foggo, was under investigation for a variety of wrongdoings and later pleaded guilty to corruption in steering a CIA contract to a friend. The investigation included an FBI raid in mid-May 2006 on his office at CIA and one on his home. Foggo eventually ended up serving several years in federal prison.

Foggo was a West Coast wheeler-dealer—so the new CIA director, Mike Hayden, had probably wanted someone with my Midwestern straight-arrow image to try to restore respect for the office. After all, in addition to being in charge of administration, budgets, IT, security, and HR, I was also in charge of maintaining good order and discipline at the Agency.

Foggo, only a mid-level officer when he was promoted to the top of the Agency, had gotten the job by taking very good care of congressional staffers when they visited him in his previous assignment at an overseas post. Foggo treated the staffers well (two weeks after I started in the new job, I found twenty to twenty-five bottles of expensive liquor in a credenza in my office, a special treat for the "right" visitors to Foggo's office) while bad-mouthing his director George Tenet and the other senior leaders of the Agency. Great guy.

* * *

Two days after I started, one of the Agency's senior attorneys paid me a visit. He said he needed to "read me into [brief me on] a compartmented program." That is CIA-speak for being brought into the circle of trust on a sensitive operation—in this case the Agency's detention and interrogation programs. The programs involved the Agency's establishment, after 9/11, of several secret prisons around the world and the use of harsh interrogation techniques to obtain critical information from the most senior and hardened al Qaʻida leaders that we kept in those prisons. The programs had been in place since 2002.

After I signed a document—essentially saying that I understood I could go to jail if I ever disclosed the information in an unauthorized way—the attorney briefed me on the locations of the Agency's secret detention facilities. He also briefed me on the "enhanced interrogation techniques" (or EITs—CIA's name for the harsh techniques) designed to teach detainees that they had resisted as much as they could, that they were helpless to resist further, and therefore that it was acceptable for them to answer our questions thoroughly and truthfully. He explained each technique in detail. I remember thinking that a few of the techniques, in particular waterboarding, were extraordinarily harsh, but I also learned that of the ten techniques that had originally been authorized only six were still in use, including grabbing detainees to get their attention and depriving them of sleep. Waterboarding was no longer authorized and, in fact, had not been utilized in over three years.

Over the coming years, I would learn that only 119 people had ever been detained by CIA and that only a third had been subjected to enhanced techniques. I would also learn that only three had been waterboarded—the last session having taken place in 2003—that EITs were used for only a short time on many detainees, and that interrogations became gradually less coercive as the program gained experience with the various techniques and as the Agency amassed more information on al Qa'ida that could be used to elicit missing pieces of the puzzle from detainees. Finally, I learned that CIA leaders repeatedly sought legal and policy affirmation for the use of the techniques and had suspended their use—including at the time I was briefed on the program—whenever questions arose about the legal or policy basis for them.

* * *

On November 4, 2008, the country elected Barack Obama to be our forty-fourth president. His victory was decisive. Obama received 53 percent of the popular vote, the most for a Democrat in over half a century. And he won 365 electoral votes to John McCain's 173. In terms of the new president's beloved sport, basketball, it was a blowout.

Obama wanted to bring considerable forward-looking change to America, but one thing that his victory unleashed was an un-relenting look backward at some of the counterterrorism tools that the Bush administration had used in the aftermath of 9/11. Among those, and by far the most controversial, were CIA's rendition, detention, and interrogation programs (often lumped together by the acronym RDI). Renditions, a long-standing practice and the key counterterrorism tool used by the Clinton administration, involved CIA's transporting terrorist suspects from where they were captured to their countries of origin or elsewhere, where they were wanted on charges or otherwise put into a legal process.

The new president had made his position on these programs

clear during the election campaign. He had called for an end to renditions, calling the practice "shipping away prisoners in the dead of night to be tortured in far-off countries." He'd likewise called for an end to "secret prisons to jail people beyond the reach of the law." He'd labeled harsh interrogation techniques "torture." And he'd suggested that all these practices were inconsistent with American leadership in the world and its commitment to humanity, decency, and respect for all individuals.

* * *

Months before the election, the intelligence community began preparing for a new president, and the director of national intelligence at the time, Mike McConnell, asked me—at the time serving as CIA's director for intelligence, the Agency's chief analyst—to play a large role in the transition. As had been done historically, the intelligence community offered national security briefings to the candidates. Along with a team, I briefed John McCain—who, given his long service in Congress, particularly on the Senate Armed Services Committee, did not need a briefing. He knew as much as we did about national security.

And, along with another team, I provided Sarah Palin with her first-ever national security briefing. I was impressed with Governor Palin's interest in what motivated individual foreign leaders, and it was clear she had a natural understanding of people and how to deal with them. But her knowledge of the world was diametrically opposed to that of her running mate. She knew almost nothing about the key foreign policy and national security issues of the day. In contrast to the many questions she asked about people, she asked almost none about the issues themselves. She was in over her head, she seemed to me to know it, and it was not her fault. I felt sorry she had been put in that situation.

In addition to giving oral briefings to the candidates, we prepared briefing papers for the senior officials that the new president would bring along with him. We also prepared two briefing packages for the president-elect himself—a package on CIA's most sensitive programs (of which fewer than ten copies were made) and a book of short biographies of all the world leaders who were likely to call the winner to congratulate him.

We also prepared—with the permission of the Bush White House—to start providing the President's Daily Brief to the winner as soon as possible after the election. But the White House added a crucial caveat—only the president-elect and those he had already publicly named to a senior national security post could receive the PDB. No one else.

This was not the White House playing politics. This was President Bush continuing his eight-year practice of limiting the number of people who received the PDB, in order to protect the information in it. During my one year briefing the president, it had fallen to me on several occasions to make the case to add someone to the dissemination list. Bush would always ask tough questions about the person's need to know—and these were senior officials in his own administration. In each case he would say to me, "The more people who receive the PDB, the more you will water it down." He was right. That was exactly the way it worked.

McConnell also requested that I go to Chicago—or Phoenix, if McCain had won the election—for the transition, to be the on-scene coordinator for getting the president-elect up to speed on intelligence matters. McConnell had chosen two senior analysts to be the newly elected president's daily intelligence briefers, but McConnell wanted me in the room as well. In a reversal from my Bush briefing days, I would now be doing the color commentary, while others would be doing the play-by-play.

With Obama's victory, McConnell said that he wanted to do the first two briefings himself for the president-elect—they were set for Thursday and Friday, November 6 and 7, starting just two days after the election. McConnell requested that I and one of the two daily briefers join him, so that he could introduce us. The briefing was set for nine a.m. in a secure conference room at the FBI's field office in Chicago.

Just before nine the president-elect walked in, all smiles, accompanied by several of his aides who had handled national security matters during the campaign and who were destined for top jobs in the administration. The group included Denis McDonough, Mark Lippert, and Jim Steinberg. After introductions and congratulations, McConnell apologetically made it clear that his instructions were that only Obama was to receive the briefing, not the others. The president-elect in turn made it clear that he wanted his team in the room. I appreciated the president-elect's position. What he was asking for made perfect sense: he wanted to have conversations with his senior aides about the policy implications of what he was reading and hearing. McConnell, however, stuck to his White House guidance—although I was thinking, "Now is the time to be flexible, let them all in the room, and ask for forgiveness from the White House later. This is about building relationships that will last for the next four or eight years."

The smiles and sunny attitudes disappeared. Neither side wanted to budge. Obama and his team caucused in a nearby office, with the president-elect eventually returning and saying, "OK, I'll take the briefing today, but from tomorrow on you can just send it to me to read myself—until you include my guys." The intelligence community had gotten off to a very bad start with its new boss.

While the plan had been for McConnell to stay in Chicago for one night and for me to stay for several weeks to oversee the daily PDB sessions and facilitate other substantive briefings for Obama during the transition period, that no longer seemed to make any sense, since he had no desire to take any in-person briefings without his team. So McConnell and I decided to fly home, but the Air Force jet that had brought us to Chicago had departed and it was not due back till the next day.

We improvised. Although the DNI's security detail did not like it, McConnell decided that we would fly back to D.C. on a commercial jet—it would save us time and save the taxpayers money. McConnell and I—and two of his security agents—were whisked through O'Hare Airport security and put on the plane before the other passengers boarded. On the plane we met two federal air marshals who happened to be assigned to the flight to Washington's National Airport. A conversation ensued between the marshals and McConnell's security detail. The marshals asked, "Are you guys armed?" Answer: "Yes." The marshals went on, "Well, just so you know, we are armed as well, and so are both the pilot and copilot of the flight." I was thinking, "If anyone tries to hijack this plane they are in for one helluva surprise!"

A couple of weeks later the Bush administration relented and agreed to allow a couple of designated Obama aides to be present for the briefings. I returned to Chicago and, working with McDonough and Lippert, began to coordinate a wide-ranging series of briefings for the president-elect and his team on matters such as counter-terrorism, counter-proliferation, Middle East peace, and regional hot spots. I worked hard to improve relations that had turned as frosty as a Chicago winter, and ended up spending the better part of a month in the Windy City.

I found the president to be reserved in many of the briefings, asking few questions. McDonough and Lippert, on the other hand, asked many questions in front of their boss and shared their views on issues. The president-elect listened intently to what they had to say. It struck me that they felt comfortable enough with their boss to talk for lengthy periods and even to take over the conversation. To me this signaled that Obama was willing to listen to the views of others and to create an environment where his subordinates felt they were welcome to speak—incredibly important traits, I believe, in any decision-maker.

* * *

One of the briefings I organized, held on December 9, was the president-elect's first orientation about the most sensitive operations of the intelligence community—covert action. These are operations conducted by CIA with the express written authorization of the president through the use of a presidential finding. They are among the most sensitive and secret actions of the US government, and any new president needs to be briefed on them before being sworn in—because they are his programs and he needs to be comfortable with them. This brought the rendition, detention, and interrogation issues to the table for the first time with the new president.

While I was unable to attend—I was back in Washington—the briefing was led by my boss, CIA director Mike Hayden. As part of the agenda, Hayden gave the president-elect and his team their first in-depth briefing on enhanced interrogation techniques. Hayden, hoping that the session would ease the president-elect's opposition to the program, explained that there was much misinformation about these techniques. Hayden stressed the valuable intelligence gained by the program and emphasized that only six enhanced techniques were available for use; he also emphasized that those still authorized, like the original list of ten, had been deemed by the Department of Justice not to be torture. To make the point he demonstrated one of them, the open-hand facial slap, on Deputy DNI David Shedd.

Several months later I heard from several of Obama's top aides that the president-elect had reacted to the briefing in a way quite different from what Hayden had intended. It actually convinced the president of the impropriety of the techniques and cemented his view on what to do about them. On January 22, 2009, President Obama's second full day in office, he signed an executive order banning the use of all the enhanced techniques and ordering that any future interrogation by any government agency follow the rules laid out in the Army Field Manual. He also directed CIA to close any remaining detention facilities (which had been emptied in 2006) and never operate them again. Although it went largely unnoticed by the media, the president did an about-face on the practice of rendition. He subtly endorsed the continued use of renditions—calling them "short-term transfers"—but in doing so he required greater oversight from the executive branch.

In announcing the new approach to renditions, detentions, and interrogations, Obama made clear that he did not want to look backward at what the Bush administration had done. He wanted to move forward. He wanted to put the past behind us. Indeed, he had told George Stephanopoulos a few days before signing the executive orders that he was not interested in a broad investigation of Bush-era interrogation programs.

* * *

It quickly became clear that not looking in the rearview mirror was wishful thinking. Obama's first choice to be CIA director was John Brennan, the co-leader of the president-elect's transition team for the intelligence community and an advisor on national security issues to Obama when he was on the campaign trail. But Brennan had been the number four in the Agency's hierarchy when the detention and interrogation program was established in 2002, and human rights groups came out strongly against his nomination.

Brennan, not wanting to subject the president to an early nomination fight, withdrew his name from consideration. Obama instead brought Brennan into the White House to be his counterterrorism czar, a position that did not require Senate confirmation.

Obama then turned to Leon Panetta to be his chief spy. In his confirmation hearing to become the new CIA director, liberal members of the Senate Select Committee on Intelligence (SSCI) insisted on asking Panetta if he thought that waterboarding amounted to torture. Panetta said yes. CIA officers who had been involved in the program, and who had been assured by the Department of Justice that waterboarding was legal and not torture, were not happy. Panetta eventually won over these officers, but it was a rough start.

The look backward would continue in March 2009, when the SSCI decided by a vote of fourteen to one to do a review of CIA's defunct detention and interrogation program. Chairman of the Committee Dianne Feinstein and Vice Chairman Kit Bond, in a joint press statement, said that the purpose of the review was "to shape detention and interrogation policies in the future." They noted that the review would include a close look at documents, as well as interviews of Agency officials. Feinstein later told me that she was motivated by a strongly held view that it was morally wrong for the Agency to have used EITs, and that the Agency should never do so again, no matter who the president is. Feinstein said that she wanted the committee's report to be the nail in the coffin. The timing of the investigation reflected the fact that Feinstein had become chairman of the committee in January 2009.

* * *

Senator Feinstein is someone I got to know well during my time as deputy director. She has strongly held opinions on many issues. I have deep respect for her passion about national security and the importance of intelligence to keeping the country safe. There are few members of the Senate who can match her in these regards. She is also innovative. During Panetta's early tenure as director, she began what would become a series of "coffees" with the committee. Instead of the members' sitting on a dais with the director or me at the witness table, we would all sit around a table together. The atmosphere was much more informal and the dialogue much richer. Feinstein even brought coffee and doughnuts—Krispy Kreme glazed—to the sessions. These sessions were so successful in keeping the committee fully informed that the concept spread to the House Intelligence Committee.

I cannot overstate the importance of congressional oversight. Since CIA is a secret intelligence organization operating in a democracy, it is vitally important that CIA's two oversight committees—the Senate Select Committee on Intelligence and its House counterpart—satisfy themselves and make clear to the American people that CIA is operating within the law and that it is operating effectively.

During my seven-and-a-half years on CIA's senior leadership team, I saw ups and downs in our relationship with the committees for a variety of reasons. I believe it is the responsibility of both the leadership of CIA and the leadership of the committees to make the relationship work, but at the end of the day the onus is on the CIA director.

I saw the relationship work best under Leon Panetta. Panetta's approach was that he, I, and the rest of the leadership team—indeed, the entire Agency—should be completely open and forthcoming with the committee. When Congress believes—either accurately or inaccurately—that CIA is trying to hide something from them, things go downhill. Panetta also did the small things to help the relationship—for example, a phone call just to touch base or hosting a dinner in the director's dining room—all of which paid dividends.

* * *

Director Panetta, although opposed to the committee's study about CIA's detention and interrogation program, nonetheless gave the committee unprecedented access to Agency files. In short, the committee had access to almost everything—millions and millions of documents. But in return Panetta requested that the committee review the documents—analytic pieces, intelligence reports, operational cables, e-mails, and more—in CIA spaces. The documents contained some of CIA's most sensitive information—including information that possibly could lead someone to identify our sources. Thus began a bipartisan congressional review of the program.

A few months later, in August 2009, Attorney General Eric Holder joined the fray of those looking backward. DOJ's Office of Professional Responsibility (OPR) had just handed him a report—based on an independent review it had begun in 2008—that sharply criticized the legal judgment of the DOJ attorney who had written the memos authorizing the Agency's enhanced interrogation techniques, as well as the legal judgment of the attorney who had signed off on the memos. OPR had recommended to Holder that he take steps to hold the attorneys accountable for their poor work. Additionally it had recommended that he reopen earlier DOJ decisions not to pursue the prosecution of the handful of cases regarding potential abuse in the program that CIA had referred to the Bush Justice Department.

Holder had delegated the first recommendation to one of his senior aides to decide on (the attorney general eventually decided not to take any action against the attorneys), but he'd accepted the second recommendation. And on August 24 Holder announced that he was opening a preliminary investigation into whether any federal laws had been violated in CIA's interrogation of detainees. It was another blow to putting the entire episode behind us, and it felt like a punch in the stomach to the officers of CIA who had earlier had cases sent to the Justice Department for review. This certainly felt like double jeopardy, although it did not meet the legal definition.

Holder's decision also had an important impact on the SSCI review. Because the DOJ would be undertaking a criminal investigation, Director Panetta made clear that he would not compel current CIA employees to submit to interviews by the SSCI. This was exactly the right call on Panetta's part, but it meant that the SSCI would likely not hear from current CIA officers who had firsthand knowledge of how the programs had been managed and operated—although the committee still could have asked employees to voluntarily appear for interviews, and could have done the same with former officials, including Directors Tenet, Goss, and Hayden. But the committee never asked in either case, and it never asked to speak with employees after the DOJ investigation was completed—well before the committee's work was done.

The Republican minority on the committee, believing a thorough and fair review could not be done without interviews, pulled its staff off the review team. None of this did anything to dissuade the majority, and the committee's investigation continued. The study, at that point, ceased to be a committee effort; it was now only a Democratic majority effort.

In a somewhat reassuring development, Holder let it be known that no one would be prosecuted for actions that had been consistent with legal advice provided by the previous administration. His focus would be on anyone who might have gone beyond those authorities. Holder appointed John Durham as the special prosecutor. Durham knew the subject matter because he had been appointed by the Bush Justice Department to investigate an issue involving the destruction of videotapes of some of the Agency's debriefings of senior al Qa'ida operatives. But now he would be given access to an enormous amount of Agency records—every document ever produced regarding the detention and interrogation program—and to anyone whom he wanted to interview. There were now two separate inquiries under way about the detention and interrogation programs—which no longer existed.

* * *

The videotapes were the issue about which I first found myself thrust into the EIT issue. When EITs were first employed in the field, CIA officers, for reasons that have never been quite clear, decided it would be a good idea to videotape them. The officers soon decided, however, that videotaping was not such a wise plan and requested permission to destroy the tapes. The staff in the Counterterrorism Center and their bosses in the Directorate of Operations were in favor of destroying the tapes—but lawyers at CIA and the White House as well as other senior officials (eventually including CIA director Porter Goss and Director of National Intelligence John Negroponte) said, "Not so fast." This became a source of frustration and concern for a couple of years. CTC was worried because the faces of Agency officers were shown on the tapes; if the tapes ever leaked or were ever released, those officers' personal security could be in jeopardy. Also, during this time ugly images from Abu Ghraib prison made their way into the news. Although there was no similarity between the actions of rogue army reservists in Iraq and those of CIA officers employing fully authorized interrogation techniques on a handful of known terrorists, the distinction would be lost if the CIA images became public. There was no doubt that waterboarding did not make a pretty picture, and publication of those images would have had a devastating effect on CIA, damaged the reputation of the United States abroad, and undermined the security of US officials serving abroad.

Frustrated by the lack of action, on November 8, 2005, Jose

Rodriguez, the head of CIA's operational arm, the National Clandestine Service, took it upon himself to order that the tapes be destroyed. Two Agency lawyers had told him that there were no legal obstacles to doing so and that whether he did or not was a policy call. So, despite the opposition from his superiors—Goss and Negroponte—and from the senior lawyer at CIA and senior lawyers at the White House, Rodriguez ordered the destruction and then told the chain of command. Almost exactly two years later, news of his action leaked to the *New York Times*, and the subsequent firestorm of criticism in the media and in Congress led to the appointment of a special prosecutor, John Durham, to investigate the matter. After a three-year investigation Durham ruled that he did not have grounds to prosecute Rodriguez, as Rodriguez had been told he had the legal authority to destroy the tapes. Durham concluded, however, that such legal authority had not existed and that Agency lawyers had erred in their legal judgment. Durham recommended that CIA conduct an internal "accountability board" to examine the performance of the attorneys in the matter and to assess Rodriguez's performance as well.

CIA director David Petraeus gave the first task to the Agency's general counsel, and gave me, his deputy, the second task. Specifically, he asked me to chair an accountability board of senior officers to sit in judgment of Rodriguez's action. But given Rodriguez's past seniority, the ordeal he'd gone through while being investigated by Durham over three years, and the complexity of the subject, I elected to handle the assignment solo. That he was being subjected to another review came as something of a surprise to Rodriguez, who'd thought that Durham's decision ended the matter. I chose to break the news to him over a drink at a nearby hotel. I explained what the director had asked me to do, and how I'd decided to handle it. Rodriguez told me that he appreciated the way I was handling the matter and answered all my questions about what he'd done and why with thoroughness and honesty.

After reviewing the matter extensively over the course of a month or so, I had Rodriguez come to my office on December 21, 2011, to hear my decision. I told him that, although I knew he believed that he'd done the Agency and its officers a service by ordering the destruction of the tapes, I believed his action had been inappropriate. I told him that the written record made it clear that he'd known that his bosses, not to mention the White House counsel, did not want the tapes destroyed and that "no organization can function if its officers ignore the wishes of their superiors and just do what they think is right." I went on, "Jose, you would not have stood for it if people working under you took actions that they knew you were opposed to." I told him that, given all this, I had decided to issue him a letter of reprimand in order to send a signal to the workforce that the chain of command is sacrosanct. He thanked me again for the manner in which I'd handled the matter, but made it clear to me that he still believed his actions had been necessary and justified and therefore appropriate. I know he continues to believe that to this day. (Because this was an internal personnel matter, I asked for and obtained the permission of Rodriguez to tell this story.)

* * *

The first of the two inquiries to reach closure was the Justice Department's. In late June 2011, Attorney General Holder announced the results of the preliminary investigation by John Durham. Holder said publicly what I had already known via private conversations— that Durham had examined every single interaction that CIA had had with any detainee and that his review had examined whether any unauthorized interrogation techniques had been used by CIA officers, and if so, whether such techniques had constituted a violation of the torture statute or any other applicable statute.

After two years of investigation, Durham decided that only two matters—the deaths of two detainees—required a full criminal investigation. These cases are well known publicly, but for legal reasons I am not permitted to discuss them here. Importantly, Durham determined that an expanded criminal investigation was not warranted in any other interrogation matter.

Just a year later—in August 2012—Durham concluded the investigation into the two detainee deaths, announcing that he would not be filing any charges in either case. But this was not a complete exoneration—as not only had two people died, but Durham told Director Petraeus and me that if the statute of limitations had not run out, he would likely have brought criminal charges in the two cases (even though DOJ had declined prosecution in these two cases when the deaths were first brought to its attention years earlier).

Next was the SSCI study—still very much a Democratic staff report. In the late fall of 2012, after more than three years of effort, committee staffers declared that they were done. A six-thousand-plus-page report and a five-hundred-plus-page "summary and conclusions" were submitted to the committee. Chairman Feinstein wanted to vote on the report in December. The timing was critical. While almost all Republicans on the committee were opposed to the way the investigation had been conducted, and therefore to the report itself, Senator Olympia Snowe, a Republican from Maine, was supportive of it. But she was going to retire at the end of the then-current Congress, only days away. So Senator Feinstein wanted to hold a vote while Snowe was still in office so that an endorsement of the investigation could not strictly be called a "party line" vote.

Feinstein left nothing to chance and invited Harry Reid, who as senate majority leader was an ex officio member of the committee, to attend and address the assembled senators. This was a highly unusual move. Indeed, I am not aware of another case where the

senate majority leader has attended a committee meeting. I have
been told that Reid advised the assembled senators that the report—
which neither he nor many (if any) of the other members had read
in full—was the most important piece of intelligence oversight since
the Pike Committee report in the 1970s. I have also been told that
the senate minority leader, Mitch McConnell, was unaware that
Reid had been invited and was later furious that he had not been
extended the same courtesy. The report was approved by a vote of
nine to six—along strict party lines, with the exception of Snowe.

Sitting in my office over a weekend, I read the summary and
conclusions of the report. It was stunning both in its scope and in
the depth of its condemnation of CIA activities involving al Qa'ida
detainees. It made a number of significant charges, including that
(1) the interrogations during which enhanced interrogations were
employed did not produce intelligence of unique value; (2) CIA had
frequently gone beyond the techniques authorized by the Department of Justice; (3) CIA had mismanaged the program throughout
its history; and (4) CIA had repeatedly misled the White House, the
Justice Department, Congress, and the American public about the
program (the report's unstated implication was that the CIA lied).
I remember thinking, "If even half of this is true, this is awful."
The report was compelling—well written, its judgments seemingly
backed up by facts, and heavily footnoted. It made me wonder what
the truth really was, as the allegations did not sound like the Agency
where I had worked for thirty years and was then leading. I vowed
to withhold judgment until I saw the Agency's review of the report.

Our response was well considered. I was acting director at the
time and I put our best officers on the project—but no one who
had been personally involved in the program. I took my own chief
of staff, Greg Tarbell, one of the most analytically brilliant officers
at the Agency, off-line for several weeks to thoroughly scrub our
response. Greg had large sheets of paper taped to the walls of his

office in his attempt to keep track of the all the facts in each of the SSCI's conclusions and case studies.

As our officers were coming to closure on their views of the report, I was beginning to receive updates on what they were finding—and it was not flattering to the authors of the SSCI study. They found that the report had correctly pointed out that the Agency had not managed the program well in its early days, which had resulted in the mistreatment of some detainees and the death of one. But they also found that the report had failed to credit the Agency for the steps it had taken to investigate and correct these management problems. And they found serious flaws in most of the report's other conclusions. In particular, they concluded that the committee's analysis about the effectiveness of the program was seriously flawed and that the Agency had indeed generated a treasure trove of intelligence.

I believe that the SSCI staff that produced the committee's study did a great disservice to the committee, the Central Intelligence Agency, and the country. It appears to me that the staffers wrote the report that they thought their political masters wanted to see. Their prosecutor's brief was intended to figuratively go for the death penalty. I believe they fell in love with material that appeared to confirm what they wanted to see and found ways of explaining away facts that did not fit their narrative.

Senator Feinstein also bears significant responsibility for the many flaws in the report. She made her very strong views on the appropriateness of CIA's program known to her staff—a step that undoubtedly made it difficult for those writing a report to be objective. This is an error that even the most junior of managers of analysis at CIA would never make. And Senator Feinstein was told on numerous occasions about the serious flaws in the report—including by me several times. At one meeting, I walked her through specific examples in the report of errors of fact, errors of logic, and errors of context (the latter situation is where the presented facts are accurate but other missing facts are necessary to understand the issue). And I pointed out that the examples were just the tip of the iceberg. I told her the report was riddled with such mistakes.

Errors of fact: Page six of the report's Findings and Conclusions reads "The CIA restricted access to information about the program from members of the Committee beyond the chairman and vice chairman until September 6, 2006..." Wrong. The CIA did not restrict access; the White House did. There is also an error of context here: Although the report's declassified Executive Summary includes a 17-page section on CIA's interactions with Congress, nowhere does it make clear that some of the committee leaders who were briefed, including SSCI Chairman Pat Roberts and HPSCI Chairman Porter Goss, supported limiting knowledge of the program only to the leadership. They did not want their members briefed either.

Errors of logic: The report's very first finding reads: "The CIA's use of its enhanced interrogation techniques was not an effective means of acquiring intelligence or gaining cooperation from detainees." Here is the first example provided to support that judgment: "... seven of the 39 CIA detainees known to have been subjected to the CIA's enhanced interrogation techniques produced no intelligence while in CIA custody." Hmm. Does that mean that thirty-two of thirty-nine did produce intelligence? Sounds like an argument that EITs worked, not the other way around.

Errors of context: In arguing that the CIA impeded congressional oversight of the program, the report states "The CIA did not brief the leadership of the Senate Select Committee on the CIA's enhanced interrogation techniques until September 2002, after the techniques had been approved and used." That is true, and it sounds bad. But the report conveniently left out some other interesting facts that shed a different light on this issue. The report does not say that

EITs were first used on Abu Zubaydah just a month prior to the first Congressional briefing, *while the Congress was on summer recess.* Although CIA can and does occasionally brief urgent issues to select Congressional leaders during recesses, it is not hard to understand why CIA decided to wait just a few weeks until those leaders could be briefed face-to-face on such a complex and sensitive issue. Hardly withholding information from Congress.

These multiple types of errors occur throughout the report's thousands of pages. Most of the errors are ones that even a smart high school student would not make. Many, including me, have said publicly that the report is deeply flawed. These are the reasons why. The report is not *the* history of the program that Senator Feinstein has said it is; it is one of the worst pieces of analysis that this thirty-three-year veteran of analysis at CIA has ever seen.

* * *

Never has a program generated such controversy and debate. Was it legal or was it torture? Was it effective or not? Was it necessary or not? Was it the right thing to do or not? Given that the program was one of the CIA's main responses to 9/11 and to the further threat posed by Bin Ladin and al Qa'ida, I would like to weigh in on the subject.

The first point to make is that we are actually talking about two different programs. One is the detainee program—CIA's establishment of secret prisons around the world where we held high-value detainees. And the second is the use of enhanced interrogation techniques—harsh measures—to extract information that detainees were otherwise unwilling to provide. This is an important distinction because you can have the detention program without the EIT program. To blur this distinction, as the Committee's report does, is to do history a disservice. Each needs to be addressed separately.

The second point is that context is everything. In order to thoughtfully consider the program, it is very important to understand what the key decision-makers at the time—President Bush, National Security Advisor Condi Rice, and Director Tenet—were facing every day.

My last official action aboard Air Force One on 9/11 was to brief President Bush regarding an intelligence report that George Tenet's staff at CIA had just sent me. While the credibility of the source was unknown, the information itself was stunning but believable given what had occurred fewer than twelve hours earlier. The report, provided to us by one of the many foreign intelligence services with which we work closely, indicated that al Qa'ida had prepared a second wave of attacks. This possibility was already in everyone's mind, but here it was in black and white. The president read the report very closely, handed it back to me, and simply said, "Thank you, Michael."

This report began what became an avalanche—literally thousands—of intelligence reports in the months following 9/11 that strongly indicated that al Qa'ida would hit us again in the homeland.

Some of these reports talked about the possible use of weapons of mass destruction by al Qa'ida—chemical weapons, biological weapons, and even crude nuclear devices. This too was believable, as it matched pre-9/11 reporting on the group's interest in such weapons and was consistent with post-9/11 reporting about Bin Ladin meeting with Pakistani nuclear scientists, and with what we were learning from now having access to al Qa'ida's former training camps in Afghanistan. What we were finding there included hands-on research into poisons and crude chemical weapons and, most worrisome, work on producing anthrax, a deadly biological weapon. Just a small amount of anthrax—a single gram—contains a hundred million lethal doses. If produced and disseminated effectively, a small amount of anthrax released in the fast-moving air of a subway system could kill hundreds of thousands of people.

It was the longest sustained period of significant threat reporting that I experienced in my fifteen years of working the al Qa'ida issue. We were certain we were going to be attacked again. During the five-minute walk from Tenet's "downtown" office in the Old Executive Office Building to the West Wing of the White House, Tenet and I, aware of all the intelligence, would routinely ask each other, "Is today the day we get hit again?" I seriously thought a nuclear detonation in New York or Washington was a possibility—to the point of telling my wife (we were living near Dulles Airport at the time, some thirty miles west of D.C.) that if such an attack were to happen in Washington to put the kids in the car and start driving west and not stop. It was surreal.

This reporting—reinforced by Richard Reid's attempt to bring down an American Airlines flight from Paris to Miami in late December 2001—put tremendous pressure on the White House in general and on CIA in particular to prevent another attack. Most important, it was impossible to forget for an instant that three thousand people had been killed in a little over an hour by only nineteen terrorists. And now we had reporting that another such tragedy, or even worse, might be right around the corner.

This deluge of threat reporting coincided with the capture of Abu Zubaydah in March 2002. Zubaydah had extensive knowledge of al Qa'ida personnel and operations. While briefly cooperative, Zubaydah, under standard interrogation techniques, later became defiant and evasive. It was clear that he was holding back information—information that could foil attacks and possibly save lives.

It was in this context that professional intelligence officers in CIA's Counterterrorism Center came to the leadership of the Agency and recommended using a set of harsh interrogation techniques. In short, they walked into the director's office and said, "If we do not use these techniques, Americans are going to die." This statement was not hyperbole. It was exactly what our officers thought, and there was good reason to think it. Once convinced, George Tenet had a similar conversation with the White House, and the interrogation program was born.

Where did the idea originate for using the particular set of techniques that was the program—attention grasp, walling, facial hold, facial slap, cramped confinement, insects, wall standing, stress positions, sleep deprivation, and waterboarding? They came from two psychologists—contractors working for the Agency—who helped train US servicemen to resist harsh interrogations if captured on the battlefield and who, in providing such training, learned that certain techniques were effective in getting people to a state of compliance in responding to questions. These were the techniques that the contractors suggested to CIA when it became clear that the most hardened and ideologically committed al Qa'ida operatives would not cooperate.

* * *

The CIA detention program—the creation of our own prisons, known as "black sites"—occurred somewhat earlier. We and our allies were capturing individuals we believed were aware of future plots, as well as the whereabouts of other senior leaders who were plotting against America. We needed to be able to hold terrorists indefinitely and question them in secret, controlled interrogations during which we could use information from other sensitive sources of intelligence, especially from other detainees, as leverage. No other options considered at the time filled the bill, so we proposed a new option: create our own detention system, where we could ask them any question we wanted at any time. We could also monitor them continuously to acquire any intelligence they might disclose in conversations with other detainees. The sites were set up with the knowledge and cooperation of the host governments, who wanted our thanks, some financial support, and our silence. While we delivered on the first two promises, we, as a country, were not able to deliver on the third.

* * *

The second point is that the detention and interrogation program was not some rogue CIA operation that might be depicted in a Hollywood movie. CIA proposed the program but undertook it only with the explicit approval of the White House.

In a conversation with Senator Feinstein after her staff completed its report on the program, she was surprised when Director Brennan and I told her that President Bush had been aware of the program. After the Senate committee spent tens of millions of dollars and four years on its investigation, its leader was unaware that the president of the United States had signed off on the program. Her staff had gone through millions of documents, but somehow no one had thought to read President Bush's memoirs, where he states clearly that he approved the detention and interrogation program.

CIA also briefed Congress on the program—initially only the leadership of the intelligence committees and then later the entire committees. There were roughly forty separate briefings with Congress. Through early 2005, none of the leadership who was briefed (eight different members over time) opposed the program (one member wanted to make sure that the White House had indeed approved the program). There was either approval or in some cases concern that CIA was not going far enough in trying to obtain information from detainees. When CIA in early 2004 temporarily stopped the use of EITs because it wanted to ensure that the program was still legal in the face of changes in the law (which the Agency did several times), Senator Jay Rockefeller, the ranking member on the Senate Intelligence Committee, scolded the Agency for being risk averse.

I believe the reason members of Congress reacted the way they did was because they understood the threat picture. They were briefed on it regularly. They felt the threat from al Qa'ida as acutely as did the Bush administration. Senator Rockefeller told Wolf Blitzer on CNN following the capture of KSM, "He'll be grilled by us... I'm sure we'll be very very tough with him... He does have the information. Getting that information will save American lives. We have no business not getting that information."

And Senator Feinstein herself, who was not one of the members of Congress initially briefed on the program, said in 2002, "I have no doubt that had it not been for 9/11... that it would have been business as usual. It took that real attack, I think, to kind of shiver our timbers enough to let us know that the threat is profound, that we have to do some things that historically we have not wanted to do to protect ourselves."

The third point is about the legality of the program. Were EITs legal? As the review by DOJ's Office of Professional Responsibility showed, whether the Department of Justice's Office of Legal Counsel (which is charged with providing legal advice to the president and all executive branch agencies) made the right legal call at the time is open to debate. It is hard to know with any certainty what the Supreme Court would have said if the matter had come before it. But what is very important to remember is that, at the time the EITs were being used, the Department of Justice told CIA that they were legal. Period. Full stop. The techniques, including waterboarding, were deemed by the Department of Justice not to be a violation of domestic law or US treaty obligations. They were deemed NOT to be torture. So, from a legal perspective, to call what CIA officers did at the time "torture" is wrong and does those officers a great disservice.

And the legal judgment by the Department of Justice was not just a one-time decision. This judgment was reinforced again and again through *multiple* legal opinions—many of them sought by the Agency as the legislative landscape changed and senior CIA leaders worked to assure that the Department of Justice and White House agreed that CIA and its officers were operating within the law.

The fourth point is about effectiveness. There is no doubt in my mind that the enhanced techniques were effective. Why do I believe this? Because of the SSCI report and the Agency's response to it, my last months as deputy director involved my studying this issue in great detail. I read case study after case study in which detainees, before being subjected to EITs, provided limited, vague, and general information, and after being subjected to EITs became cooperative, providing much more specific and detailed information.

The best example is that of 9/11 mastermind Khalid Sheikh Mohammed. KSM's demeanor and cooperativeness before and after enhanced interrogation techniques could not have been greater. Before EITs, he was fiercely defiant and unwilling to talk. After the techniques, he was more cooperative and willing to talk, which allowed knowledgeable debriefers and analysts to elicit valuable information despite his lingering efforts to evade and dissemble.

The result was a treasure trove of critically important information. KSM provided information regarding a number of plots he had been working on prior to his capture. One was a plot to blow up the Brooklyn Bridge. After he became cooperative, KSM revealed al Qa'ida's longstanding interest in bringing down suspension bridges in the United States. He specified the methods of destroying such bridges that al Qa'ida taught its recruits. And, most important, he said he had instructed Iyman Faris, a naturalized American citizen from Kashmir, to destroy the Brooklyn Bridge. KSM's information helped debriefers elicit more detail on Faris from another detainee, and all that information was fed to the FBI. Bureau agents already had Faris on their radar, but they were now better armed to press him about his terrorist plans and connections. He was eventually arrested, indicted, and convicted on terrorism charges. He is serving a twenty-year sentence.

Then there is the Bin Ladin operation. The first person to tell us about Abu Ahmed, the person who harbored Bin Ladin at Abbottabad, was a terrorist who was being detained by another country. This led us to ask our detainees about Abu Ahmed, and both CIA detainees subjected to EITs and those not subjected to EITs talked about him. But there is no doubt in my mind that information generated by EITs led us to push Abu Ahmed to the top of the list of leads we were pursuing on Bin Ladin. The most specific information on Abu Ahmed came from a detainee after he was subjected to EITs. And it was KSM and Abu Faraj's dissembling about Abu Ahmed—after they had been subjected to EITs and were more willing to talk—that really put the spotlight on Abu Ahmed. At a time when they were willing to provide information about the roles of various al Qa'ida personnel, especially when they could see that we already knew something about them, the fact that they were going out of their way to lie about Abu Ahmed led us to figure that he must be *really* important.

To put it bluntly: without the overall detention program, we would not have caught Bin Ladin the way we did. The detention program was a necessary condition for the success of the Bin Ladin operation. And the enhanced interrogation program resulted in our putting more resources on the lead than we would have otherwise. Whether EITs were essential or not, I do not know. But they certainly helped focus attention on the man who would eventually take us to Bin Ladin's doorstep.

In addition to information that helped disrupt specific plots and bring senior al Qa'ida operatives to justice, detainees—particularly KSM—also provided a large amount of information on the organization itself—allowing analysts to better understand al Qa'ida, and giving our operatives clues to what would undermine the group and its capabilities.

The fifth point is about necessity. While effective, were EITs necessary to get this critically important information or were there other, perhaps less harsh, ways to do so? Although the CIA officers on the front lines in this program believe that EITs were absolutely necessary, the Agency, including when I was acting director, has repeatedly said that this is something we will never know for sure. In retrospect, I believe this refrain is too cute by half. Yes, of course, necessity is an unknowable thing. But it is, I think, almost an irrelevant point as necessity is almost always unknowable, including with regard to tough national security decisions. Was detonating atomic bombs over Hiroshima and Nagasaki necessary to force Japan's timely surrender in World War II? We will never know for sure. Was Abraham Lincoln's suspension of habeas corpus necessary for the North to win the Civil War? We will never know for sure. As with these issues, historians will debate the necessity of EITs for quite a long time, and they should indeed do so.

This brings us to the last point. While the techniques were legal, effective, and at least thought to be necessary, were they the right thing to do? Was it moral to subject another human being to harsh interrogation techniques—even though they were considered not to be torture by the Department of Justice? This is a question on which reasonable people can disagree.

The Senate report on EITs gives the reader the impression that no one in the Bush administration ever considered this difficult question. That is wrong; it was considered. Senior CIA officials at the time knew, with certainty, for example, that they would face tough criticism someday because of the harshness of the techniques but they thought them necessary to protect the country. And, at one meeting of the president's national security team in early 2003, the Agency's senior lawyer, Scott Muller, raised the question of whether people were comfortable with EITs given the administration's public statements that the United States was treating detainees humanely. After the meeting, Muller wrote, "Everyone in the room evinced understanding of the issue. CIA's past and ongoing use of enhanced interrogation techniques was reaffirmed and in no way drawn into question."

When it comes to EITs, there are two key aspects to the morality question. Is it moral to subject other human beings, no matter how evil they are, to harsh interrogation techniques, particularly when done by the country that stands for human dignity and human rights in the world? At the same time, what is the morality of not doing so? What is the morality of believing that, if you do not use the harsh techniques, you may well be making a decision that leads to the death of Americans in a terrorist attack that you could have otherwise prevented? These are complicated and extremely tough difficult questions. Some people make them sound easy. They are wrong. The Senate report did not, in any way, address this most difficult of issues.

* * *

People frequently ask me what I would have done had I been the decision-maker, had I been the director of CIA at the time. The honest answer is that I do not know. And I don't believe those who say that they know with certainty that they would have said no. I think it is very difficult for those who were not in the situation at that time to know what they would have done when confronted by the same set of facts with which President Bush, Condi Rice, and George Tenet were presented—because the situation was so unusual. I think that people who say that they know exactly what they would have done are not being honest with themselves.

Shortly after leaving government, I gave an interview to the television news show *60 Minutes* in which my views on this complex subject were boiled down to a couple of sentences. I said in the interview that the EITs were not torture but that the techniques were inconsistent with American values and that for that reason I didn't think they should have been done. As is often the case with television, a simple sound bite cannot convey a highly nuanced view.

In the interview I was referring to one specific technique—waterboarding. I was not referring to the entire suite of techniques. I believe that one has to have the morality discussion about each individual technique, and that is exactly what the Bush administration did. After CIA presented a range of possible techniques to the White House, National Security Advisor Rice told us one of the techniques crossed the White House's moral line and it was not to be used. The judgments on the morality of individual techniques will, of course, vary from person to person.

I am personally troubled by waterboarding. When I served as acting director and deputy director, I made decisions about right and wrong in a very simple way. I would say yes to a CIA operation only if I believed I could, as an American, be proud that CIA had conducted the operation if it leaked and was on the front page of the *Washington Post*. With this litmus test, I believe the less severe techniques were perfectly appropriate. For example, I could in good conscience tell the American people that grabbing senior al Qaʿida terrorists by the collar when they were not paying attention during an interrogation session, or even denying them sleep for prolonged periods, were the right things to do. At the same time, I have doubts that I could in good conscience tell the American people that waterboarding someone was the right thing to do. So in terms of the techniques, I believe—but again I cannot say for sure—that I would have drawn the line in a different place, all the time knowing that others, using the same litmus test, might draw it in yet another place.

But here is my moral dilemma. Based on my review of the program—done as I oversaw the Agency's response to the Senate report—I believe that waterboarding was one of the two most effective of all the harsh techniques (the other being sleep deprivation). That complicates things. Doesn't it?

* * *

After months of wrangling among the White House, CIA, and the Senate Intelligence Committee over how much of the committee's executive summary could be released without putting national security at risk, the report was finally made public on December 9, 2014.

The press coverage was as ugly as it was predictable. Most of the attention was devoted to the most graphic descriptions of activities at some of the secret prisons. Little notice was given to the fact that most of the examples of mistreatment were those few cases where CIA officers had gone beyond what the Justice Department had authorized. In all these cases, CIA reported the mistreatment to its own inspector general, to the Department of Justice, and to Congress a decade before. Each had been investigated by DOJ—twice. The Senate report gave the impression that such mistreatment was widespread, occurred throughout the eight years of the program, and had been uncovered by Senate investigators. All of these impressions are wrong.

What was especially troublesome to me was the fact that most news organizations paid scant attention, if any, to either the report of the SSCI minority or to the CIA report—both of which debunked much of what the SSCI majority staff had written, most important its judgments about the efficacy of the program and the honesty with which CIA spoke about the program to the rest of the executive branch and to Congress. In short, most of the media, including reporters, commentators, and editorial writers, accepted the Senate's findings as the truth—without any questioning. It was not the fourth estate's finest hour.

In addition, there was little interest on the part of the media in two key issues that were not discussed or inaccurately portrayed in the Senate report—the circumstances that led the Bush administration and CIA to believe that harsh techniques were necessary or the lengthy paper trail that showed that the White House, Justice

Department, and Congress were fully briefed on it. A history of CIA's interactions with the rest of the executive branch and with Congress on the issue of EITs that was released by the CIA at the same time as the committee's report was completely ignored by the media.

A number of senior CIA alumni—notably former director Mike Hayden, former deputy director John McLaughlin, former senior attorney John Rizzo, and former clandestine service chief Jose Rodriguez were active in the media trying to set the record straight against a narrative that Senate staffers had been preparing the press to hear for months (the committee staff actually provided the report to reporters several days before its release so that the reporters could have their first pieces ready to go following Senator's press conference on the issue). Other former officials, led by George Tenet, created a highly trafficked website called CIASAVEDLIVES.com that brought together in one place key documents about the program. They continue to add materials to the website.

For their part, the American people shrugged the whole thing off. In polls taken after the Senate report was released and after days of the media hyping its findings, the majority of Americans said that they supported the use of harsh interrogation techniques in order to protect the lives of their fellow citizens. This view was consistent across a number of polls that were conducted.

*   *   *

The sun was setting on Florida's Gulf Coast. It was late afternoon, and I was at a beach party in Naples, Florida, where my in-laws live. It was my first Christmas holiday after retiring from CIA. It was my first family trip in years without a team of security officers and communications officers. I was not thinking about CIA, national security, or any aspect of my past life.

I tend not to like parties because I do not enjoy reception-style small talk. But on this particular evening, I was introduced to someone quite interesting. One of the guests at the party was a long-time constitutional law professor from one of the nation's most elite law schools. He had taught constitutional law for decades. Knowing that I had recently participated in President Obama's Review Group on Intelligence and Communications Technologies, the professor asked me a number of questions. He was very interested in the National Security Agency's telephone metadata program and our group's recommendations regarding it.

But I was interested in his views on enhanced interrogation techniques, which were also in the news as a result of the brewing controversy over the SSCI report. In one of the most interesting conversations I have ever had on the issue, the professor told me that he thought some of the techniques were indeed unlawful and that the Department of Justice had erred in its judgment. He also told me that he thought that many of the techniques were inconsistent with America's support for human dignity and America's leadership role in the world. And so, he concluded, he was opposed to the use of the techniques. Then came the punch line. He said "Opposed, that is, unless I were the president of the United States, and someone walked into my office and said this is the only way to prevent a massive terrorist attack that might kill hundreds or thousands of Americans. In that case, if the decision were placed on my shoulders, I would say go for it. And then I would stand up and tell the American people the decision I had made and why I made it and accept the consequences."

To me, the law professor was in a sense describing a Lincoln moment. During the Civil War, President Lincoln violated a number of the first ten amendments to the Constitution—principles in which he believed deeply—because he thought it necessary to save the Union. What must be stressed is that these perilous decisions cannot be made at low levels. In the case of the EITs, they were not. The highest levels of the US government in both the executive branch and Congress were engaged—as they should have been.

* * *

In discussing the EIT issue, a senior British official recently told me about an incident that occurred in World War II. In June 1940 a ship named RMS *Lancastria* was evacuating British troops and civilians from France. An estimated six thousand to nine thousand people were aboard when a German bomber sank the ship, killing four thousand to seven thousand people. Prime Minister Winston Churchill directed that the news be withheld from the British people and the official records were ordered sealed until the year 2040. Clearly, hiding so many deaths was not the right thing to do—and Churchill knew it, but he felt that the British people could not withstand that much bad news, and for the good of the country, he kept it from them. While the decision to employ the EITs was a much different matter, I understand why those making the decision believed it was the right thing to do.

CHAPTER 12

Breach of Trust

An employee of the Central Intelligence Agency liked to frequent chat rooms. His online persona was TheTrueHOOHA. Here is a chat from January 2009:

> **TheTrueHOOHA:** HOLY SHIT
> http://www.nytimes.com/2009/01/11/washington
> /11iran.html?_r=1&hp
> [a reference to a *New York Times* article on purported US operations in Iran]
>
> **TheTrueHOOHA:** WTF NYTIMES?
> Are they TRYING to start a war?
> Jesus Christ
> They're like wikileaks
>
> *User19:* they're just reporting dude.
>
> **TheTrueHOOHA:** They're reporting classified shit.
>
> **TheTrueHOOHA:** moreover, who the fuck are the anonymous sources telling them this?
>
> **TheTrueHOOHA:** those people should be shot in the balls.

TheTrueHOOHA: I wonder how many hundreds of millions of dollars they just completely blew?

TheTrueHOOHA: these are the same people who blew the whole "we could listen to osama's cell phone" thing the same people who screwed us on wiretapping and over and over again. Thank god they're going out of business.

User19: the NYT?

TheTrueHOOHA: Hopefully they'll finally go bankrupt this year.
Yeah.

An exchange a few minutes later:

User19: is it unethical to report on government intrigue?

TheTrueHOOHA: VIOLATING NATIONAL SECURITY. No

User19: meh.
national security

TheTrueHOOHA: Um, YEEEEEEEEEEEES

TheTrueHOOHA: that shit is classified for a reason

TheTrueHOOHA: it's not because "oh we hope our citizens don't find out"

TheTrueHOOHA: it's because "this shit won't work if Iran knows what we're doing."

TheTrueHOOHA was the online persona of Edward Snowden.

* * *

In the preface to this book, I explained how my final weeks as deputy director were consumed with a credible and serious threat from al Qaʻidaʼs number one franchise—AQAP. Along with that threat, my final weeks in the job were also filled with another major issue. On June 5, 2013, the UKʼs *Guardian* newspaper carried a report claiming the NSA was collecting the phone records of millions of Verizon customers daily. This, of course, was a reference to the now-declassified telephony metadata program, which operates under provisions of the Patriot Act.

Under this program the telephone companies, operating under a broad court order, provided to the NSA the following information for calls made to and from US phone numbers—the number that initiated the call, the number that was called, the time of the call, and the duration of the call. The phone companies did not provide the NSA with the identities of the callers or the content of the call—what was actually said in the conversation. It was akin to sharing what is on the outside of a letterʼs envelope—minus any names—without sharing what is inside the envelope.

The next day the *Washington Post* ran a story saying that the NSA was intercepting the e-mail communications of persons overseas as the messages passed through the United States. This program, which operates under Section 702 of the Foreign Intelligence Surveillance Act, focused on collecting foreign-to-foreign communications that, because of the nature of the Internet, ran through the United States.

Within four days the *Guardian* revealed that its source had been a young man named Edward Snowden. Through the *Guardian*, Snowden told his story—saying that he had become increasingly concerned about the massive NSA surveillance aimed at the public both in the United States and overseas, that he wanted there to be an open debate on the issue, and that he had taken documents from his job at the NSA in order to demonstrate his concern. Snowden said he had fled to Hong Kong on May 20.

Snowden had been an NSA contractor since 2009, working as a systems administrator. His most recent job had been at an NSA facility in Hawaii. And although he was an NSA contractor at the time of his flight to Hong Kong, we quickly learned that Snowden had worked for CIA from 2006 to 2009. Prior to that he had worked as a security specialist at the Center for Advanced Study of Language—a partnership between the University of Maryland and the intelligence community. This is where he received his first security clearance.

At a briefing in mid-June, Director Brennan and I made clear that we needed to know a number of things—as soon as possible. One, were there CIA documents or information in the materials that Snowden had stolen from the NSA? Two, had he stolen any classified information when he served at CIA? Three, how had he gotten a job at CIA and what were the circumstances of his departure in 2009, when he left to become a contractor for the NSA? And four, was Snowden working with any foreign intelligence service— either wittingly or not?

The first issue—had he stolen any CIA information while at the NSA—proved maddeningly difficult at first. Snowden's principal victim, the NSA, was understandably distraught at the massive security breach and initially refused to let CIA officers be part of its security review. It took a phone call from me to Chris Inglis, the NSA deputy director at Fort Meade (the NSA's headquarters), to break through that barrier. Inglis, an outstanding intelligence officer and friend, understood the importance of my request immediately, and simply said, "I'll take care of it." Once CIA officers were given access, the news was not good. Snowden, a clever but relatively low-level computer systems administrator, had figured out how to access millions of documents. It was not clear what documents had been taken—but the scope and range of the potential loss was enormous. And as Agency officers sifted through the information to which Snowden had had access, they discovered that among the documents at risk were not just NSA secrets but CIA secrets as well.

On the issue of whether Snowden stole classified information while he worked at CIA, I am not permitted to provide the answer that was briefed to me, because of concerns about the national security implications if this information were disclosed.

I can say more about the questions involving Snowden's CIA employment. Amazingly, in 2006, this high school dropout with a GED and less than five months in the US Army Reserve—where he did not complete basic training—was hired by CIA to be a telecommunications support officer, or TISO (pronounced *tee-so*)—an important job that ensures that our officers can communicate securely with one another no matter where they are on the planet. Snowden had self-taught computer skills but little else going for him. At the time the Agency was still in the middle of a massive buildup in the aftermath of 9/11, and one of the areas of greatest need was TISOs. This is why Snowden got hired.

Snowden's employment application, work performance, and behaviors created concerns at the Agency—including security concerns. Snowden was aware of this, and he departed the Agency before they could be resolved and before the Agency could take any action against him. So the guy with whom CIA had concerns left the Agency and joined the ranks of the many contractors working in the intelligence community—before CIA could inform the rest of the IC of its worries. He even got a pay raise. He was working on the rolls of Dell and later Booz Allen Hamilton for the NSA.

On the fourth major question for us—the issue of possible foreign intelligence involvement with Snowden—we learned some very interesting things that I am not permitted to share. I can say that when Snowden stopped first in Chinese-controlled Hong Kong and later in Russia there is no doubt that the intelligence services of those countries had an enormous interest in him and the information he had stolen. Both the Chinese and the Russians would have used everything in their tool kits—from human approaches to technical attacks—to get at Snowden's stolen data as well as simply what he knew about the intelligence community.

My own view on this question is that both Chinese and Russian intelligence officers undoubtedly pitched him—offering him millions of dollars to share the documents he had stolen and to answer any questions they had about the NSA and CIA. But my guess is that Snowden said, "No, thank you," given his mind-set and his clear dislike for intelligence services of any stripe. My concern, however, is that Snowden may have unwittingly led the Chinese or, more likely, the Russians to his treasure chest of documents. Snowden thinks he is smart, but he was never in a position in his previous jobs to fully understand the immense capabilities of our Russian and Chinese counterparts and therefore not smart enough to realize when and how he might be being used.

This is not even to mention the interest that the Chinese and Russians would obviously have in the reporters to whom Snowden provided classified information. They too are undoubtedly targets of the Chinese, Russians, and others. To their credit, these reporters have refused to publish some of the most sensitive information in their possession. But not publishing it and protecting it from intelligence services are two completely different things. How well they have protected such information is open to question. They too do not understand the capabilities of our adversaries.

* * *

In my last week as deputy director I got a call from Denis McDonough, who in early 2013 had been promoted to be the president's chief of staff. "The president is thinking of putting together a commission to look into some of the issues raised as a result of the Snowden leaks. He'd like you to be a member." I promised to give the request some thought, and I discussed it with one of my mentors, a veteran of the intelligence community.

"Are you nuts?" the mentor asked. "You are about to become a civilian for the first time in thirty-three years." The last thing that I ought to do, he suggested, was agree to join a presidential commission. "Denis promises that it won't be that onerous," I told the mentor. "Yeah, that's what they always say," he advised. "Somebody needs to do this job, Michael, but as your friend, I'm telling you that it does not need to be you."

I did not follow my mentor's advice. In the end I decided that I could not say no to the president and to McDonough. And I could not say no given the enormous damage that Snowden had done to national security. So I found myself, before I was even off the government payroll, serving as a member of the president's Review Group on Intelligence and Communications Technologies. Joining me on the group were three renowned law professors—Geof Stone from the University of Chicago, Cass Sunstein from Harvard, and Peter Swire from Georgia Tech. Also on the panel was Dick Clarke, a former senior government official with immense experience in terrorism, cyber security, and other national security issues. My mentor, of course, had in large measure been right. The panel soon took up much more time than McDonough had promised.

Operating from a federal office building on K Street in D.C., I began digging into the issue. The first thing that struck me was that there were a handful of causes of the "Snowden affair," which I defined as Snowden's successful theft over time of vast amounts of significant information coupled with the sharp negative reaction at home and abroad to the NSA's work. The first cause was, ironically, the enormous success of the National Security Agency in collecting information. Government agencies usually get in trouble for failing to do their jobs. In this case the NSA got in trouble, at least in part, for doing its job, as Snowden had in part been motivated by the breadth and depth of the NSA's collection capabilities.

I would argue that in the decade after 9/11, of all the agencies that make up the US intelligence community, none was more successful than the National Security Agency. And that is a significant statement for a CIA officer to make, because there is a bit of professional rivalry among intelligence organizations. In fact, I was a little chagrined by how well the NSA was doing relative to the Agency. The amount of critical intelligence the NSA was collecting was staggering, and that agency was—and remains—the collector of some of the most important pieces of the intelligence puzzle presented to the president and national security decision-makers every day.

It is important to note that all of the NSA operations that resulted in this treasure trove of intelligence collection were approved by the executive branch and overseen by Congress. Some of the operations were even overseen by the Foreign Intelligence Surveillance Court, made up of federal judges appointed by the chief justice of the Supreme Court. And the NSA did not disseminate anything to the rest of the intelligence community and to policy-makers that they had not been asked to collect by a rigorous requirement process managed by the director of national intelligence (DNI). In short, the NSA was not in any way acting as a rogue agency. Rather, it was doing the job that the DNI had given it and it was doing that job well.

Another cause of the Snowden affair was that, despite its great success, the NSA had two internal problems—one of which had contributed directly and one indirectly to Snowden's ability to steal the amount of information he did. The first problem was that the NSA—the world's most capable signals intelligence organization, an agency immensely skilled in stealing digital data—had had its pocket thoroughly picked. You would have thought that of all the government entities on the planet, the one least vulnerable to such grand theft would have been the NSA. But it turned out that the NSA had left itself vulnerable.

At its facility in Hawaii, where Snowden had gone to work every day, the NSA did not have the audit functions on its computer network that would have made Snowden's theft all but impossible. Like the audit function on personal credit cards, such software raises flags when people access information outside their normal pattern of type and volume. In fairness, the NSA had safeguards at its headquarters at Fort Meade—but it was vulnerable at the outer regions of its network, in places like Hawaii, where it had not yet installed the latest security technologies. It was simply an issue of the timetable for which NSA facility received security upgrades at what time. Hawaii was low on the list.

The second internal problem was that the NSA—an organization renowned for its secrecy—was remarkably transparent among its own people. The culture at the NSA was for personnel to freely talk among themselves about issues on which they were working. The NSA had its own wikis where its employees could post, for their colleagues to see, information about their projects—including those on which they worked hand in hand with CIA officers. The idea was to spread knowledge and learn from the successes of others, but it created an enormous security vulnerability, given the always-existing risk of an insider committed to stealing secrets. Snowden took advantage of this vulnerability, scooping up much of the information on these wikis. This kind of internal openness was anathema to the typical attitude in the intelligence community that information should be shared only with those who have a legitimate need to know.

The final cause of the Snowden affair was the failure of some in the media to accurately describe what they were seeing in the Snowden documents. Many of them went to the darkest corner of the room, and it had political impact. This was sloppy reporting. On June 6, CNN led with a story titled "Spying on Your Calls," and the story contained the following line: "When you call Grandma in Nebraska, the NSA knows." Fox noted that "NSA knows your calling habits." MSNBC said that NSA is "screening your calls." The Associated Press said, "The government knows who you are calling. Every day. Every call." Glenn Greenwald, the reporter who broke the initial story, wrote, "Do you want to live with a government that knows everything you are doing?"

All of this was complete nonsense, but you could forgive the average citizen for not knowing that. Such reporting created the impression that NSA surveillance in the United States was much more intrusive than it really was. Media accounts created the impression that the NSA was listening to phone calls and reading e-mails—neither of which it was doing. Polling makes it clear that these inaccurate perceptions were immensely influential in shaping the ensuing political debate.

As I continued to read in our K Street office, the second thing that struck me was that the fundamental problem with which we were dealing was a loss of trust on several fronts—the loss of trust by a significant percentage of Americans in their own government, the loss of trust by some of our allies in the United States, and the loss of trust by overseas customers in a number of US companies—customers who were now concerned that the NSA had secret deals with these companies to compromise their products by placing "back doors" in their software and hardware.

To be clear, I was much less concerned about the loss of trust on the part of our allies than I was in the other two issues. Governments typically act in their own interests, and I was confident that the citizens of friendly nations would get over the temporary insult and that their governments were realistic enough to know that they too collect intelligence on friend and foe alike. Spying is the world's second-oldest profession and most of our allies have been at it since long before our nation was formed. A little harrumphing would be necessary for domestic political consumption—but this was not a major hurdle. From my time at the Agency, I am not aware of a single spying scandal that has had a long-term impact on a bilateral relationship, and I was convinced that the Snowden disclosures would not do so either.

The Review Group offered forty-six recommendations. Because of the strong public reaction to the Snowden leaks, I became convinced that our panel would have to make a number of strong recommendations if the country was to begin taking the first steps toward restoring public support for our government. If we had conducted a comprehensive review of NSA programs prior to the wholesale dumping out of intelligence secrets, I would have been in favor of just a few changes to the way the NSA was doing business. But in light of the public outcry, modest steps would never work now. We would have to make some dramatic proposals if we were to have any hope of regaining lost support.

Two recommendations stood out to me as much more important than the rest—and I believe we would have made these recommendations with or without Snowden. The first was the group's recommendation about the 215 metadata program—that the government no longer hold the data and that it be required to obtain a court order prior to querying the data each time, as opposed to the then-current situation in which the NSA was holding the data and could query it at will under a broad court order. This recommendation, and the president's acceptance of it, was absolutely necessary, I thought, to winning back the trust of the American people and keeping the program alive. Without winning back that trust, I was concerned that Congress would kill the entire program—in essence throwing the baby out with the bathwater.

And it also made sense. While the NSA did nothing illegal and committed no abuses under the 215 program, the group's law professors, particularly Geof Stone, convinced me that such power in the hands of the government creates the potential for abuse, and that we therefore had to recommend steps that would make it much harder for future administrations—or even rogue elements within administrations—to overstep their bounds.

The second recommendation that made great sense to me was

to put in the hands of senior policy-makers decisions on what intelligence to collect and how to collect it—particularly for collection that carries significant political, economic, or foreign policy risks. The NSA had largely been collecting information because it could, not necessarily in all cases because it should. To be sure, some oversight was already in place, but it was not broad enough to cover all the collection activities that carried special risks, and it rarely dealt with the question of how intelligence would be collected. The best example of such risky activity, of course, is spying on the senior leadership of allies. Only senior policy-makers looking at all the benefits and risks can make decisions on what to collect and how. At the end of the day, only senior policy-makers can decide on the "should."

There was also a set of recommendations that I thought absolutely critical—not for winning back trust but for making sure that another Edward Snowden does not happen. These recommendations—outlined in a chapter of our report called "Protecting Data"—received no media coverage. In this chapter we recommended two fundamental changes—that the government move from assessing the security risks of its employees every five years to doing it continuously, and that classified computer networks have state-of-the-art security software. It turns out that the best network security is not in the intelligence community—it is on Wall Street. This, of course, should not be surprising, as Wall Street is protecting something very important—your money.

But this chapter also called for another change—a revolutionary change that is not likely to see the light of day. Our Review Group felt that the tightest security practices should apply not only to intelligence community employees and networks but also to any government employees with access to secrets—including political appointees in the White House and elsewhere—and any computer networks that contain classified information. After all, Private Chelsea Manning was not an IC employee and was not operating on an

IC computer network when she stole information and passed it to WikiLeaks. All of these steps are necessary in order to ensure that another Snowden or Manning affair does not happen. And they are essential to ensure that secrets stay secrets. If our recommended changes are not implemented, I fear it will happen again.

I worked hard when we were crafting our recommendations to see that there was language attached that would permit reasonable accommodation for the business of intelligence, albeit generally with more oversight. My colleagues were very supportive of this. After all, the balance we were trying to strike was in winning back trust—and advancing privacy and civil liberties—without doing damage to the intelligence community's ability to do its critically important job.

The Review Group was surprisingly unified in its recommendations. Very little argument, very little drama.

In the end the president was supportive of a large majority of the Review Group's recommendations. He accepted 70 percent of the recommendations—including the two that I saw as the most important; he agreed to study 15 percent; and he rejected 15 percent. The ones he rejected had to do with the organizational structure of the NSA. And while I did not disagree with these recommendations, I did not see them as integral to the effort to win back trust. How many of our recommendations ultimately get adopted and the extent to which they help restore public confidence in the NSA, intelligence community, and government remains to be seen.

In the aftermath of the public release of the report, I felt that the media generally mischaracterized both the breadth of the report and our key recommendations regarding the 215 program. A number of media outlets were calling the recommendations "sweeping reforms of the intelligence community," and they were saying that the Review Group had recommended an end to the 215 program. Neither was true.

While our recommendations were many, they were not sweeping. Where we suggested change, it was most often a recommendation to add layers of scrutiny and review—making certain kinds of operations more cumbersome, but not impossible.

The 215 program was the best example. We saw real value in the program and we recommended to the president a change in approach, not a wholesale rejection of the program. We recommended that the 215 database should be taken out of the hands of the government and each query should require an individual court order.

Although we did not discuss it as a group, I also thought the database should actually be expanded to include all calls made in the United States and should include e-mails as well. Today the database does not contain the metadata from *all* calls and does not contain the metadata from *any* e-mails. It should. Imagine a scenario in which AQAP in Yemen sends multiple operatives to the United States to conduct attacks, and the intelligence community learns of the plot and runs a search of Yemen-based phone numbers against the 215 database. But the search is a dry hole—because AQAP is using a phone system outside the 215 program. Imagine the outrage of the American public when these facts became public following a successful attack.

* * *

Two final thoughts—one on the damage done by Snowden and the other on Snowden as an individual. I believe that the Snowden disclosures will go down in history as the greatest compromise of classified information ever. Period. Full stop. The damage done has already been significant and it will continue to grow. While great attention and angst have been devoted to the loss he created by exposing the 215 telephony metadata program, Snowden damaged a much more important program involving the collection of e-mail information from foreign-based terrorists, the 702 program mentioned earlier.

Within weeks of the leaks, terrorist organizations around the world were already starting to modify their actions in light of what Snowden disclosed. Communication sources dried up, tactics were changed. Terrorists moved to more secure communication platforms, they are using encryption, and they are avoiding electronic communications altogether. ISIS was one of the terrorist groups that learned from Snowden, and it is clear his actions played a role in the rise of ISIS. In short, Snowden has made the United States and our allies considerably less safe. I do not say this lightly: Americans may well die at the hands of terrorists because of Edward Snowden's actions.

The damage caused by Snowden is not limited to terrorists' adjusting their tactics. Foreign intelligence services have been studying the tremendous amount of intelligence data now available to them in the media and deriving work-arounds to thwart US collection efforts. You can bet that outfits like the Iranian MOIS—Iran's CIA—have cells of smart young people studying the news articles and working on countermeasures. What is more, we know that foreign intelligence services will export their lessons learned. Outfits like the Russians and Chinese will study our tactics and then go to other, less sophisticated foreign intelligence services and offer tips about how to frustrate the American collection effort. In return they will be given access and influence that will only add to our woes.

One of the most troublesome leaks in this regard was the publication in the *Washington Post* of the intelligence community's Congressional Budget Justification Book (CBJB) for Fiscal Year 2013. This is the IC's so-called black budget. It lists where we are putting our priorities, where we think we are having our greatest intelligence successes, and where we still need to do more work. For our enemies, having it is like having the playbook of the opposing NFL team. I guarantee you that the SVR, the Russian foreign intelligence service, would have paid millions of dollars for such a document. Instead they didn't even have to invest $1.25, the cover price of the *Washington Post*, since the document is available free online. To its credit, the *Washington Post*, at the request of the DNI, did not publish the document in its entirety—protecting the most sensitive secrets—but still the damage was enormous.

This just refers to the material that has been disclosed. We don't know what other documents Snowden and his media allies have in their possession that they will publish at some point. It is a good bet that there is more to come—and therefore more damage (material from the Snowden leaks was still being published at the writing of this book—in early 2015—eighteen months after Snowden walked away from the United States). And we do not know what information foreign intelligence services have already acquired of what was stolen but not yet disclosed.

One more word about damage and that relates to the earlier point about a loss of trust on the part of foreigners in American products. As a result of that lack of trust, US information technology companies have lost hundreds of millions of dollars in sales overseas. People now shy away from US IT products over a concern that the US government is using those products to collect intelligence. This will be the hardest loss of trust to restore. Apple's move in the fall of 2014 to encrypt all data on its products so even Apple can't get at it is a response to that loss of trust. We can only hope, for the sake of the American economy, that US firms will win that trust back.

What were Snowden's motives? One thing I am sure of is that he was not acting out of a simple desire to protect the privacy and civil liberties of Americans or even citizens overseas. And this takes any idea that he was a whistle-blower off the table. The vast amount of information he stole and disclosed to journalists had nothing to do with privacy. Legitimate arguments can be had about how far our intelligence community should go in collecting information that potentially could touch US citizens. I would suggest, however, that the appropriate place for those discussions to occur is before the congressional oversight committees. Every one of the hundreds of thousands of people who have access to classified information cannot be allowed to individually decide to disclose information just because they do not like a particular program. If Snowden felt that privacy rights were being trampled, there were avenues available for him to make his concerns known to our elected representatives of Congress. If he didn't trust congressional overseers, departmental ombudsmen, and inspectors general to act, he could have easily taken one or two documents that solely addressed the privacy issue, put them in a plain brown envelope, and mailed them to the *Washington Post* (an action I am in no way endorsing, by the way). Instead he backed up a virtual tractor trailer and emptied a warehouse full of documents—the vast majority of which he could not possibly have read and few of which he would likely understand. Then he delivered the documents to a variety of international news organizations and God only knows who else.

So if his primary motivation was not the protection of privacy and civil liberties, what was it? I don't know for sure, but I strongly suspect that his actions were all about his favorite subject: Edward J. Snowden. It is clear that Snowden has an enormous ego—one that had to be quite large for him to convince himself that he knew better than two presidents (of different parties), the intelligence committees of multiple congresses, the Justice Department of two administrations, and tens of FISA court judges appointed by the chief justice of the Supreme Court. That is arrogance.

A full answer to the question of why he did what he did would require that he sit down for months with counterintelligence debriefers and top-notch psychologists. But my hunch is that Snowden is someone who felt underappreciated and insufficiently recognized for his self-perceived brilliance while working for CIA and the NSA, a feeling that left a huge chip on his shoulder. This is a classic attitude that intelligence officers try to exploit among the enemy. You find someone working for the other side and tell him that he is not receiving the recognition, pay, and honors due him, and you provide those in return for the individual's betrayal of his country. This was the psychology that led Aldrich Ames and Robert Hanssen to commit espionage. Let me stress that I am not suggesting here that Snowden was encouraged by a foreign intelligence service to act as he did—only that the same psychological dynamic can motivate someone to act alone and still do as much damage. In short, I think he wanted to show the world how smart he was by crippling the agencies that did not recognize his brilliance.

As big as his ego was in June 2013, it must have grown exponentially since. The media and international organizations have relentlessly pumped hot air into his inflated self-esteem. Institutions ranging from the European Union to politicians musing about putting him forward for the Nobel Peace Prize have undoubtedly added to his sense of worth. Some news organizations have awarded him icon status. I recall seeing one media outlet seek his wisdom on what foreign intelligence targets would be appropriate for the United States to collect against. The absurdity of this is stunning. It would be like going to the equipment manager for the Dallas Cowboys and asking him what plays the team should run on Sunday.

* * *

On June 21, 2013, the US Department of Justice charged Edward Snowden with espionage. If I could have a conversation with Snowden, I would ask him only one question. That question would be, "Edward, you had enough trust in the American people that you thought they could and should judge for themselves the right balance between liberty and security. If you really believe that, then surely you must believe that those same Americans could and should judge your behavior with regard to the disclosures you made possible. So why don't you come home and be judged before a jury of your peers?"

I know some readers will think, "Of course you say bad things about Snowden because he exposed systemic wrongdoing by the intelligence community, a place you worked for thirty-three years." My answer is that the programs he disclosed were legal and approved at the highest levels of the US government and that the damage he did was huge. As someone who was uniquely positioned to evaluate that damage, I can tell you that the costs of Snowden's actions will be enormous. If he truly thought his actions were those of civil disobedience, the honorable approach would have been to take his stand and then accept the consequences.

* * *

Throughout this entire affair, the people I have worried most about are the men and women of the National Security Agency. The media and some politicians have demonized the organization for which they work and, to an extent, the officers of the NSA themselves. They do not deserve this. They go to work every day for a government salary, they work long hours for no public acclaim, and they execute tasks that keep the country safe and that literally save lives. They are talented, professional, and dedicated.

In collecting intelligence, the NSA and its officers in no way did anything wrong. The NSA never undertook a program without the approval of the executive branch and the oversight of the congressional intelligence committees or the courts. The NSA never broke the law and never abused the power that it had been given in the 215 program. In short, the NSA and its officers were doing the job that they had been asked to do.

NSA officers are patriots. Edward Snowden is a traitor.

CHAPTER 13

The Long War Ahead

On the morning of September 11, 2001, the chaplain of the New York City Fire Department, Father Mychal Judge, was told that a plane had just crashed into the World Trade Center. He changed from his Franciscan habit into his chaplain's uniform, donned his fire helmet, and joined the rush of brave men and women to the Twin Towers. When he arrived, Mayor Rudolph Giuliani saw him. The mayor grabbed Father Mychal by the arm and asked him to pray for the city. Father Mychal looked at the mayor with his usual big grin and said, "I always do." Only moments later, as Father Mychal was heading straight into danger to minister to his firemen, falling debris from the collapsing South Tower struck him down. An iconic photograph captured the moment when firemen and first responders carried Father Mychal's limp body from the debris. Father Mychal was the first victim recovered at the scene, making him the city's first officially recorded fatality of the attacks.

At almost exactly the same time that Father Mychal fell, Kevin Shaeffer, a young officer in the Naval Operations Center in the Pentagon, was following the terrible events in New York. With no warning, his workplace exploded in an orange fireball as Flight 77 crashed through the building. At the moment of impact, Kevin was thrown across the room. He would later learn that all twenty-nine of his coworkers had perished in that instant. The intense heat melted his name tag, but, perhaps foreshadowing what was to come, did not touch the ribbons on his uniform. Remembering his emergency training, Kevin smothered the flames engulfing his clothes and hair. Breathing in jet fuel and thick black smoke, Kevin crawled through water gushing from pipes and past live electrical wires toward the blue sky he glimpsed through gaps in the wreckage. He called out for help, and, at first, no one answered.

Nearby, an army sergeant first class named Steve Workman heard the explosion and ran toward the burning Ops Center. He found Kevin and immediately recognized the severity of his injuries. Steve helped Kevin to safety, and he prevented Kevin from going into shock by raising his legs. Steve helped Kevin into one of the first ambulances on the scene and rode with him to Walter Reed Army Medical Center. Along the way, Steve asked Kevin about his life, his family, and his hobbies, anything to keep him conscious. At the hospital, the best trauma doctors on the planet gave Kevin a fifty-fifty chance of surviving. He had third-degree burns over almost half his body and extreme difficulty breathing. In the following weeks, Kevin battled infections, fluid buildup in his lungs, and the pain of the burns. During surgery in early October, Kevin went into cardiac arrest and died twice on the operating table, but he was brought back to life each time. After many months, seventeen operations, and countless hours of torturous physical therapy, Kevin recovered. He was among the last of those injured on 9/11 to be released from the hospital.

* * *

Why tell these stories? Because they underscore two extremely important points: one, the world is a very dangerous place, and two, it takes heroes to protect us from those dangers—US diplomats, intelligence officers, military personnel, and federal law enforcement officers, not to mention local police officers and fire fighters. And there is little doubt in my mind that the world is going to become an even more dangerous place in terms of international terrorism, and that our need for heroes—like Father Mychal, Kevin, and Steve—is, unfortunately, only going to continue to grow.

* * *

In February 2013, as President Obama was considering options for a US military presence in Afghanistan after 2014, Tom Donilon, the president's national security advisor, had a request for Matt Olsen, the Director of the National Counterterrorism Center, and me, the acting director of CIA. He asked that we have a conversation with the president about what the threat from international terrorists—primarily al Qa'ida—would look like in the years ahead, so that the president could think about Afghanistan in a broader context. It was a great question, and to prepare for the meeting I huddled for two hours in my office with CIA's best and brightest experts on international terrorism.

As always, the smartest and most insightful person in the room was the director of the Counterterrorism Center, Roger (because he is undercover I cannot use his real name). Roger is the hardest-working and most dedicated officer with whom I have worked at the Agency. He has run the center for several years—longer than anyone before him—and he has produced results. He is tough to work with because he sets the bar very high, but there is no better person to be protecting the country from al Qa'ida. My last official act—literally five minutes before my successor took over as deputy director—was to call Roger and simply tell him that I thought he was the most talented operations officer with whom I had ever worked. There was a long silence on the other end of the phone, then a quiet "Thank you."

Roger presented the most insightful ideas during the prep session, and I went home that night and wrote out what I wanted to tell the president. I presented CIA's thoughts to the president on February 21, 2013. I talked about how we saw the extremist threat at the moment, how it had changed since 9/11, and how we thought it would evolve in the years ahead. In addition, I outlined the state of our overseas partnerships that are so critical to dealing with the threat. The overarching theme of my presentation—almost two years ago to the day of the writing of this book and well before the rise of ISIS—was that the war against Islamic extremism was far from over and that this war would be one that would be fought by multiple generations. I told the president that my children's generation and my grandchildren's generation would still be fighting this fight.

* * *

Twenty years into my career I was asked to be George W. Bush's first intelligence briefer, and I spent several months of that time providing unspecified warnings that al Qa'ida was about to hit us somewhere. Those briefings, of course, included the August 6, 2001, piece *Bin Ladin Determined to Strike in the United States*. Thirty years into my career I was asked to become a member of the Deputies Committee of Barack Obama's National Security Council by serving as the deputy director of CIA. In that capacity I would provide many briefings to the president over the next three and a half years about al Qa'ida, our successes against it, and the many threats it still posed. This included the February 21, 2013, briefing requested by Tom Donilon.

In this chapter I want to give you—the readers of this book—a briefing on the terrorist threat we are facing, and I will do it as if I were speaking to a president of the United States, albeit with unclassified information. The key questions are what is the threat today, where is it going, and what should the United States do about all of this? Because CIA does not recommend policy, this latter question is not something an intelligence officer would normally brief to a president, but, given the importance of the issue, I will do it here in this book.

* * *

Let's start the briefing with two overarching points. First, extremists inspired by Usama Bin Ladin's ideology consider themselves to be at war with the United States and they want to attack us—and neither one of these two facts will change anytime soon. It is important to never forget that—no matter how long it has been since the last attack here in the homeland.

Second, in the post-9/11 fight against these terrorists, we have scored a great victory but so have the extremists. Our great victory has been the severe degradation and near defeat of al Qa'ida's core leadership, still located in the tribal areas of Pakistan, the group responsible for the terror that occurred on that beautiful, bright sunny day in September 2001. The degradation has been so severe that al Qa'ida in Pakistan no longer has the capability to conduct a 9/11 style attack—multiple, simultaneous, complex attacks that kill thousands.

Al Qa'ida's great victory has been the spread of its ideology, its franchising, across a geographic area that now runs from northern Nigeria north into the Sahel, primarily in northern Mali, and across North Africa from Morocco to Algeria to Tunisia to Libya and Egypt; that includes parts of East Africa, primarily in Somalia but also in Kenya; that stretches across the Gulf of Aden into Yemen and up to Iraq and Syria, still in South Asia (Afghanistan, Pakistan, India, and Bangladesh), and in some parts of Southeast Asia. All told, some 20 countries now have groups of terrorists inside their borders espousing the jihadist ideology.

This spread began because of Bin Ladin's successes in East Africa, Yemen, and the United States (the embassy bombings in 1998, the *Cole* bombing in 2000, and 9/11). These al Qa'ida victories created a following for Bin Ladin across the Muslim world. He became a role model. The spread was given a boost by the operatives who fled South Asia after 9/11 and by Muslim opposition to the Western interventions in Iraq and Afghanistan—just as Bin Ladin had hoped. But the spread of the al Qa'ida brand has been given perhaps its most significant lift as a result of the Arab Spring, which created safe havens in which al Qa'ida could operate and that provided the franchises with much-needed recruits, money, and weapons.

This geographic dispersion is important because it stretches the diplomatic, intelligence, and military resources of the United States—at a time when the available resources are shrinking. The State Department has never been given—by any of a number of administrations and different Congresses—the resources it needs to do its job around the globe. The intelligence community and the US military were given an infusion of resources in the aftermath of 9/11, but those budgets have been falling for the last few years and they will likely continue to fall. But these cuts are in no way automatic. They are a conscious choice that the administration, Congress, and the American people are making.

These two "victories"—one for the good guys and one for the bad guys—have altered the threat landscape in significant ways. The change is defined by a reduction of the threat from the original al Qa'ida organization but a significant expansion of the threat from the emerging groups, a reduction in the threat of large, spectacular attacks but a skyrocketing rise in the threat of small-scale attacks. And this is playing out. Jim Clapper, the Director of National Intelligence, told Congress in July 2015 that "when the final accounting is done, 2014 will have been the most lethal year for global terrorism in the 45 years such data has been compiled."

* * *

So, this is the threat from a general perspective. What about the threat posed by individual terrorist groups? That is the next issue to cover in this briefing

ISIS. The Islamic State of Iraq and Greater Syria (ISIS) is a very good place to start because the group has grown faster than any terrorist group we can remember and because the threat it poses to us is as wide-ranging as any we have seen.

ISIS was born of al Qa'ida. When the United States invaded Iraq in 2003, al Qa'ida made a calculated choice to confront us there. It built its organization in Iraq around Abu Mus'ab al-Zarqawi, who trained with al Qa'ida in Afghanistan before 9/11 and who led an Islamic extremist organization in northern Iraq prior to the war. He had an on-again, off-again relationship with Bin Ladin: he did not like being managed from Pakistan, but he shared Bin Ladin's ideology fully. He also had the benefit of the many foreign nationals who raced to Iraq to join the jihadist fight against the West.

Zarqawi's organization, called al Qa'ida in Iraq (AQI), pursued a fiendish strategy of attacking not only coalition and Iraqi government targets but also Shi'a targets. The goal was to start a civil war and to significantly undercut the stability of Iraq, making our job that much more difficult. Regrettably, AQI was assisted by two decisions by the Coalition Provisional Authority (the temporary governing entity established by the United States following the invasion of Iraq). The edicts were made in the early weeks after the cessation of combat operations. The decisions—to remove anyone who had been a member of Saddam's Baath Party from a position inside the Iraqi government, and to disband any organization with close ties to the Baath Party—resulted in the collapse of the Iraqi military and security services. The resulting vacuum was filled by Iraqi Sunni insurgents, Shi'a militias, and AQI.

The United States, together with its coalition partners and the Iraqis, worked over a period of years to get Iraq under control in general and to destroy AQI in particular. Great success was achieved by the end of the Bush administration in January 2009, with AQI on the ropes. That progress continued through the end of 2011, when the last US troops were withdrawn from Iraq. AQI, however, benefited from the military vacuum—both because there was less military and intelligence pressure on the group but also because Prime Minister Nouri al-Maliki, without the United States in the country, felt emboldened to move even more aggressively in an authoritarian direction, alienating and disenfranchising Sunnis at every turn. Moderate Sunnis began to support AQI.

AQI also benefited from its involvement in Syria (it was when AQI joined the fight in Syria that the group changed its name to ISIS). ISIS added Syrians and foreign fighters to its ranks, built its supply of arms and money, and gained significant battlefield experience fighting the Assad regime. Together with the security vacuum in Iraq and Maliki's alienation of the Sunnis, this culminated in ISIS's successful blitzkrieg across western Iraq in the spring and summer of 2014, seizing large amounts of territory. ISIS now controls more territory—in Iraq and Syria—than any other terrorist group anywhere in the world.

It is interesting to note that ISIS is not the first extremist group to take and hold territory. Al-Shabab in Somalia did so a number of years ago and still holds territory there, al Qa'ida in the Islamic Maghreb did so in Mali in 2012, and al Qa'ida in Yemen did so there at roughly the same time. I fully expect extremist groups to attempt to take—and sometimes to be successful in taking—territory in the years ahead. But no group has taken so much territory so quickly as ISIS has.

Although there is a deep rift between the leadership of al Qa'ida and the leadership of ISIS, it is important to note that ISIS is effectively al Qa'ida. ISIS shares Bin Ladin's long-term goal of establishing a global caliphate, it sees both the West and its allies in the Middle East as it its primary enemies, and it sees violence as the most effective means of achieving its goals. The only reason that ISIS is not formally part of al Qa'ida is that the group does not want to have to follow the guidance of Zawahiri. It's an issue of "who should be calling the shots," not an issue of a different vision.

ISIS poses four significant threats to the United States. First, ISIS is a threat to the stability of the entire Middle East. ISIS is putting the territorial integrity of both Iraq and Syria at risk. And a collapse of either or both of these states could easily spread throughout the region, bringing with it sectarian and religious strife, humanitarian crises, and the violent redrawing of borders, all in a part of the world that remains critical to US national security.

Second, ISIS's success on the battlefield and its Madison-Avenue quality messaging on the Internet is attracting vulnerable young men and women to travel to Syria and Iraq to join its cause. At this writing, at least twenty thousand foreign nationals from roughly ninety countries have traveled to Syria and Iraq to join the fight. Most have joined ISIS. This flow of foreigners has outstripped the flow of fighters into Iraq during the war there a decade ago. And there are more foreign fighters in Syria today than there were in Afghanistan in the 1980s working to drive the Soviet Union out of that country. These foreign nationals are getting experience on the battlefield, and they are becoming increasingly radicalized to ISIS's cause.

There is a particular subset of these fighters to worry about. Somewhere between 3,500 and 5,000 jihadist wannabes have traveled to Syria and Iraq from Western Europe, Canada, Australia, and the United States. They all have easy access to the US homeland.

There are two possibilities here to worry about. One is that these fighters will leave the Middle East and either conduct an attack on their own or conduct an attack at the direction of the ISIS leadership. The former has already happened in Europe but not yet in the United States (but it will). In spring 2014, a young Frenchman, Mehdi Nemmouche, who went to fight in Syria, returned to Europe and shot three people at the Jewish Museum of Belgium in Brussels.

The latter—an ISIS-directed attack—has not yet occurred either, but it will as well. Today, such an attack would be relatively unsophisticated (small scale) but over time ISIS's capability to conduct a more complex attack will grow. This is what long-term safe haven in Iraq and Syria would give ISIS, and it is exactly what the group is planning to do. They have announced their intentions to attack us—just like Bin Ladin did in the years prior to 9/11.

Third, ISIS is building a following among other extremist groups around the world—again, at a more rapid pace than al Qa'ida ever enjoyed. This has occurred in Algeria, Libya, Egypt, and Afghanistan. More will follow. This makes these groups, which are already dangerous even more dangerous because they will increasingly target ISIS's enemies (including us) and they will increasingly take on ISIS's brutality. We saw the former play out in early 2015 when an ISIS-associated group in Libya killed an American—in an attack on a hotel in Tripoli frequented by diplomats and international businessmen. We saw the second play out just a few weeks later when another ISIS-affiliated group in Libya beheaded twenty-one Egyptian Coptic Christians.

And, fourth, ISIS's message is radicalizing young men and women around the globe who have never traveled to Syria or Iraq but who want to commit an attack to demonstrate their solidarity with ISIS. Such an ISIS-inspired attack has already occurred in the United States—an individual with sympathies for ISIS attacked two New York City police officers with a hatchet. Al Qaʿida has inspired such attacks here—the Fort Hood shootings in late 2009 that killed thirteen and the Boston Marathon bombing in spring 2013 that killed five and injured nearly three hundred.

We can expect more of these kinds of attacks in the United States. Attacks by ISIS-inspired individuals are occurring at a rapid pace around the world—roughly ten since ISIS took control of so much terriroty. Two such attacks have occurred in Canada—including the October 2014 attack on the Parliament building. And another occurred in Sydney, Australia, in December 2014. Many planning such attacks—in Australia, Western Europe, and the United States—have been arrested before they could carry out their terrorist plans.

AQAP. Al Qaʿida in the Arabian Peninsula, al Qaʿida in Yemen—the group most tightly aligned to the al Qaʿida leadership in Pakistan—poses an even greater threat to the US homeland than does ISIS, at least for now. The last three attempted attacks by an al Qaʿida group against the United States—the Christmas day bomber in 2009, the printer cartridge plot in 2010, and the nonmetallic bomb plot in 2012—were all AQAP plots. Two of these came close to being great successes for al Qaʿida. To put it bluntly, I would not be surprised if AQAP tomorrow brought down a US airliner traveling from London to New York or from New York to Los Angeles or anywhere else in the United States. Not surprised at all.

And one AQAP senior leader is more dangerous than the rest—Ibrahim al-Asiri, a Saudi by birth and AQAP's chief bomb maker. Asiri is the mastermind behind new explosive devices designed to evade security checks. He is smart and creative, and he is training a new generation of AQAP bomb makers. He undoubtedly has

trained dozens over the past couple at years. He may well be the
most dangerous terrorist alive today. He is a master at his craft and
he is evil.

He built a rectum bomb and recruited his younger brother,
Abdullah, to use it in an attempt to assassinate Saudi Arabia's
most senior security official, Prince Muhammad bin Nayef, the
country's minister of the interior and now deputy crown prince.
Abdullah pretended to be a repentant terrorist, and in a meeting
with Prince Muhammad designed to symbolize the sincerity of his
change of heart, he detonated the device. The two were sitting on
pillows on the floor, shoulder to shoulder, when Abdullah hit a button on a cell phone, detonating the explosives. Abdullah was killed
instantly—pieces of him were scattered all over the room, including
the ceiling—but Prince Muhammad, sitting just inches away, survived with only minor injuries. He did not even spend a night in the
hospital. Scientists explain Prince Muhammad's survival in terms of
the physics of the blast, but the prince does not accept this explanation. He thinks that God saved him for a purpose—to continue to
help keep his country safe from terrorism, particularly from AQAP,
an organization located on the same peninsula as the Kingdom of
Saudi Arabia. I find the prince's reasoning compelling.

Asiri's bomb exploits go well beyond killing his own brother.
Asiri was the mastermind behind young Nigerian Umar Farouk
Abdulmutallab's underwear bomb, which nearly brought down an
airliner flying from Amsterdam to Detroit. Asiri also built a bomb
hidden in a printer cartridge that, once the cartridge was placed in a
printer, was nearly impossible to find. The goal was to bring down a
cargo plane—or multiple cargo planes. The printer cartridge bomb
could not be found on traditional airport scanners, and dogs trained
to identify explosives could not find it either. He also built a nonmetallic suicide vest, again designed to bring down airliners, and

he has experimented with surgically implanting explosive devices inside human bodies.

AQAP's capabilities were on full display in Paris in January 2015, when two brothers attacked the offices of the satirical weekly newspaper *Charlie Hebdo* over the media outlet's lampooning of the Prophet Muhammad. The attack, which killed twelve, was methodical and demonstrated planning, organization, and precision. The brothers escaped the scene, were found two days later twenty miles northeast of Paris, took hostages, and were finally gunned down by police after a nine-hour siege. At the same time the siege was underway, a third individual conducted a sympathy attack, taking and killing four hostages at a kosher market in Paris, before the police killed him as well. The assault on *Charlie Hebdo* was the largest terrorist attack in France since 1961. It dominated the news for several days.

One of the brothers in 2011 had traveled to Yemen, where he attended a terrorist training camp run by AQAP. He met with a leading operative of the group, an American named Anwar al-Awlaki, who was intent on conducting attacks in the United States and Western Europe. During the operation in Paris, the brothers announced their allegiance to AQAP, and subsequently AQAP claimed to have directed the brothers to attack *Charlie Hebdo* and to have provided them with funding. If AQAP's claims are true—and I think they are—this would represent AQAP's first successful attack in the West and the largest al Qa'ida attack in Western Europe since the London bombings ten years earlier.

AQSL. So where does the threat to the US homeland from al Qa'ida in Pakistan, the al Qa'ida senior leadership, stand today? Al Qa'ida in Pakistan still has the ability to carry out attacks in the United States, but only small-scale attacks—a singular event that might kill a hundred or fewer. I do not want to understate the significance of such an attack, but al Qa'ida in Pakistan no longer has the ability to conduct a 9/11-style event.

It had that capability twice—in the period just before 9/11 and from 2006 to 2010. It was taken from the group the first time by the US paramilitary and military intervention in Afghanistan and by Pakistan's decision to work with CIA against al Qa'ida. And it was taken from the group the second time by the aggressive CT operations begun by President Bush in August 2008 and continued by President Obama.

But just because it does not have that capability today does not mean it will not get it back someday. And that could happen. Indeed, it may even be likely to happen, given trends in Afghanistan. Even in a best-case outcome for Afghanistan post a withdrawal of US forces, in which the government controls Kabul and most cities, the Taliban will control swaths of Afghan territory in the south and east. (The worst-case outcome is that the Taliban will be knocking on the door of Kabul within eighteen months of the departure of US forces.) The al Qa'ida leadership in the FATA, if not defeated by then, will find safe havens with the Taliban. Some members will stay in Pakistan, but many will move back across the border into Afghanistan. And if the United States cannot or chooses not to contest al Qa'ida there, the group will rebound, it will resurge, and it will eventually again pose a 9/11-style threat to the homeland. If this were to occur, it would mean that all of our efforts in Afghanistan over the past fourteen years—the longest war in American history—would have been for naught. What a terrible thing that would be.

And, as in Yemen, there is one particular terrorist in South Asia whom I worry the most about—Farouq al-Qahtani. The al Qa'ida leadership in Pakistan sent al-Qahtani to Afghanistan as a backstop so al Qa'ida could regroup if it lost its sanctuary in Pakistan. Al-Qahtani took his men to one of the most inhospitable places on the planet—Afghanistan's Kunar and Nuristan Provinces, where steep mountain peaks and narrow river valleys make movement extremely difficult. There al-Qahtani has developed a following among the Taliban and the locals, and his al Qa'ida branch has grown as more operatives have joined his group.

Al-Qahtani, a Qatari by birth, is a US counterterrorism expert's worst nightmare. He is smart and operationally sophisticated. He is also a charismatic leader. He is one of the few al Qa'ida leaders I worry might have what it takes to replace Bin Ladin. I worry more about al-Qahtani than I do about the current leader of al Qa'ida, Ayman al-Zawahiri.

* * *

Zawahiri became al Qa'ida's new leader, its emir, in June 2011, six weeks after Bin Ladin's death. Zawahiri was born in Egypt in June 1951 and comes from a prominent family. His father's uncle, Rabi'a al-Zawahiri, was the grand imam of Cairo's al-Azhar University. His maternal grandfather was a highly regarded academic who served as the president of Cairo University and founded King Saud University in Riyadh. During his teenage years, Zawahiri began a lifelong association with Islamic extremism—to the point where he and some fellow students discussed overthrowing the regime of President Nasser. In 1980, like other ideologically motivated extremists, Zawahiri spent time in Peshawar, a Pakistani city near the Afghan border, where he met and connected with a young Usama bin Ladin. In 1981, after returning from Pakistan, Zawahiri would be implicated, tried, and thrown in prison for allegedly participating in the assassination of Egyptian president Anwar Sadat. Some years later, Zawahiri was released from prison and became the new leader of Egyptian Islamic Jihad (EIJ), a group which the United States believes helped participate, along with al Qa'ida, in the 1998 embassy bombings in East Africa. Just two years later the collaboration between Bin Ladin's al Qa'ida and Zawahiri's EIJ became a full merger of the two organizations, with Zawahiri taking on the role of second in command.

Zawahiri is a less charismatic leader than Bin Ladin, possibly one of the reasons that he was not publicly named as al Qa'ida's new leader until six weeks after the Abbottabad raid. Since assuming his leadership position, he has presided over the group's global expansion, but this has been much more a result of the regional affiliates' actions than Zawahiri's leadership. Zawahiri in 2013 publicly expelled ISIS, suspending its franchise and stripping it of its status as part of the al Qa'ida global enterprise, because it had disregarded Zawahiri's order for ISIS to stay out of Syria. Zawahiri, like Bin Ladin and al Qa'ida's other senior leaders, places great importance on maintaining unity, so the move to expel ISIS can be read as a significant step by Zawahiri—but also a failure on his part to bring ISIS into line.

* * *

The Khorasan Group. ISIS is not the only terrorist group in Syria. The first jihadist group there to rise against President Assad was Jabhat al-Nusra. While ISIS grew out of the old al Qa'ida in Iraq, al-Nusra was formed from an old organization of Syrian extremists, who had helped to facilitate the movement of foreign fighters into Iraq, via Syria, during the initial rise of AQI during the US occupation of Iraq. Unlike ISIS, al-Nusra is fully in the camp of the al Qa'ida leadership in Pakistan. Al-Nusra is an official affiliate of al Qa'ida, and al-Nusra accepts guidance from Zawahiri.

Early in the fight against Assad, Zawahiri sent a group of his own operatives from Pakistan to Syria. Zawahiri had two objectives for the group: one was to assist al-Nusra in its fight against Assad and the second was to use Syria as a base of operations for attacks in the West, to include attacks against the United States. This group of operatives from Pakistan is called the Khorasan Group. Like AQAP and AQSL, the Khorasan Group has the capability to conduct successful attacks in the United States. And, like with ISIS, the more safehaven al-Nusra has in Syria, the more potent their attack capability against the West will become over time.

Boko Haram. Finally, I worry about Boko Haram. While the group has not yet focused on the US Homeland or on Western Europe, it could do so in the years ahead. And if it does, Boko Haram would pose a particularly worrisome threat because of its savage approach to its cause (Boko Haram kills roughly a thousand Nigerian civilians a year and in 2014 kidnapped two hundred Nigerian school girls because it believes girls should not be in school) and because the worldwide Nigerian diaspora would allow Boko Haram operational advantage. That is, Boko Haram's operatives could hide in plain sight among the many Nigerians living outside of Nigeria.

Other Groups. There is a long list of other jihadist groups, largely in Africa—but also more broadly—who pose a local threat to US interests and our allies. These groups regularly conduct attacks—three of the best known are the September 2012 attacks in Benghazi against our diplomatic facility, an attack in September 2013 in Nairobi, Kenya, involving a number of terrorists from the al Qa'ida–affiliated group al-Shabab assaulting an upscale mall, and the January 2013 attack in In Amenas, Algeria, which involed terrorists from Mali taking hostages at a natural gas facility in eastern Algeria operated by British Petroleum and Norway's Statoil. In these three attacks, terrorists killed over a hundred people, including seven Americans. The risk to Americans living and traveling overseas has never been greater.

* * *

The final part of the "this is not over" warning is the most important part of the briefing. Al Qa'ida, if given a safe haven for some length of time, will again try to acquire weapons of mass destruction.

Al Qaʿida's groups in various locations and at various times have shown an interest in acquiring nuclear weapons, radiological devices, chemical weapons, and biological weapons. And they will try again.

A recent reminder of this desire was the acquisition by the moderate Sunni opposition in Syria of an ISIS computer. ISIS left the computer behind after retreating from a January 2014 firefight with the opposition. The laptop contains 35,347 hidden files, and these files contain a treasure trove of information on the group, including documents that make clear ISIS's interest in acquiring a biological weapons capability. A nineteen-page document explains how to develop biological weapons, including how to weaponize the bubonic plague from diseased animals, and a twenty-six-page document justifies on religious grounds the use of weapons of mass destruction. The first document states, "The advantage of biological weapons is that they do not cost a lot of money, while the human casualties can be huge." The second document notes, "If Muslims cannot defeat the unbelievers in a different way, it is permissible to use weapons of mass destruction—even if it kills all of them and wipes them and their descendants off the face of the Earth." While some of these documents are dated—going back to Bin Ladin's pre-9/11 days—they underscore the desire of extremists to get their hands on the world's most dangerous weapons.

*   *   *

Now, to the last part of the briefing, which tries to answer the toughest of questions: how do we deal with the problem of terrorism and how do we end this menace?

The most important concept that policy-makers—and the American public—must accept is that, if we are to keep the homeland and Americans overseas safe, we must maintain pressure on al Qaʻida. Always. This concept needs to be the basis of our policy toward al Qaʻida wherever it takes root.

But that is not the same thing as saying the United States needs to be the sole actor in putting that pressure on al Qaʻida. Quite the contrary: it is best if other countries take the lead when they have the necessary capabilities and that we act only when there is no other option. Not only does this make sense from the perspective of not playing into al Qaʻida's narrative about the United States, but it also has the best chance of being accepted, long term, by the American people.

What does this mean in practice? First, the US intelligence community and military must—along with our allies—expend resources and effort to build the intelligence, security, military, and rule of law capabilities of the frontline states against al Qaʻida—particularly those who have been historically weak and those that have been weakened by the Arab Spring. This is a long-term effort, but it has to be systematic, it has to be sustained, and it has to be funded.

Second, having the capabilities is not enough—a willingness of the frontline states to use them against extremist groups is also required. And here American diplomacy must take the lead. The State Department needs to be active in convincing countries to fight terrorism within their borders. And the president and his or her senior national security team must actively support this diplomacy. Third, we need to have global partners who are willing to take action outside their own borders when necessary—so that we are not the only country doing so. That's another job for our country's diplomats, including our top diplomat, the president of the United States. For example, this is what France did in Mali in January 2013.

The French government, growing increasingly concerned about the threat from al Qaʻida in the Islamic Maghreb (AQIM), took action. AQIM, reinforced with thousands of weapons from the Libyan stockpile, had taken advantage of a security vacuum in the north caused by the political crisis in Mali. As a result AQIM was able to seize control of a large swath of territory approximately the size of Texas, imposing shari'a law and opening training camps for jihadists of all types. Understanding that France would be AQIM's number one target, the French responded, putting thousands of troops on the ground and going toe-to-toe with the enemy, killing hundreds of terrorists, driving them back into the mountains, and denying them a vitally important safe haven. The US military supported this effort. The French are to be commended for this action. It is a model for what we need our other allies to do from time to time.

The Kenyans and Ethiopians took a similar step in Somalia in 2011. Deeply concerned about the growth of al-Shabab, an al Qa'ida–associated terrorist group in Somalia, both countries acted in concert—the Ethiopians directly with their own troops, and the Kenyans using a surrogate force. As in Mali, this intervention was successful in killing hundreds of terrorists and taking valuable territory from them. Al-Shabab is weaker today as a result. The United States was less supportive of this venture—we had doubts about whether it would work or not—but now that it has, we should be providing as much support as possible.

Fourth, the United States needs to act when no one else is able. Whether the action is air strikes from manned or unmanned assets, action from Special Forces personnel on the ground either alone or in close support of others, or even the use of conventional military forces, the United States needs to be willing and able to act. And the leadership of the executive branch and Congress must explain to the American people why this is important. Leadership is not about following public opinion. Leadership is about guiding public opinion to a place that best serves American interests over the longer term.

* * *

All of the above is necessary, but it is not enough to win the war over the long term, as more and more terrorists are created every day. To win the war over the longer term, we and our allies must address the issues that create terrorists in the first place. We must address the disease as well as the symptoms. We must undermine the jihadist appeal to disenchanted young Muslims. We must discredit the terrorists' narrative that hatred and violence are the only mechanisms for dealing with the modern world and the resulting pressures on Islam. This effort essentially requires winning the war of ideas. But it also requires minimizing the number of disenchanted young Muslims through economic and social development. Counter-radicalization is a two-part effort.

Counter-radicalization has not been a major focus of the United States since 9/11, but action on this front is just as important as action on the intelligence, law enforcement, and military fronts. There have been steps in this direction, but much more needs to be done. Developing the policies to get at the root causes of why young men and some women join terrorist groups has never really gotten off the ground. For every hour that I spent in the Situation Room talking about counter-radicalization, I spent a thousand hours talking about dealing with young men who had already become radicalized. The dollars spent by our government on programs related to counter-radicalization are an infinitesimally small percentage of the government's overall CT budget.

It is not unreasonable to ask, "Why have we not attacked the problem at its roots?" The answer is twofold. First, the priority will always be on those individuals who are trying to attack the United States. That will always take precedence over the longer-term issues. And, second, the issues involved in counter-radicalization are numerous and complex, and require a number of countries to take the right steps. The issues involve good governance; anti-corruption; economic development; social service provision, particularly education; religious tolerance; and a host of other issues. Most important, for every narrative of al Qa'ida's, there must be a counter-narrative delivered loudly and widely—by the United States and our allies, by governments in countries where young people are radicalized, and by Islamic scholars and clerics.

One of the best examples of success in this area is Indonesia—the home to the largest Muslim population on the planet. Between 9/11 and 2006, Indonesia suffered sixteen terrorist attacks, resulting in more than three hundred deaths. In the next eight years, there were only five attacks, causing fourteen deaths. And, as of early 2015, only about 150 Indonesians had gone to fight in Syria, a remarkably low number for its population and for its terrorist past. While excellent intelligence and law enforcement work have played a role—and these tools will remain vital, particularly as many terrorists will be released from prison over the next few years—so have the Indonesian government's counter-radicalization programs.

At the core of Jakarta's program is a willingness to work with any entity that can reach young people with the right messages. The program is systematic and reaches almost every part of Indonesian society. The messages are essentially two—that the extremist interpretation of Islam is not consistent with the Koran, and that there is great value in tolerance.

Religious organizations in Indonesia are popular within society and are therefore an important channel for delivering the government's counter-narrative to al Qa'ida. Jakarta, for example, works with imams and mosques to offer a variety of perspectives on Islam, particularly to youth and student groups. Schools are also a focus—courses emphasize inclusion and tolerance. All the world's religions are now studied, not just Islam, and schools are working to provide multiple perspectives on some of the issues that have played a role in radicalization, such as the relationship between Israel and the Palestinians.

Popular culture is also used. The government communicates with young people through popular musicians who communicate carefully crafted messages aimed at counteracting radical ideas. Music with lyrics about tolerance as an alternative to extremism has become popular in Indonesia and indeed throughout Southeast Asia. All of this is supported by a variety of media—books, articles, newsletters, the Internet, television, and radio. TV and the Internet focus on urban populations. Radio stations reach rural areas.

All of this, of course, requires focus, effort, and resources. It needs to be done throughout the Muslim world. It needs to be led by the governments in question. And it needs to be supported by the United States.

* * *

To me this is the most important chapter in the book, because it is about the threat from al Qa'ida going forward and what we need to do to deal with it. But in sharing my thoughts in this chapter, I do not mean to imply that international terrorism is the only national security issue facing the United States. Quite the contrary. Terrorism is only one of many security issues we are facing as a country. Al Qa'ida, as dangerous as it is, is only one of the things that keeps me up at night.

I believe national security issues can be put into two bins—national security threats and national security challenges that, if not managed effectively, could become threats. In addition to terrorism, the threats we face include "cyber"—cyber espionage, cyber crime, and cyber warfare—Iran, North Korea, narcotics and human trafficking, the intelligence activities of our adversaries, and others. The challenges we face are also many and include the rise of China, the Cold War–like behavior of Russia, the future stability of key countries like Pakistan, and historic change in what is still the most important place on the planet—the Middle East.

Of the threats, two stand out to me—"cyber" and Iran. The online world of cyber is now the preferred method that intelligence services use in stealing national defense secrets. Several nations have the capability to attack our critical infrastructure—transportation, finance, energy, etc.—in a way that could literally bring our nation to a standstill. Cyber is used by both foreign governments and foreign companies to steal the intellectual property of American companies—to the tune of hundreds of billions of dollars a year. Cyber crime, largely committed by organized crime groups, is now generating as much money as the illegal drug trade. And all of this is going to get worse as cyber tools spread to more adversaries and as even more advanced tools are developed.

On Iran, it is very easy to go immediately to the nuclear issue, but our problems with Iran are much deeper. Iran wants to be the hegemonic power in the Middle East; it wants, in short, to reestablish the Persian Empire, which at its height in 500 BCE controlled 45 percent of the world's population. Moreover, many Iranian leaders believe that Israel should be wiped off the face of the earth. Iran itself practices terrorism as a tool of statecraft, and Iran supports terrorist groups that target Israel, including the most significant ones—Hezbollah and Hamas. Iran supports insurgent groups in the Persian Gulf that want to overthrow the governments there. It supports the Houthi insurgency in Yemen, which in early 2015 overthrew the legitimate government of Yemen. And on top of all that, is Iran's nuclear program. Iran is going to be a problem for the United States for a long time to come.

Among the national security challenges, none is more important than China. The US-China relationship is the most important bilateral tie in the world. There are two sides to the relationship—one positive and one negative. The positive includes the economic relationship between China and the United States, which is vital to both countries' futures. In addition, based on meetings I had with my Chinese counterparts, there are more global national security issues where our interests overlap than where they are in tension, creating opportunities to work together. The negative side includes the fact that China is a rising power relative to the United States—and that China wants a greater say and greater influence in East Asia, where the US is currently in the driver's seat; it also includes the fact that each country needs to prepare for war against the other (because our militaries are in close proximity to each other). Each plans for such a war, each trains for it, and each must equip its forces with the modern weaponry to fight it. Both of these trends on the negative side of the equation lead to tension in the relationship. The key question—the key challenge—is how to mitigate the downsides while taking advantage of the upsides to push the relationship forward. This will be a major task of the next president. President Obama began this agenda with his Asia-Pacific rebalancing and in his conversations with Chinese president Xi, and our next president must aggressively move the agenda forward.

The United States, of course, is going to have to deal with all these problems, and doing so successfully is going to require many things—including first-rate intelligence. Why? Because intelligence has never been more important than it is today. That is because without intelligence, policy-makers cannot understand many of these issues, cannot make policy on them, and, in most cases, cannot carry out the policy they establish. Just think about it this way: almost any expert, using open sources, can provide real insights on the eurozone crisis, German politics, or the Japanese economy. But only the intelligence community can provide insights on the plans, intentions, and capabilities of al Qa'ida, the status of the Iranian nuclear program, or the capabilities of North Korean missiles. In short, this is a critical time to be an intelligence officer.

Dealing with these issues will also require educating our allies and adversaries alike on what the United States is all about. I was struck during my thirty-three-year career how many misperceptions there are of the United States and our policies. The Supreme Leader in Iran and the leadership of North Korea, for example, both believe that the United States wants to overthrow their regimes and is working to do so. That is not true. Russian president Putin believes that the United States was behind the protests in the streets of Kiev that began the Russia-Ukraine crisis. That is not true. The number of misperceptions and even conspiracy theories is large and worrying—because it both creates threats and makes managing them difficult.

* * *

I remember visiting with Afghan president Karzai in Kabul in late 2010 only a few weeks after WikiLeaks, an online organization that publishes secret information, posted on its website and disseminated to several news organizations thousands of US State Department cables. The documents were provided by Chelsea Manning, who was serving with the US military in Iraq. Many of the cables reported on discussions that US diplomats had with foreign leaders as well as our diplomats' thoughts on a large variety of foreign policy issues. The damage to US foreign policy was immediate and significant.

When I walked into Karzai's office that day, the first thing he said to me was "Congratulations, Michael." I said, "Mr. President, congratulations for what?" "For WikiLeaks," he said. I said, "Mr. President, I don't follow you. I don't understand." He said, "WikiLeaks was a brilliant CIA operation. Now foreign leaders will not talk to the State Department; they will only talk to CIA. Great job." I jokingly responded, "If only we were that good." But to Karzai this was not humor. He really believed it. He really believed that CIA had leaked thousands of classified State Department documents to get a leg up in the bureaucracy. It was an example of the kind of misperceptions and conspiracy theories that abound in the world.

* * *

Successfully dealing with the national security threats and challenges facing the United States also requires US leadership. No other country on the planet has the resources or the credibility to play that leadership role. American leadership is a necessary condition for mitigating the many threats and dealing with the many challenges we face. And policy-makers—most important the president and the leadership in Congress—have a responsibility to educate the American people on the threats and the important role required by the United States.

Policy-makers must approach the threats and challenges this country faces with the same sense of urgency as the officers I worked with from our Counterterrorism Center. There is a sign as you enter an important office in CIA's Counterterrorism Center. The sign is a picture of the burning Twin Towers on 9/11, and there are words printed at the top. Those words are "Today is September 12, 2001." That is the mind-set with which CTC does its job today and it is the mind-set with which CIA combats all the threats I just talked about.

And finally, we can only mitigate the threats facing us and deal with the challenges if we are strong as a nation, and we can be strong only if our political leaders make decisions that move our economy and our society forward. Because at the end of the day the most important determinant of a nation's national security is the health of its economy and its society. That is why it is vital for our leaders to come together, discuss the tough issues, compromise, and make decisions. Nothing is more important to our future security as a nation.

* * *

Let me come back to the two stories that opened the chapter. First, Steve and Kevin.

For his courageous actions on 9/11, Steve earned the Soldier's Medal, the highest peacetime award for valor. In the immediate aftermath of the attacks, he became a casualty assistance officer, helping others through their times of grief. He continues to serve our country today at the Defense Intelligence Agency.

Following his recovery Kevin went on to serve on the 9/11 Commission, and he worked for CIA in our Counterterrorism Center, helping to keep our country safe from other attacks. He worked there until after Bin Ladin was brought to justice, and then he felt he could finally move on.

One more word about Kevin. In those early hours on September 11, the doctors were not sure Kevin would live. And for many months they were not sure that he would ever be able to have children. But Kevin and his wife eventually had three beautiful children, and, of course, they named their son Steve.

And finally, Father Mychal Judge, who, like Kevin and Steve, acted when he needed to act. On September 10, 2001, Mychal Judge gave his last sermon at the dedication of a renovated firehouse in New York City. He said,

> That's the way it is. Good days. And bad days. Up days. Down days. Sad days. Happy days. But never a boring day on the job. You do what God has called you to do. You show up. You put one foot in front of another. You get on the rig and you go out and you do the job—which is a mystery. And a surprise.

*You have no idea when you get on that rig. No matter how big
the call. No matter how small. You have no idea what God
is calling you to do. But he needs you. He needs me. He needs
all of us.*

Father Mychal, Kevin, and Steve. I believe that all three were
heroes, that all three are true leaders, and that the actions of all
three speak to us about the importance of the United States's taking
a leadership role in the world to deal with the very difficult issues
that we are facing today, and will continue to face for a long time to
come.

CHAPTER 14

Carved in Stone

I worked for the Central Intelligence Agency for thirty-three years. From day one I was motivated by the mission of the Agency—keeping the country safe—and that motivation only grew over time as the significance of what I was doing expanded. I was also driven by the dedication of the men and women who undertook the task of keeping the country safe each and every day. Early in the morning, around seven a.m., almost half of the Agency's parking lot is already filled. And late into the evening, at seven p.m., still half of the parking lot is filled. I had officers turn down well-deserved promotions or spend months away from their families and friends because they were so committed to a particular operation or initiative.

I have never worked with more dedicated people. People frequently ask me about specific movies and television series about the Agency. "Is *Homeland* real?" they ask. "Did *Zero Dark Thirty* get the story right?" My answer is always the same: "No, not really, with one exception, and that exception is the passion that CIA officers bring to the job." I usually explain that the passion for getting the job done that is demonstrated, for example, by the character Carrie in *Homeland* or Maya in *Zero Dark Thirty* is a dead-on accurate portrayal of the passion of many CIA officers, particularly those who work in our Counterterrorism Center.

That dedication, I think, was captured simply and beautifully in the written answer to a question on a job application by the son of one of the finest scientists in the history of CIA. The question was "If you had the opportunity to meet someone from the past or present, who would it be and why?" His answer: "If I had the opportunity to meet anyone, past or present, I would elect to meet the man my dad becomes when he goes to work every day at CIA. I love my dad because he is the very definition of fatherhood: stoic, strong, capable. His career at CIA has always been out of my view, save for the awards and promotions he has brought home. My father is one of the countless unsung heroes of the clandestine service. I would love nothing more than to meet my dad at work, because as far as I'm concerned, I would be meeting Superman."

* * *

Throughout my career I found particular inspiration and motivation from the men and women who made the ultimate sacrifice—those CIA officers who lost their lives in the line of duty. The most special place at the Agency is the north side of the main lobby at CIA headquarters—the location of our Memorial Wall, with stars etched into the marble, one star for every hero who made that sacrifice. I worked by a simple motto—that what I did every day needed to live up to the sacrifices represented by those stars. And I posed that challenge to the new officers when I led them through their oath of office on their first day at the Agency.

When I became deputy director in May 2010, I insisted that we move the swearing-in ceremony to the main lobby at the main headquarters building, so we could hold it in front of the stars. I was given many bureaucratic excuses for why we could not do so—"It will take too much time to move the class back and forth between buildings," "We will have to shut down the main entrance for an hour," "We will have to set up chairs and a podium for each swearing in"—and on and on. In response to each attempt to push back on my directive, I simply said, "I don't care. Just do it." After several days of this routine, the opposition got tired of my refrain and gave up, and the swearing-in ceremony moved to the lobby, where it is still held today, with all new employees raising their right hands and taking the oath while facing the Memorial Wall.

In my speech to the new employees before administering the oath of office, I would tell them, "I want you to know that you are not about to join just any company, not just any government agency." It was important, I said, that they fully appreciate that they were about to join an organization that conducts espionage as a business, stealing secrets around the globe and making sense of them for the president of the United States—all with the goal of making our nation safer. "There is no other agency like this in the United States government," I would say. And I would tell them that what they would do every day would be extremely relevant because intelligence "has never been more important than it is today."

I would finish by telling them that I wanted them to be obsessed with quality. "*Good enough* is not a phrase we use at CIA," I would tell them. "Pursue excellence in everything you do," I would add. "The president, the taxpayers, and the stars on the wall deserve nothing less."

Toward the end of my tenure at the Agency, not only did the new employees hear those words but so did their spouses and partners. When I became a member of the CIA leadership team, my wife, Mary Beth, became even more involved in the Agency and in its efforts to support the families of our officers. When I became deputy director, she had the idea that spouses and partners should be in the room when their loved ones take the oath of office. It was a brilliant idea—an important first step in binding an employee's family to the Agency. When I retired, Director Brennan awarded Mary Beth the Agency Seal Medal, the highest CIA award a non-officer can receive, and her passion for including spouses and partners in the swearing-in ceremony was one of the reasons for the award. I am very proud of her.

Today the swearing-in ceremony, with spouses and partners in attendance, is regularly led by the director—which is relatively new for the Agency. When I was the number three at the Agency, from 2006 to 2008, I presided over the oath of office. When I became deputy director in 2010, I insisted on taking on the task again, although my duties at the White House would often preclude me from doing so. But when Dave Petraeus arrived at the Agency in September 2011, he insisted on doing the ceremony. He believed that there was no better day to start imprinting the values of the organization than hearing from the director on day one. John Brennan continues that practice to this day. While I was disappointed that the responsibility had been taken from me—a job I truly loved—I thought the idea of the director's conducting the swearing-in ceremony was exactly right. On November 30, 1980, on my first day at the Agency, I was sworn in by a mid-level official, the director of personnel, in a classroom. I do not remember who that person was or even the room where the ceremony took place. But today's new employees will always remember that they were sworn in by the director, standing in front of the most important wall in the Central Intelligence Agency.

* * *

The Wall was meaningful not only for new employees. It was also important to me personally. I found it a place to clear my mind. On days when things seemed to be at their worst, on days when nothing seemed to be going right, I would wander down to the Wall (I had a method of sneaking out of my office without my security detail seeing me and therefore following). After a few minutes everything would come back into perspective. No matter how bad my day, it paled in comparison to what the family and friends of our fallen officers had gone through and would continue to go through for the rest of their lives. I would always return to my office with a renewed sense of purpose. I would also go down to the Wall on the one day each year when the engraver came to the Agency to add the new stars. Standing and watching from afar as the chisel chips away marble and slowly creates a star is one of the most meaningful and moving experiences an Agency officer can have.

As of this writing there are 111 stars on the Wall, and certainly more will be added in the years ahead. They date back to the founding of the Agency in 1947. The stars are accompanied by the Book of Honor, a simple list of the names of the officers killed in the line of duty. Some of the entries are blank, as even in death the officers' affiliation with the Agency cannot be revealed. Eighty of the stars were added between 1947 and September 11, 2001. And thirty-one stars have been added since 9/11—almost all represent officers who were in some way involved in the fight against al Qa'ida.

Mike Spann was the first of the thirty-one. Mike was the first American to die in Afghanistan in our country's response to the 9/11 attacks. On November 26, 2001, I arrived at work at one a.m. to prepare for my daily briefing of the president. I found on my desk, seemingly placed and centered there with care, a cable from our officers in Afghanistan. It reported the death of an Agency officer. I sat down and started to read, and I read every word of the cable. Mike and a teammate had been visiting a Northern Alliance prison near Mazar-e-Sharif in northern Afghanistan on Sunday, November 25. It was one of the places the Northern Alliance took Taliban and al Qa'ida prisoners when they were captured on the battlefield.

It was a routine mission that went bad. Mike's job was to gain from the prisoners any intelligence that might speed the Taliban and al Qa'ida's defeat, as well as any information about further terrorist plotting against the United States. One of the prisoners Mike talked to that day was an American citizen, John Walker Lindh, who had decided to fight for the Taliban. Late that morning a riot broke out among the prisoners and the Afghan guards lost control. The prisoners overran the prison and went right after the Americans. Mike fought with his AK-47 until it ran out of ammunition, drew his pistol and fought with that until it emptied, then resorted to hand-to-hand combat before being overwhelmed by the large numbers of prisoners. Mike's body was recovered on the morning of November 27, after Northern Alliance troops and US and British Special Forces, backed by US air strikes, reestablished control at the prison.

I put the cable down, drew in a deep breath, and said to myself, "I'm showing this to the president; he will want to see this." I highlighted sections of the text of the cable with a yellow highlighter. President Bush and I had an unspoken understanding that if he read only what I had highlighted, he would get the gist, the main points, of a piece. I tried to highlight as little as possible of the ten-page cable without losing the story. I placed it in the front of his PDB binder, before the analytic articles specifically written for the president to see that day and before two or three intelligence reports that I thought he needed to see.

I met Director Tenet, as usual, in his office in the Old Executive Office Building to prepare for the briefing of the president. The director's briefer had already shown him what I planned to use with the president. Tenet took one look at me and said, "You're not showing the Mike Spann cable to the president. He does not need to know that." I pushed back, saying I was certain that he would want to know about our loss of Mike, the first American killed in combat on his watch as commander in chief, and certain that he would also want to read about the details. One of the many great things about Tenet was that he listened and was open to changing his mind. He relented by simply saying, "I hope you are right."

Tenet and I walked into the Oval Office and greeted the president. He was already sitting in his chair next to the vice president. I handed him his book and distributed books to Dick Cheney, Andy Card, and Condi Rice. As I was handing out the books, Tenet told the president that we had lost an officer in Afghanistan overnight. Tenet told the president that I had put the reporting cable in his briefing book but that "it simply boiled down to a case of being in the wrong place at the wrong time." The president did not say anything in response. He just started to read. It quickly became clear to me that he was not just reading the highlighted text; he was reading the entire cable. And he was not skimming; he was reading every word carefully. It took him almost twenty minutes to finish the cable. The president closed his briefing book without reading anything else in it and asked if Mike had a family. Tenet said, "Yes, Mike has a wife named Shannon, who is also an Agency officer, and three children." The president looked at Card and said, "I want to call Shannon." I was fighting back tears.

* * *

The prison near Mazar-e-Sharif was the location of CIA's first post-9/11 casualty, but the CIA base near Khost, Afghanistan, near the border with Pakistan, was the site of our heaviest post-9/11 casualties. There, on December 30, 2009, a suicide bomber—who had pretended to be a CIA source and who had said he might be able to pinpoint the location of Ayman al-Zawahiri, the number two of al Qa'ida—detonated his vest filled with explosives, killing seven CIA officers and severely wounding several others. It was the first time in the history of the Agency that someone who was a source—or at least pretending to be a source—had killed his CIA case officers.

At the time I was serving as the director for intelligence, the Agency's chief analyst. My family and I had spent the Christmas holiday in Florida, returning to Washington late on Wednesday, December 30. On the morning of the thirty-first, an official government holiday, I came to work to catch up. As I often did, I stopped in Deputy Director Steve Kappes's office on the way to my own. When I walked into his office, he and several senior officers from the operations directorate were sitting together. I immediately sensed that something was terribly wrong, as the mood in the room was deeply somber. I sat down and they told me what had happened. I was stunned—not only because of the size of the loss and the nature of the tragedy but because I knew one of the victims, base chief Jennifer Matthews, very well. We had served together for three years earlier in our careers.

Just a few days later Panetta asked the Agency's senior leadership team to attend with him the dignified transfer of the remains at Dover Air Force Base. We were met there by the commanding officer of mortuary services. He briefed us on what would transpire. He explained that the families of the seven fallen officers were in a large room not far from where we were, adding that we would meet with them first. He said that there were nearly one hundred people in total—mothers, fathers, aunts, uncles, spouses, and children. He told Panetta to say a few words to the entire room; then we should all mingle and talk to the families. He added, "Many people in your shoes worry about what you should say in a situation like this. Don't. Realize that they are still in shock and will not remember what you say. What they will remember is that you were here." He finished by explaining that after about an hour with the families, we would move to the tarmac for the transfer.

While perhaps the families do not remember what he said, Panetta was masterful. To the large group and then in the small groups, he told the families about the work of the Agency at Khost and about its importance. He told them about the potential of this particular operation, going into detail about why we'd been so interested in the person who had turned out to be a suicide bomber.

In similar circumstances since then, I have learned that the families of fallen officers want desperately to know three things. They want to know that the work of their loved one was important to the security of the nation. They want to know that their loved one was good at that work, that he or she made a difference. And they want to know that their coworkers respected and loved him or her. When I became deputy and then acting director, I would pore over the personnel files of the fallen, so I could give the families specific examples of these three simple, yet powerful, points.

The dignified transfer involved the CIA leadership team standing on the flight line as seven metal caskets were carried, one at a time, from the back of a C-17 to vehicles that would transport the caskets to the base mortuary. A single transfer would begin with a prayer by a chaplain over the casket in the back of the C-17 and the saluting of the flag-draped casket by the white-gloved eight-man transfer team. As the transfer team lifted the casket and started down the ramp of the C-17, the commanding officer would call, "Present arms." This was the order to render honors—military officers going to the salute position, civilians putting their right hand over their heart. The transfer team would then carry the casket the hundred feet or so to the transfer vehicle. Each transfer took about ten minutes; the entire event took well over an hour. It was bitterly cold—with a temperature just below freezing and the winter wind gusting.

Over the next several weeks, I attended with Panetta the funerals and memorial services of our officers. Each was special but two have been seared in my memory. The first, a funeral for Harold Brown, was in a small town outside Boston. The funeral mass was beautiful, but what occurred after the mass was extraordinary. As we left the church for the cemetery, I saw a family of five—a mother, a father, and three children—standing on their front porch, at attention, with their hands over their hearts. A few blocks more brought additional people standing in honor—in driveways, at intersections, and along the road. Families, scout troops, civic groups, and lone individuals. The crowds grew as we got closer to the cemetery. In the thirty-minute ride, there were hundreds—perhaps a thousand—Americans standing to honor our officer. They stood in fifteen-degree weather, holding American flags of differing sizes, many with hands on their hearts, some with signs that simply read "Thank you for keeping us safe." Panetta said, "I wish every member of Congress could see this." I was thinking, "I wish every American could see this."

The same day, a few hours later, I attended a memorial service in my hometown of Akron, Ohio, for another of our fallen colleagues. This officer, Scott Roberson, had left behind a wife and an unborn daughter, whom Scott and his wife had already decided to name Piper. One of the eulogies was given by one of Scott's close friends, a military officer. At the end of this eulogy, this military officer said that he had a vision of the future. He said that he saw a young woman, her husband, and her children standing in front of the Memorial Wall in our lobby at CIA. He said that this young woman had her hand on one of the black stars on our Memorial Wall as she told her family about Scott, about his life, and about his service to his country—his contribution to freedom. He said that in his vision, this young woman—named Piper by her parents—was as proud as she could be of the father she had never met.

* * *

One of my first overseas trips as deputy director was to Afghanistan, where the Agency had many officers deployed. I insisted on visiting the site of the attack at Khost. I saw the scars that were still visible from that awful day. In particular I saw small holes in the corrugated roof over a patio—and even one in a steel I beam—made by the ball bearings that had burst with extreme force from the suicide vest. And I saw the plaque that Director Panetta had dedicated a few months before. The plaque contains a few verses from Isaiah chapter eight: "And I heard the voice of the Lord saying, 'Whom shall I send, and who will go for us?' Then I said, 'Here am I. Send me.'"

* * *

I met the vast majority of the families of the thirty-one officers who have perished in the line of duty post-9/11. And, through the emotion and the tears, I would always tell them the same thing—that the Agency would forever be there for them and that if they had a problem, they needed only to pick up the phone and call me. A few days after I decided to retire, I awoke in the middle of the night with the thought "Who is going to take care of these families going forward, who is going to live up to the commitment that I made, who is going to be on the other end of the phone?" I reached for the pen and pad of paper on my nightstand and simply jotted down, "Transfer responsibility for the families to the new leadership team." This note became two actions for me as my days at the Agency wound down. First, I wrote letters to the families to whom I had made the commitment and I told them that my departure would have no impact on my commitment to them. "The Agency will always be here for you," I wrote.

At the very end of the speech I gave at my retirement ceremony on the evening of my last day on the job, I challenged the senior leadership team. I told it about the meetings that I'd had with the families of many of the fallen, about the commitment that I had made to them, and about the letter I had just sent. I explained that I was passing on to the members of that team the responsibility to keep that commitment. I concluded by reading aloud the names of the officers and the locations where they'd fallen in the line of duty. You could have heard a pin drop. I have no doubt that my colleagues are meeting the challenge.

* * *

The CIA Officers Memorial Foundation is an organization that assists the families of Agency officers who die while on active duty. The Foundation was created in the immediate aftermath of the death of Mike Spann. Its primary mission is to fund the educational expenses of the children and some of the spouses of such officers. In addition it provides financial assistance to families immediately after a tragic loss. Nearly eighty students have benefited from scholarship grants amounting to more than $3.1 million since the program's inception. The Foundation has identified over one hundred people who, over the next seventeen years or so, will be eligible to apply for scholarships and related assistance. Among those who have already benefited from the Foundation's generosity is Alison Spann, Mike Spann's oldest daughter, who received her bachelor's degree from Pepperdine University in 2014.

A share of my proceeds from this book will be donated to the CIA Officers Memorial Foundation. For more information visit http://www.ciamemorialfoundation.org/.

* * *

I would like to close by telling the story of how I came up with the title for this book. When I retired, many different offices in CIA gave me gifts—small, medium, and large plaques and other mementos. For the last month or so of my service as deputy director, I was taking home three or four such gifts every night. I placed them in a closet in our attic, vowing to appreciate them fully at some point. One such plaque came from the Counterterrorism Center, the organization within CIA that I had worked most closely with during my time as deputy director and acting director, and a group of people I deeply admired and respected. No one was more committed to their mission than the women and men of CTC. But even that plaque went into the closet.

Two years earlier, during the daily meeting with my personal staff, one of my executive assistants had said that a nine-year-old boy with a complex genetic disease had a dream of becoming a CIA officer. Some of the people in our Office of Security had heard about it and wanted to make his dream come true—at least for a day. They had invited him—along with his parents—to visit the Agency and were hoping I would spend a few minutes with him. "Absolutely," I told the EA. I did not know it at the time, but this young boy and his family would become close friends of my family and me.

Brandon has mitochondrial disease. Mitochondria are components of every cell in the body, except red blood cells, and they are responsible for producing 90 percent of the energy in the body. In those who suffer from the disease, the mitochondria do not function properly, which robs the body of the energy it needs to sustain life and maintain growth. Depending on the particular mitochondria that are malfunctioning, symptoms of the disease can include muscle weakness and pain, gastrointestinal disorders, swallowing difficulties, poor growth, developmental delays, susceptibility to infection, heart disease, liver disease, and many others.

Brandon has long suffered from some of these symptoms, but the disease has not diminished his amazing spirit. Nor had it dampened his desire to visit the Agency and "catch bad guys," a request that we gladly granted. Brandon spent hours at the Agency. Analysts from the Counterterrorism Center put together mock intelligence reports that Brandon pieced together to uncover a terrorist plot, identify the terrorists, and pinpoint their location. Then our security officers suited up Brandon in fatigues (to size) and a battle helmet and led him on a raid that resulted in the capture of the "terrorists." His final responsibility was to come to the deputy director's office to brief me on what he had accomplished. I met him at the door to my office and he introduced himself with a strong handshake, looking me straight in the eyes. I led him to the sofa in my office and offered him some of the fresh chocolate chip cookies that the director's dining room had prepared for the visit. Brandon, ignoring the cookies, said, "Sir, I am here to brief you." Without touching a cookie, he proceeded to walk me through the analysis, the preparation for the operation, and the operation itself. I told Brandon that his was one of the best briefings ever in my office, and I meant it. I was immensely proud of what my officers had done to make Brandon's visit to the Agency so memorable for him.

Brandon struck me immediately as special. He was whip-smart, inquisitive, kind, and full of love. I certainly fell in love with him. Since his initial visit to my office, my family and I have spent many hours with Brandon and his family—when he was feeling well and not so well. But he is always full of life; he always has something new to show us, something new to share.

When the news broke about the president's selecting John Brennan to lead CIA, I got a personal note from Brandon. It read as follows:

Dear Mr. Morell,

It's me Brandon. I wish you had got the job of Director of the CIA. I was really rooting for you. You will always have my vote! I know that being Deputy Director of the CIA is still a very important job and one of the most important in the world. You are my hero! I can't wait to see you!

Your friend,
Brandon

Shortly after I retired, my family and I were at Brandon's house the evening the CBS program *60 Minutes* aired an interview with me in which I commented on Syria. I was nervous; it was my first time on television. Brandon told me over and over again that it was going to be OK. It was. Before we left that night I mentioned to Brandon that I had received many gifts from my former colleagues as I was leaving the Agency. I invited him over to see "my loot." His big black eyes lit up.

Brandon's visit coincided with a time when I was agonizing over what to title this book. I shared a number of possible titles with family and friends and none of them worked. Fault was found with every one—major fault with many, and all of those were my ideas. I was stuck. On the morning of the day that Brandon was to come and see my gifts, I decided to go into the closet in the attic, go through the gifts, and bring out the really special ones for Brandon to see—a pistol that had belonged to Confederate officers in the Civil War, a dagger that had been carried by officers of the Office of Strategic Services during World War II, a knife that had been used by the Polish resistance fighting the Nazis, and much more. As I was rummaging through the closet, I came across the gift from CTC. It was a reminder of a significant victory in the fight against al Qa'ida when I was acting director, following Leon Panetta's departure for the Department of Defense. The plaque read "Thank you for your unconditional support to the Team in the Great War of Our Time." It hit me instantly. I had the title.

* * *

In addition to the CIA Officers Memorial Foundation, a portion of my proceeds from the book will go to the Brandon Heschel Leach Research Fund of the United Mitochondrial Disease Foundation, which is working hard to cure the disease that afflicts my very good friend Brandon.

Acknowledgments

Perhaps the most difficult part of writing this book is crafting this passage, which will attempt to thank the many people who played important roles in helping me accomplish whatever successes I have enjoyed in my career, who helped me survive when I experienced failures, and who helped me write this book. The process of thanking people is fraught with peril because I don't want to leave anyone out but I know that I inevitably will.

While it is impossible to know where to stop in thanking people, it is easy to know where to start: with my parents—Joseph and Irene Morell. Neither went to college—my father was a blue-collar worker at Chrysler and my mother a homemaker—but they gave me two great gifts that I am absolutely certain were largely responsible for whatever success I've enjoyed at CIA and in life.

My mother gave me the gift of hard work. She taught me to work hard at whatever I was doing. She would not rest until all her work was completed. She modeled this behavior, for example, by not sitting down to eat dinner with the family, instead getting a head start on cleaning the kitchen as soon as the meal had been served. Odd? Perhaps. A powerful lesson in how hard work is done? Absolutely.

My father gave me the gift of pursuing excellence at whatever I do. He insisted—sometimes bringing me to the point of tears as I was growing up—that I always do my best. I remember, as a young boy, building a birdhouse in my father's elaborate carpentry shop in our basement. He repeatedly looked at my effort and said, "Not good enough. Try again." When I protested, he took a hammer and smashed what I had done. I started over, and when I was finally done, I had a near-perfect birdhouse. Was he tough on me? You bet. Did he teach me to pursue perfection in whatever I did? Absolutely.

Put these two lessons together and you have a very powerful combination—hard work and the pursuit of excellence. Nothing has been more responsible for my success.

Once I began my professional career there were countless people whom I worked for who took the time to mentor me, to demonstrate the joy of hard work and to take the hammer to any of my efforts that were inadequate—much as my mom and dad had done. Some of those mentors have previously been mentioned in this book but many more have not. I owe enormous debts of gratitude to Jim Clapper, George Tenet, Mike Hayden, Leon Panetta, Dave Petraeus, John Brennan, Scott Redd, John McLaughlin, Steve Kappes, Hugh Turner, Jami Miscik, Winston Wiley, Dave Cohen, Mike Barry, Marty Petersen, Tom Elmore, Mary Meyer, Kent Harrington, Jim Harris, Len Litke, Gary Coene, and Deane Hoffman. All of them taught me a great deal.

There were innumerable coworkers as well. They were not bosses, but people I worked alongside who called *me* boss. I will never be able to cite all or even most of them, but a few cannot go unthanked because they gave me the great gift of telling me when I was wrong. (I will use only first names and last initials, even for the one or two who have been mentioned elsewhere in the book.) These are my special assistants when I was acting director and deputy director, Lisa O. and Brenda O.; my chief of staff, Greg T.; and my immediate subordinates Meroe P., Sue B., Fran M., Glen G., Mike S., John B., Frank A., John P., and Sue G. These are some of the strongest leaders that CIA ever produced.

I also want to specifically thank the following groups of people, without whom I could not have done my job: my daily intelligence briefers, who kept me up-to-date on the latest intelligence and who routinely provided me with my most enjoyable meeting of the day; my executive assistants, who put up with my endless requests and my varying moods; and the many members of my security detail, who were always at my side. Over my three and a half years as acting and deputy director, these dedicated and talented security officers became members of my family and role models for my children. I owe them a great deal. Likewise, the officers of the Agency's protocol staff, led by Sheila S., and the officers of the Agency's dining room staff did their job of supporting me with the utmost skill and professionalism.

I cannot write this chapter without thanking the men and women who served or still serve in CIA's Counterterrorism Center. No one works harder at keeping the country safe. No group worked more directly with me during my three years as deputy. They were and are an inspiration to me. Two of those officers deserve special recognition—the longtime chief of the center, Roger, and the long-time chief of one of the Center's key units, Emma. The country owes them a huge debt of gratitude—because no two individuals have done more to protect the country from another attack than they have.

In my thirty-three years at CIA I worked for six presidents. I was privileged to get to know two of them very well. I will be forever indebted to President George W. Bush and President Barack Obama, who gave me incredible opportunities to serve them and our country in ways I would never have dreamed of. I am grateful for their confidence and leadership. Both men have their critics—but for the most part, those critics have no understanding of the complexity of the issues that come before presidents of the United States. I can say with absolute certainty that both George W. Bush and Barack Obama always had the interests of the United States at the very top of their priority list.

My time in government was certainly an adventure and so too has been my new life in the private sector. My transition has been made infinitely easier by Mike Hayden, who gave me invaluable advice and who introduced me to many in the private sector; George Tenet, Peter Corsell, John Scarlett, John Cushman, Mel Immergut, and Glenn Gerstel, who offered wisdom, guidance, and friendship; Tom Donohue Sr., the CEO of the Chamber of Commerce; his son Tom Donohue Jr., the CEO of Adelphi Capital; Rich Kramer, the chairman and CEO of Goodyear Tire and Rubber; Jeff Fager and David Rhodes, the chairman and president, respectively, of CBS News; Steve Feinberg, the managing partner of Cerberus Capital Management; Josh Mayne, the CEO of Orbis Operations; Mark French, the CEO of Leading Authorities; and Mark Testoni, the CEO of SAP/NS2—all of whom gave me early opportunities in the private sector.

My Agency afterlife includes hanging my hat at Beacon Global Strategies, a Washington, D.C., firm specializing in helping US companies navigate the never-ending geopolitical complexities of our world. Beacon is managed by four former US government officials, Michael Allen, Jeremy Bash, Philippe Reines, and Andrew Shapiro, who each dedicated more than a decade of their professional lives to national service both as individuals and in support of their bosses: Michael for President George W. Bush on his NSC staff and for Mike Rogers as his staff director on the House Intelligence Committee, Jeremy as Leon Panetta's chief of staff at both the CIA and the Pentagon, and Philippe and Andrew at the State Department for Secretary Hillary Clinton. Like me, public service is part of their DNA, and I simply love the work and team at Beacon, and the values they uphold in everything they do. A special thanks to Meredith Steen, an associate at Beacon without whom I could not function. When I contemplated returning to the administration at the end of 2014, Beacon was understanding and supportive—so long as I didn't take Meredith with me!

Graham Allison, the director of the Belfer Center at Harvard University's Kennedy School of Government, deserves special mention, as his invitation to be a senior fellow at the Belfer Center provided me with the opportunity to test many of the ideas in this book with some of our country's leading minds on national security and foreign policy. Graham was a frequent visitor to my office in Langley, where he always provided insight on key national security issues, and I am thrilled that our professional relationship continues at Harvard.

Graham also provided me with a graduate assistant to help me with the research required to produce the manuscript. Josh Stiefel, an analyst at the Department of Defense, is a brilliant student at the Kennedy School, with a very bright future in national security. Josh did extensive research for the book, as well as multiple fact checks of the document. Josh turned around my questions with a speed and a level of insight that are hard to overstate. I am indebted to him.

In addition, late in the process, as the questions were coming fast and furious, my daughter, Sarah, and her friends Jackson Akselrad and Shayan Karbassi spent hours on the Internet answering what seemed to them to be never-ending questions, and hours doing additional fact-checking. My deepest thanks to the three of them.

Many people read the manuscript and provided thoughtful critiques. At the top of the list are my family—Mary Beth, Sarah, Luke, and Peter. They read the manuscript and provided hours of valuable feedback. Luke helped in particular with the chapter titles; they are much stronger because of his assistance. My thanks to them and to the other readers of the manuscript, all of whom provided useful critiques—George Tenet, Steve Hadley, John McLaughlin, Mike Vickers, John Moseman, John Rizzo, Peter Corsell, Nick

Shapiro, Ira Rosen, Glenn Gerstell, and Sam Vinograd. Glenn and Sam in particular approached their critique with a thoroughness and thoughtfulness that are hard to overstate.

The Chicago Project on Security and Terrorism (CPOST) at the University of Chicago produced the map for the book. My thanks go to the CPOST director, Robert Pape, who is not only a fine scholar but also a fine friend, and to the two primary researchers who created the map, Keven Ruby and Vincent Bauer. They did a great job.

Writing this book has been an eye-opening experience for me. It has forced me to reflect on some of the most critical and trying periods of my time at CIA. I am indebted to Andrew Wylie of the Wylie Agency, who facilitated my introduction to the world of publishing and who, to my great pleasure, connected me with Sean Desmond and the fine professionals at Twelve Publishing, who have helped me conceptualize, craft, and deliver *The Great War of Our Time.*

With Sean's guidance I have endeavored to make this book informative, accessible, and entertaining while sharing with the public critical information about the threats the United States and our allies face from international terrorists in the years ahead. His editing made the book much more informative and readable. Throughout, Sean asked many questions to which he believed readers would be interested in knowing the answers—a process I believe has added significantly to the book. I thoroughly enjoyed working with Sean, and now consider him a friend as well as a colleague. Sean's assistant, Libby Burton, made the book better in more ways than I can count.

What can I say about my friend and coauthor Bill Harlow? It was his phone call late one morning asking if I was going to write a book that got me thinking about it. And he was with me every step of the way. He knew what questions to ask to pull thoughts from deep within my memory. He crafted prose that flowed easily from sentence to sentence and paragraph to paragraph. And his judgment about how to handle delicate issues was always right on the mark. We had only a handful of differences of opinion over the many months of writing the book together, and Bill's view was the right one in every case. I could not have written this book without him. He is a fine writer and even finer friend.

There was no doubt about how to start these acknowledgments and there is also no doubt about how to end them—with deep thanks to family and friends. My sister, Karen, has always been there for me, and she did a wonderful job taking care of our aging parents while I was working so hard. My in-laws, Peter and Susan Manion, have not only been supportive but they have been role models to me in more ways than they will ever know. And Mary Beth's and my very good friends Shannon and Joe Hynds provided not only a supportive friendship but became a second set of parents to our children.

The most significant thanks—and love—go, of course, to Mary Beth and our three children, Sarah, Luke, and Peter. For the kids, the long hours demanded of someone who works at the top levels of the national security community started when they were quite young. They paid a high price for the long hours, for the never-ending phone calls, and for the many times when my mind was far away even when I was there right next to them. Early on they did not understand why their dad missed so many events, but now they do. They now know that service to one's country is a family affair, that it requires the love and support of family. I am so proud of the young adults they have become and the fascinating directions in which they want to take their lives.

On our first date, Mary Beth told me that she wanted a life of adventure. Well, I think I delivered—indeed, more than she bargained for. She bore the brunt of all the challenging jobs in which I served—managing the affairs of the family and my many job-related mood swings. I could not have done my job protecting our country without her. Mary Beth also served the Agency with distinction herself—working to improve the lives of Agency families, particularly those officers and families overseas and those families here at home whose loved ones were serving in war zones. I was very proud of the Agency Seal Medal that Director Brennan gave to her. I always said that she deserved a medal for putting up with me, and she got one. I love her very much.

Index

About the Authors

MICHAEL MORELL, former acting director and deputy director of the Central Intelligence Agency, is one of the country's most prominent national security professionals, with extensive experience in intelligence and foreign policy.

BILL HARLOW is a writer, consultant, and public relations specialist. He spent seven years as the top spokesman for the Central Intelligence Agency. He coauthored George Tenet's #1 *New York Times* best-seller, *At the Center of the Storm*.